THE
EVERYTHING.
GUIDE TO
COPING WITH PERFECTIONISM

Dear Reader,

It is a cosmic stroke of luck that I have been invited to share with you some thoughts, experiences, and discoveries about the slippery topic of perfectionism. For me, being perfect at many things brought momentary pleasure, even honors, prizes, and awards, but at what cost? As I've gone through situations where it is important to cooperate with others, as in a marriage, child-parent relationship, working within a group or with a client, I see that doing things perfectly is not such a great asset.

Being 100 percent on top of things makes others uncomfortable. Always being on time or a few minutes early makes latecomers nervous. Always having a good answer can make others feel incompetent or unimportant. It can be an act of grace to be an accepting, attentive presence and smooth out the kinks later on.

If you have a monster within you that shouts you're not doing things fast enough, perfectly enough, or whatever else enough, this book can help quiet that voice. We can work together to lighten up unrealistic expectations, and in the process, open the door to the incredible wonder of life and people around you, however quirky and flawed.

Appreciatively,

Ellen Bowers, PhD

Welcome to the EVERYTHING® Series!

These handy, accessible books give you all you need to tackle a difficult project, gain a new hobby, comprehend a fascinating topic, prepare for an exam, or even brush up on something you learned back in school but have since forgotten.

You can choose to read an Everything® book from cover to cover or just pick out the information you want from our four useful boxes: e-questions, e-facts, e-alerts, and e-ssentials.

We give you everything you need to know on the subject, but throw in a lot of fun stuff along the way, too.

We now have more than 400 Everything® books in print, spanning such wide-ranging categories as weddings, pregnancy, cooking, music instruction, foreign language, crafts, pets, New Age, and so much more. When you're done reading them all, you can finally say you know Everything®!

QUESTION

Answers to common questions

FACT

Important snippets of information

ALERT

Urgent warnings

ESSENTIAL

Quick handy tips

PUBLISHER Karen Cooper

MANAGING EDITOR, EVERYTHING® SERIES Lisa Laing

COPY CHIEF Casey Ebert

ASSOCIATE PRODUCTION EDITOR Mary Beth Dolan

ACQUISITIONS EDITOR Kate Powers

ASSOCIATE DEVELOPMENT EDITOR Eileen Mullan

EVERYTHING® SERIES COVER DESIGNER Erin Alexander

Visit the entire Everything® series at *www.everything.com*

THE EVERYTHING® GUIDE TO COPING WITH PERFECTIONISM

Overcome toxic perfectionism, learn to embrace your mistakes, and discover the potential for positive change

Ellen Bowers, PhD

Adams media
Avon, Massachusetts

The Everything® Guide to Coping with Perfectionism
is dedicated to my friends, family, clients, and coworkers
who have tolerated my own perfectionism. Thank you.

An Everything® Series Book.
Everything® and everything.com® are registered trademarks of F+W Media, Inc.

Published by Adams Media, a division of F+W Media, Inc.
57 Littlefield Street, Avon, MA 02322 U.S.A.
www.adamsmedia.com

ISBN 10: 1-4405-5160-X
ISBN 13: 978-1-4405-5160-4
eISBN 10: 1-4405-5182-0
eISBN 13: 978-1-4405-5182-6

Printed in the United States of America.

10 9 8 7 6 5 4 3 2 1

Library of Congress Cataloging-in-Publication Data
Bowers, Ellen.
 The everything guide to coping with perfectionism / Ellen Bowers.
     p. cm.
 Includes bibliographical references and index.
 ISBN-13: 978-1-4405-5160-4 (pbk. : alk. paper)
 ISBN-10: 1-4405-5160-X (pbk. : alk. paper)
 ISBN-13: 978-1-4405-5182-6 (ebook : alk. paper)
 ISBN-10: 1-4405-5182-0 (ebook : alk. paper)
 1. Perfectionism (Personality trait) 2. Interpersonal conflict. 3. Adjustment (Psy-
chology) I. Title.
 BF698.35.P47B69 2012
 155.2'32–dc23
                                        2012030651

This book is intended as general information only, and should not be used to diagnose or treat any health condition. In light of the complex, individual, and specific nature of health problems, this book is not intended to replace professional medical advice. The ideas, procedures, and suggestions in this book are intended to supplement, not replace, the advice of a trained medical professional. Consult your physician before adopting any of the suggestions in this book, as well as about any condition that may require diagnosis or medical attention. The author and publisher disclaim any liability arising directly or indirectly from the use of this book.

Many of the designations used by manufacturers and sellers to distinguish their products are claimed as trademarks. Where those designations appear in this book and Adams Media was aware of a trademark claim, the designations have been printed with initial capital letters.

This book is available at quantity discounts for bulk purchases.
For information, please call 1-800-289-0963.

Contents

Acknowledgments

The first thank you is to Kate Powers of Adams Media, who saw the tremendous need and potential for a book of this sort. Her enthusiasm and skill helped enormously to shepherd this work into fruition. The next thank you is to numerous friends and family members who contributed ideas, examples, and even begged to be case studies for the book. I am immensely appreciative of so much kindness and generosity, and I am grateful to know so many perfect people. Another thank you goes to the fabulous resources of the Glendale and Pasadena public libraries. I cannot live without you. And finally I wish to thank Fay, Orchid, Jeanine, and my stalwart Sunday group for consistent interest and support.

Top 10 Signs of Suffering from Perfectionism

1. Never feeling relaxed or at peace.

2. Always wanting to be the best, the first, the greatest.

3. Feeling driven to have the last word in arguments or conversations.

4. Feeling deeply tired much of the time.

5. Believing that your accomplishments are of little or no value.

6. Wanting to chuck everything and start over with a new job or new spouse.

7. Physical symptoms such as insomnia, heart palpitations, skin disorders.

8. High anxiety because of having so many things to do.

9. Your closest relationships lack warmth and comfort.

10. The sensation of having an enormous hole in your soul.

Introduction

MOST PEOPLE THINK of perfectionism as a good thing. What's wrong with working hard to reach lofty goals? But perfectionism can go too far—much farther than pulling all-nighters to hand in the perfect paper or cleaning the house until it shines. Toxic perfectionism can result in obsessive behavior, damaged self-esteem, depression, and even physical ailments.

Perfectionism is rampant in modern culture. The pressures of the media, working hard to sustain a career, the rising cost of living combined with dwindling job opportunities, somewhat fragmented families, and the faster pace of life all contribute to unrealistic expectations of oneself and others. The result can be a sort of dark, pervasive irritability and short-temperedness in every conversation and human exchange.

Have you eavesdropped lately on anyone ordering his or her favorite latte? More than likely, the instructions are delivered in a clipped, terse voice, and the barista is doomed if he uses 2 percent milk instead of soy. Have you overheard a young parent giving last-minute instructions to a beleaguered child as she is dropped off at school or daycare? "Don't mess up your new dress," and "Remember what I said about being friendly to little Mike who has just joined the class," or "Eat all your vegetables, and remember to phone me at four o'clock, and don't lose the cell phone." All this for a five-year-old!

The faster pace of communication, availability of infinite amounts of information in print or on the Internet, and the constant blasts of media cause people to feel that they are always behind, not quite up on the latest news, or impossibly inept at following the latest fashion trend or movie releases. It makes a person tired before he or she even begins the day. Even enormously bright, capable people are overwhelmed by the perfectionistic standards of today's society. And then there are those who simply give up trying.

Perfectionism can be a huge motivating factor for tremendous achievement. A young pianist memorizes and performs the entire repertoire of

Bach's Preludes and Fugues. An aspiring skater practices every day and competes in the Olympics. Ordinary people diet and work out in order to be a little healthier. A young, eager husband engages in therapy in order to learn more effective ways to communicate with a delicate-natured wife. A traveler memorizes dozens of sentences in a foreign language before taking an adventurous trip.

These instances are not necessarily harmful, unless other aspects of life are so neglected that something is sacrificed. If the young pianist has ulcers, the aspiring skater has no friends, the health enthusiasts are scheduled for numerous plastic surgeries, and the willing husband is lying awake at night to the point of not being able to function at work, then perfectionism is at play. Of course, people have a wide range of talents and capabilities. While an average person cannot memorize so much music, perhaps there is someone who can do so without adverse effects. The important thing is whether or not the person is truly happy with the accomplishment, and trickier still—where does the motivation come from?

A key component in identifying perfectionism in oneself is the question: "Is it important to be perfect in this situation, or am I making myself unhappy?" Getting at the root causes of the dark world of impossible, pervasive perfectionism can lead to a detective search into childhood experiences, buried traumas, and unconscious agendas. The quest is worth it, as the result is a happier, sane, pressure-free life. Perfectionism is not a curse. With enough information and a bit of curiosity and willingness, even years of perfectionistic thinking and behavior can be untangled and laid to rest. However, it will take some courage to do such an investigation, and tenacity in forming some different habits and responses. The rewards are great.

CHAPTER 1

The Basics of Perfectionism

Perfectionism is when high standards have become impossible to reach. For sometimes unknown reasons, a person is driven to be the most beautiful, top one's sales records month after month, attain perfect As in school, and become a Nobel Prize winner. Perfectionism has an element of compulsivity, and anything short of perfection is seen as a failure. Think of high standards on steroids. A desire for mastery is certainly admirable and can lead to a fulfilled life. However, perfectionism, whether in what one imagines others expect or in what is expected of a child, mate, or coworker, ultimately leads to the erosion of relationships.

Definition: What Is Perfectionism?

Merriam-Webster's online dictionary offers the following definitions of *perfectionism*:

First, there is the theological view that a perfect moral character allows a person to attain the highest good. Next, theology says that perfection is a state of freedom from sin. The third definition is more the focus of this book: a personal disposition that inclines one to see anything short of perfection as unacceptable.

Perfectionism can be broken into two types. First, there are behaviors such as checking, correcting, categorizing, and organizing. Second, one has difficulty making decisions, gives up efforts too quickly, or procrastinates. Both types are burdensome to the individual and others who live or work near the person.

Perfectionists tend to screen out positive options, almost always focusing on the negative. Perfectionists sense a host of "shoulds" careening through their mind most of the time. Perfectionists adversely compare themselves to others and make many wrong assumptions, imagining that they can read minds and that others can read their minds. There are core beliefs of not being okay, not being valuable or lovable. The result is a lot of spinning wheels and wasted time and energy.

Well, What's Wrong with That?

Perfectionism causes unhappiness—ill feelings within the self and in relation to others. It creates a life seemingly fraught with danger at every turn because the high standards believed to be important can never be met. This creates a tired, discouraged person, always on the brink of satisfaction and achievement but never quite making it. Perfectionistic parents raise nervous children, those kids who hover around the edges of something fun, afraid that they will do something wrong and get yelled at.

Perfectionistic spouses create a "walking on eggshells" atmosphere in the home, as the significant other never knows when the next verbal barb will fly. Should the car have been washed on the way home? An impromptu luncheon planned for the corporate wives? Should the carpet have been cleaned before the holiday dinner? A perfectionistic spouse can create an impossibly elusive checklist of tasks that was never discussed or agreed upon with his or her significant other. In the significant other's mind, this list becomes paramount with keeping the other person momentarily happy.

FACT

Perfectionism leads to a preoccupation with others. One's own needs get shifted to the back burner, resulting in personal neglect, even physical illness. Others may thrive on all that attention, but the self atrophies.

The Appeal of the Imperfect

Have you noticed that in recent years handmade items are very popular and indeed sought after? A hand-hewn chair may be a cherished souvenir from travels and is favored over something less expensive from an assembly line. There is something very personal and attractive in an art or craft that comes from the efforts of an individual. The flaws add to the character of the piece.

ESSENTIAL

Often the direction one is going is the only thing that is really important. Perfection is unattainable, so it makes perfect sense to simply keep taking actions in the direction of the desired goal. The results will take care of themselves.

This could be true for people, as well. The flaws in appearance or character add to the artistry of the human being. Can you imagine Frida Kahlo without her heavy eyebrows? But no biographies relate trips to the salon for waxing and tweezing.

Staying Out of the Affairs of Others

Straightening out other people is so appealing to perfectionistic people. There are so many potential projects! However, nagging and criticizing does not create happy, wholesome relationships, and one soon finds others turning the other way when one enters a room. Redirecting the focus to oneself is appropriate.

There is much to do in terms of developing a life of satisfying activities. The result is a well-rounded person who brings a relaxed glow to relationships. Such a person has a great deal of appeal, whether in romantic relationships or in a work group. Old habits may resist change, but catching that inclination to correct or fix can create a much more peaceful life.

Understanding Perfectionism and Its Effect on Your Life

Perfectionism can be a deadly detriment to enthusiasm, satisfaction, and happiness. It destroys relationships as people pick, pick, pick at each other, whether it is in a marriage or between parent and child. Children of perfectionistic parents tend to carry the mantle forward and become unreasonable taskmasters toward themselves and others, and the unhappy legacy is passed on. With perfectionistic people, often the unreasonable need to be right is lorded over others, much to the detriment of friendships and working relationships. Have you ever heard a very bright, small child lecturing someone in the sandbox about the correct way to make sand cookies? This is a future perfectionist, and someone not so easy to be around comfortably.

ESSENTIAL

It has been said that a person who isn't making mistakes isn't making much of anything. Life is constant trial and error, a series of discoveries about what works and what doesn't work. Mistakes are a natural part of the process.

What are some of the effects of perfectionism?

- Difficulty setting realistic goals and taking steps toward them
- Inability to relax and enjoy an ordinary day
- Extreme sensitivity to criticism
- Tendency to look at problems rather than solutions

- Strained relationships or inability to have relationships
- Tendency to escape into fantasy or various addictions
- A sense that life is passing by without participating
- Insomnia and other psychosomatic conditions
- Social isolation, shame, fear about even simple things
- Creating rituals to overcome the blocks to action

A tendency toward perfectionism makes it nearly impossible to even think about trying something new, let alone actually doing it. What if one has a yearning to work in a foreign country? The thought is daunting because of the impossibility of knowing the language and culture ahead of time. Not acting on desires creates a feeling of great loss. Who knows—people in that country may find it quite endearing to interact with a foreigner speaking their tongue at a toddler level of expertise. Many happy diplomatic memories could result from various blunders.

Toxic Perfectionism

Toxic perfectionism is the extreme edge of perfectionism where the person is frozen in paralyzed inaction. There is such a high degree of fear of failure that it becomes impossible to do anything because it is certain to be wrong! This state of paralysis leads to depression in fairly short order. It is difficult to reason with a person in this paralyzed state of mind, even if you are trying to convince yourself to do something differently. All you will hear is "Yes, but . . ." Even the most highly intelligent person cannot see that the way out of intense immobilization is to take any action, however lame and imperfect. This would be a good time to try something mediocre, as it releases the logjam of shame and self-recrimination.

FACT

Fear of abandonment often underlies toxic perfectionism. One is deathly afraid that if something is not done perfectly, the situation or relationship will simply fall apart. The emotions around this are akin to life-threatening terror, often based in childhood where, in fact, one might have been told that something had to be perfect in order for the child to remain in the family.

Toxic perfectionism works like an insidious poison that can wither even the most gorgeous day or luscious experience. It's like Eeyore's sighing even when the sun is shining and friends have gathered for his birthday celebration. Toxic perfectionism is like a foggy lens of perception. Everything will be musty and moldy because of the lens, not because of the nature of the actual experience or situation. This is quite difficult to understand when one is in it. It helps to have trusted people—spouse, friend, or therapist—who can point it out.

Toxic perfectionism can be especially deadly for substance abusers or those with behavioral addictions, as one is apt to totally "go for broke" when in that impaired state of thinking. The gambler will slip the last twenty dollars into the slots, even though it is part of the rent money, and the compulsive overeater will finish off the half gallon of ice cream because the diet has been ruined anyway with some small slip. The drinker will finish three bottles of wine, simply because they are there, staring at him, speaking to him for some action. The all-or-nothing, black-and-white thinking and action is the hallmark of toxic perfectionism. It is difficult to even imagine small increments of anything positive in such a state of mind.

The Lurking Culprit—Fear

Hiding behind toxic perfectionism is a huge amount of fear. It may even be hidden from the perfectionist. Though all their excuses may seem completely rational, hidden fear is their motivator. It protects the perfectionist from failure—ultimate and colossal failure of the most public sort or even minuscule mistakes that aren't worth the bat of an eyelash. Sometimes a person can sense that fear and even face it by taking one small step in the direction of the desired goal.

ALERT

A different version of the familiar adage could be, "Anything worth doing is worth doing badly." No one is an expert at the beginning of a new undertaking. Often there is much to learn in the early processes of something different, and it can be quite fun to mess around with materials or strange circumstances.

For example, if you'd like to earn your living as an artist, place a sketch pad and drawing materials near your work space and reach for it when you get a little free time. You might find that the small action of reaching for the lovely colors and textures brings on a barrage of admonitions and emotions. "No! That's a waste of time! Doing art is frivolous! You'll never amount to anything! Nobody wants to see your art!" If you can continue the positive action in spite of the negative chatter, it does subside. The positive action becomes easier and the buried fear is no longer so powerful. Sometimes the emotions are incredibly strong and scary, like that of a child in danger. Those out-of-proportion fears are a clue that the irrational beliefs about perfection were learned in childhood.

The Extremes of Toxic Perfectionism

At the farthest extreme of toxic perfectionism, people commit suicide over a large or small crisis. For example, a straight-A student gets a B and loses a scholarship. A family breadwinner suffers a large financial loss and does not see how the family can survive. If the whole identity and self conception rides on being the perfect student or the perfect provider, the situation is precarious indeed. Death may seem the only way out, as the individual is momentarily incapable of accepting that another direction could possibly become fruitful. The student could get a part-time job or the family breadwinner could ask for help and support from the spouse, or possibly consider a different career direction. These avenues would not be clearly evident to a person suffering from toxic perfectionism.

The Urge to Complete at All Costs

Perfectionism can take some strange turns, causing the afflicted person to do completely irrational things. For example, an entrepreneur has botched an investment deal, and there is considerable financial loss. He goes to the extreme of taking the rest of his money and splurging it on a wild weekend in Las Vegas.

The urge to complete at all costs shows up with eating disorders. The undereater refuses to eat at all or binges and purges so there is no nourishment for the body. The overeater goes to the extreme of eating whole cakes in the middle of the night or ordering a family-sized pizza and finishing it off while watching a video alone. It is not hunger driving the action. It is the need to completely finish it off.

Sometimes the urge to complete at all costs is found in domestic violence situations. For example, the abused spouse senses that the partner is gathering steam for a destructive outburst. She is quite aware of the nuances of behavior in herself and in the spouse, knowing that saying just the perfect crude remark will send him over the edge. At least, she thinks, the episode is finished then, even if it ends up with a visit to the emergency room. In this case, the two participants share the perfectionistic thinking and behavior, sharing responsibility for bringing the cycle to its culmination. It's perfectly horrible, but the energy between them sought completion.

A Matter of Perspective

Sometimes perfectionism is a case of misplaced emphasis. Imagine that when you are entertaining a friend for coffee, you discover that there is no creamer in the refrigerator. The perfect host or hostess would be embarrassed. However, the point of the visit is to enjoy each other's company, not to create a Martha Stewart moment. No one will remember in a month whether or not the hostess offered creamer or not.

Perhaps an individual is interested in taking on a community volunteer effort for a cause that seems really important. However, without a background in fundraising, event planning, or working on committees, it is natural to feel inept and reluctant. Truthfully, there are no Nonprofit Police gauging the degree of competence when someone takes on a new task. One is likely to find that others in the organization are quite happy to have new energy directed toward the work. Part of the enjoyment is learning the ropes of the situation. One's humanness makes an endearing contribution.

Can I Change My Mind?

The urge to complete something at all costs precludes the possibility of changing course along the way. For example, a young college student studies art history for three years, aiming for a career as a university professor. During the course of studying her required courses she finds out that art history seems a little dry, compared to the fun that the studio students seem to be having. If she changes her major, more time in college will be required. Is it worth it to shift gears? Most likely yes, as it is illogical to continue on a course that would not be enjoyable. Most probably, the additional art history background would be quite enriching to the studio artist, adding an historical depth to her work.

The Seduction of Praise

In close relationships, one has to be very careful and selective with the use of praise, as others with perfectionistic tendencies can become dependent upon it and feel quite frightened if everything is not praiseworthy. Of course, this is an unrealistic way to live, hanging on the possibility of a word from the significant other or boss. Parents who praise their children constantly may feel that it is a right thing to do, but moderation would be in order.

A steady diet of praise is like a steady diet of candy and cookies—ultimately harmful for the person. One hopes that each person within the relationship, whether adult or child, is able to generate positive reinforcement from within. The child puts away the toys because it is the accustomed thing to do in that family. The family chef prepares a nice meal out of loving kindness, not for the dangling carrot of syrupy thank-yous.

Classical conditioning says that intermittent reinforcement is the most powerful way to shape attitudes and responses. An occasional comment of gratitude is much more powerful than a constant stream of praise. Praise makes the other person dependent on that feedback, leading to false behaviors of all kinds and too many perfection-motivated actions.

Certain very strong individuals are impervious to praise or criticism, understanding that often the other person has an underlying motive to control. You might think that praise would always be welcome, but not if the intent is to manipulate. It might be an interesting idea to try, even for only one day, to be oblivious to others' comments of praise and criticism, to simply be secure within oneself no matter what is said.

The Symptoms of Perfectionism

To err is completely human, but perfectionistic people have surreal, completely different standards, behaviors, and beliefs. Some of the following are typical symptoms of perfectionism:

- Anxiety
- Fear of making mistakes
- Depression
- Procrastination
- Fear of criticism
- Critical of self and others
- Overemphasis on minute things
- Great difficulty prioritizing relative importance of tasks
- Interpersonal difficulties
- Persistent negative thinking
- Social phobias
- Substance or behavioral addictions

Other difficulties may include being unusually slow in one's tasks or not doing them at all, having seemingly well-thought-out excuses for not doing what is expected, and behaving in irrational, emotional ways when the situation does not require such.

But It's Important to Do It Right!

Perfectionism can be an elusive difficulty to understand, as the American culture rewards hard work, commitment to results, putting in long hours, and high achievement. However, striving for excellence is different from striving for perfection. Perfection is hopeless; it is virtually unattainable.

It is easy to forget that perfection is a matter of fantasy. French writer Nicolas Chamfort quipped that bachelors' wives and old maids' children are always perfect.

Excellence is a different matter—simply bringing all that is possible to the task at hand and then letting it go, assuming that it is completely acceptable. A person who is not perfectionistic is able to view herself as a completely worthwhile individual, regardless of what is attained or not. The perfectionist, however, has a deeply felt belief that one has to be perfect in order to be acceptable as a person. Of course, this almost never happens, resulting in fragile self-esteem.

FACT

There is a belief among Navajo weavers that perfection provokes the wrath of the gods. For that reason, an intentional mistake is cleverly woven into each beautiful rug. Thus, the gods are appeased for the moment. The hidden knot is generally only known by the weaver.

Struggles with Negativity

The perfectionist is rarely happy. There is a persistent undercurrent of dissatisfaction with oneself and life. Whatever achievements there are bring only fleeting joy. Then they are dismissed as trivial or marginal. There is the element of control with perfectionism, where one is provoked to seek particular outcomes, even when they are impossible. Food addicts often have ritualistic, controlling behaviors around their meals and food, veering into perfectionism, even if it means perfectly consuming all that is available at the moment. Perfectionists can exhibit extreme apathy and hopelessness, as nothing seems right or good enough. Such despair may take the form of unresolved grief.

Overcompensating

It can be tempting to try to become perfect in order to compensate for something that seems wrong or missing in life. Perhaps a young woman came from a terrible family. Her sense of security was shattered by her parents' difficult divorce and resulting experiences of being shunted from relative to relative during her formative years. She might create a goal to have a happy family—actually a perfect family to make up for what was lost before. The unsuspecting groom does not realize that he will be playing a part in an unknown play, rather than spontaneously creating a life together based on the needs of both persons. He becomes a puppet, willed by the wife to behave in a certain way, do only certain types of work, and relate to her in specified, rigid ways.

Someone else may try to create something fantastic to overcome perceived imperfections, such as the colorful DJ played by Wolfman Jack in the film *American Graffiti*. In a *Wizard of Oz* manner, he creates a strong persona, one who is almost entirely invisible, in order to be important in the lives of the high school students in the story.

Risk

To counteract some of the effects of perfectionism it is helpful to become more comfortable with risk. Imagine life as a grand adventure, and it's up to you to explore and participate. Yes, there may be setbacks and temporary embarrassments when trying something different, but the pleasures of new experiences are mostly likely worth it. Maybe you have always wanted to shop in the markets of Kathmandu. Maybe you would like to work with a hot-air balloon crew and silently drift over the mountains, looking at miniature coyotes and rabbits below. Maybe you would like to fly in a helicopter over the Grand Canyon. These types of things entail risk but could bring new life and energy into the deadened sensibilities of perfectionism.

CHAPTER 2

The Root Causes of Perfectionism

Perfectionism doesn't spring from nowhere. People with perfectionism, if they take the time to investigate their personal history and do a careful appraisal of their environment, will see that it's no accident that they have perfectionistic tendencies. Some of the origins might be genetic, which, of course, are completely out of a person's control, and others are found in the surroundings and significant relationships that impact a person's life. If you want to discover the roots of your perfectionism, think of tracing the causes of being too perfect not as a mystery, but as a bit of an adventure.

Domestication and the Big Dream of Society

The popular writer Don Miguel Ruiz clarifies some of the struggles that modern people endure, especially in his bestseller, *The Four Agreements*. One of his helpful concepts is that strong forces act on small children to "domesticate" them, to make them fit into society in a smooth way. Well-meaning parents condition the child to act, speak, move, and believe in the ways of the prevailing culture. A Navajo child or a Korean child might be given a lot of freedom up to the age of four or five, as it is assumed that children are naturally good and don't need any serious correction. Caucasian children in Western society might be more severely directed—"Do this," "Do that"—and have to learn a lot of rules of the household, Grandma's household, school, and church in order to behave in a customary manner. The child is innocent and takes on, wholesale, the beliefs of the parents and culture as the absolute truth. It takes years of effort in adult life to examine those beliefs and accept or delete, one by one.

FACT

In the Inuit culture there is no word equivalent to the English word "discipline," as within that society it is incomprehensible that small children would misbehave. They are simply being small children, doing what babies and toddlers do in a quite natural, uninhibited way.

Ruiz's idea of the Big Dream of society helps one to understand the roots of perfectionism. The society, group, clan, or family is more or less sold a bill of goods in terms of the prevailing values of the bigger surrounding culture. This is true around the globe; otherwise, chaos would prevail. However, sometimes beliefs get reduced to the lowest common denominator and work to a person's detriment. For example, in Mexican culture a woman is often praised if she is compliant, meek, and subservient toward men. What if she wants to be an engineer or construction manager? She will have a lot of opposition and work to do to overcome the Big Dream of her society. There may be a lengthy time of ostracism while she finds a new tribe of like-minded individuals to encourage her in her life's true calling.

In terms of perfectionism, it is natural for children to want to please their parents. A child learns at a very young age what is okay with the big people and what is not. There is a strong drive to be in harmony with the caretakers, even if the situation is logically impossible. For example, if one comes from a family where higher education is revered, the children will likely make good grades in school and become literate and conversant on intellectual matters. If such a child wants to chuck everything and backpack around the world at the age of twenty, there will be a conflict of drives. She will want to complete something educational in order to please the parents but still follow her own curiosity about, say, the Great Wall of China and the exotic plants of Costa Rica rain forests. A conflict arises within the person because she is going against the Big Dream of her formative years. This can be rough to endure, sometimes leading to hopeless efforts at pleasing people when the original aim is buried but not forgotten.

ESSENTIAL

Don Miguel Ruiz's dictum of don't take things personally, no matter what, helps greatly when dealing with others who are perfectionistic. The boss may come down really hard because a report is not formatted *her* way. It's not personal. The mother-in-law may have a fit about a new career plan that's outside of the family reality, but it's not personal.

Family of Origin Causes

Dysfunctional families are fraught with possibilities for the development of perfectionism. If alcoholism or other substance abuse is present, relationship dynamics are distorted in incomprehensible ways to a child or even adults. The drinker may be sweet and accommodating during the sober times, and the child works very hard to please. When the drinking starts, the child still wants to please, possibly in order to stop or curb the drinking as it creates such chaos in the household.

The spouse in such a situation may believe that keeping the house completely clean and the children quiet will prevent drinking or at least prevent violent outbursts during the binge weekends. Such magical thinking perpetuates perfectionism in the spouse and in the children as they work very hard to control the uncontrollable. It is not a true cause-and-effect situation, but no one sees that.

High-Achievement Perfectionism

In families where high achievement is revered, but there is actually little warmth and true emotional caring, children may learn that getting a good report card will bring a fleeting bright spot of praise. This can be mistaken for love. The wrong association becomes deeply imbedded in the child's mind, and he tries harder and harder to keep the straight-A average going, even at the cost of immense stress and limited social life. Because the perfection is elusive, the distorted mind of the youngster propels the individual to keep at it, constantly grasping for the invisible goal. Such children often take a career path advised by the parents, perhaps falling into an arduous life of medicine and law, somewhat innocently, because the true interests and talents are clouded over by the dynamic of the parents' control over what is lauded and what is not.

Parents who are mentally ill, whether with narcissistic personality or other disorders, will likely unwittingly foster perfectionism in their children. For example, a man who has become a compulsive gambler recalls that his mother attempted suicide several times during his young years. He never knew whether she would survive or not. Such an insecure atmosphere makes the individual grasp at straws, believing that the next big win will solve all his problems and he'll have a perfect life. He can even put together a perfect betting plan, based on the number of tries and strategies in order to perfectly outwit the casinos.

FACT

The relationship between a daughter and a narcissistic mother can be a particularly damaging one. Such a mother sees a daughter not as a separate entity but as an extension of herself. This kind of maternal narcissism makes any genuine bond almost impossible. It also gets in the way of the daughter's ability to grow into a strong, independent, and capable woman. A narcissistic mother often sets impossibly high standards for her daughter, and the daughter's struggles to meet perfectionistic standards go unrewarded or punished. Narcissistic mothers can be envious of their daughters' youth and beauty, and this jealousy can take the form of aggression and cruelty.

Narcissistic Personality Disordered Parents

Narcissistic parents sometimes live through their children, especially if they are highly talented, and the child becomes accustomed to planning her days around the quixotic needs of the demanding parent. "Make me a cup of tea. Paint me a picture. Show me the poem you wrote. Come over here and keep me company." The litany emitting from the bottomless pit keeps the child quite busy, much to the detriment of normal development. There is always the hope that *this time* the parent will be satisfied and happy. This is almost never the case, and the child dances faster and faster, likely on a perfectionistic bent for life.

Addictions in the Childhood Home

Any addictions in the family of origin—workaholism, sex and porn, shopping, playing the stock market, overeating, overachieving, incest, alcohol, or drugs—will likely lead to a degree of perfectionism in the children, as the emotional needs are not met during the formative years. The addiction always is the most important relationship for the addict, and the family's emotional needs are a far second down the ladder. The child, however, does not understand that and wants so very much to make Daddy stay home for a while, take a few minutes away from the computer screen, or put down the beer and barbequed dinner for a while.

There becomes a drive of desperation that is the norm for the person who evolves from such a family environment. Being perfect seems, subconsciously, to right the wrong of not having enough of the right kind of attention as a child. A young professional adult can be driven to do her job so well that she will never provoke any criticisms from her supervisor or coworkers. Of course, this is an unrealistic hope, but it feels life-threatening, as the emotions are that of a child, the child who wanted to make the parents stop fighting and drugging by being the best little girl. It is, sad to say, a futile effort.

ALERT

Persons who are unmothered or unfathered may, according to Dr. Clarissa Pinkola Estes, become unrealistic in their desires for perfect high achievement, attempting to go to great impossible lengths of earning numerous PhDs or ascending to the top of Mount Everest. Being "unmothered" or "unfathered" means that the parent was not available to emotionally nurture the child. Such parents may be preoccupied with their own lives or in some manner stunted in their development. Persons who are unparented may have had parents who were physically or emotionally absent, neglectful, or abusive. The result is a gaping psychological scar.

Societal Causes

Living in present times is fraught with pressures, deadlines, and a plethora of digital and electronic gadgetry demanding maintenance. Schedules are complicated, involving multiple careers in the household and the children's round of extra activities. Financial pressures loom, and at the same time, there is the push to provide everything for oneself and one's family that seems "normal"—designer clothes, wholesome food, and enough culture and entertainment to keep up. In urban areas, traffic snarls are a predictable part of daily life and workers are often on call, tethered to unrelenting responsibilities by cell phones or the Internet. It is impossible to perfectly keep up with all this, but people try. The frantic pace is the new norm.

ESSENTIAL

Persistence, even in the face of opposition, is a good way to make progress on cherished personal goals. Imagine a woodcutter chopping down a redwood tree or Michelangelo chipping away at his sculpture of David. The first dozen attempts will have little effect, but cumulatively, each effort adds to the glorious result. The trick is to remain focused on the mundane, or, on each little action of chipping away.

Even the closest relationships are different in the twenty-first century compared to two or three generations ago. These days, everyone watches TV talk shows or reads self-help books to glean the secrets of being happy with someone. Expectations are high in terms of hoped-for happiness with a significant other. It's easy to constantly miss the mark and come up feeling not good enough, attractive enough, or clever enough for that special someone. It's hard work to be so perfect in one's romantic life.

QUESTION

Why are arranged marriages sometimes more enduring than those unions based on romantic love?
During past times in the United States and in even somewhat recent years in Asian countries, partners were chosen by the parents in terms of compatible family values and harmonious goals. The role of each person was clear, and expectations were in line with reality.

Effects of School and Church

Although the original meaning of the word *educate* meant "to draw out from what is within the student," one does not often experience that luxury in schools these days. From preschool through postgraduate degrees, time is regimented and the learning process is heavily controlled. Pressures are enormous at every stage of schooling, even to the point that some parents of preschoolers are cultivating the child's spot in an Ivy League college! The emphasis is most often on results—grades, reports, starring in a play, scoring the most in sports—and potential for perfectionism is abundant.

Education and Perfectionism

Children and youth are vulnerable. They are learning their place in the world, and school is a big part of their life during those years. Their self-esteem is fragile, and having the wrong backpack or pair of shoes can seem like the end of the world. A frown from a disgruntled teacher can ruin a child's day. Peer approval is so important and fleeting in its demands. Having the perfect app for the iPhone may be the ticket for a coveted friendship. Having access to money and a car for a teenager makes it possible to have the perfect date. It's an unwieldy house of cards, but everyone involved tries to negotiate their way through it without injury. A persona can be somewhat shaped by the right clothing, friends, and manner of speaking in order to fit in with the best crowd. The criteria are fluid, creating a lot of stress for a sensitive teenager just trying to keep up and learn what is going on.

FACT

Patience for oneself, and eventually with others, is a marvelous antidote for the effects of society, school, and church pressures. Imagine that you are your own encouraging teacher or spiritual guru, and you gently and quietly support yourself in small triumphs. Such compassion for the self is a great role model for those in your world, as societies' institutions teach quite the opposite.

For those on the highest academic track, families pressure students to perform well so they can get into good schools and perhaps bring the family acclaim. This is especially treacherous if the family is troubled and a student's success is the only way the family can feel good about itself. This leads to a hopeless type of perfectionism, as the youth takes on the burden of making the sinking ship float a little longer, producing great anxiety about one's worth.

Church and Perfectionism

Depending on a person's spiritual and religious orientation, one can feel the weight of sin and a watchful patriarchal God who is constantly assessing one's position in the scheme of things between heaven and hell. Even in adult years, one can hear the cautionary voices of the nuns and priests, or remember a smack on the hand for momentarily having a daydream or flirting with someone of the opposite sex. The church, as an institution, is a big part of the Big Dream, working diligently to keep people in line so that society will function in an orderly way.

In his book, *Perfection: Coming to Terms with Being Human*, writer Michael J. Hyde says that philosophers such as Hume were critical of the church because it used "their own esteemed notions of perfection in a fanatical way to manipulate and persecute the masses." Many philosophers of the Enlightenment period saw the church as a threat to freedom of thought. Why would churches try to control people with a perfectionistic view of God and sin? Perhaps to keep the treasury coffers full, or to simply keep the conservative aspects of society in place, preserving order.

Trying to be perfect so that one is worthy of love from God is another hopeless road to travel. It can seem life-threatening if those early influences were fraught with threat and fear. Many people go through a lengthy period of examining the true nature of their spirituality, sloughing off the punitive aspects of the early teaching. Some find it easier to stay closer to the first teachings, finding comfort in the finite predictability of it. This is a personal matter. However, if one wonders if God is angry and disapproving a good amount of the time, one can likely find perfectionistic habits and thinking going along for the ride.

FACT

One way to strengthen spirituality if one is recovering from harmful early religious influences is to read dramatically different spiritual books. Volumes by Hafiz and Rumi are chock full of celebratory love from God, completely untainted with punitive judgment. If you are interested in this topic, you might want to sample *The Gift*, by Hafiz, and *The Illuminated*, by Rumi.

It takes effort to untangle a mature spiritual value system, but it is very much worth it. Keeping family harmony with previous generations who hold conservative, set views can be accomplished if one is not too argumentative or defensive about one's new direction. Ultimately, if you are comfortable with what you believe, those around you will likely be at ease as well. After all, God created flowers and animals in enormous variety. Why not paths to enlightenment? Perfectionism will be less troubling if one cultivates a belief in some sort of higher self that is nonjudgmental, loving, embracing, and noncritical.

Effects of the Media

The hype of advertising, emphasis on celebrity, and rampant consumerism all combine to make a person feel inadequate and insecure without the particular product being touted. Think about it. An ad for a great product flashes on the TV, perhaps a breath freshener or dental whitener. It is presented as if it will be the answer to all a person's relationship challenges. The weight control industry is quite prosperous, as 50 percent of the entire Western Hemisphere slowly becomes obese. In parts of the United States, plastic surgeons advertise in elegant, slick magazines, persuading the reader to consider just one more nip or tuck in order to be more perfect.

QUESTION

Is less than perfection actually more attractive and appealing?
The famous writer, Adrienne Rich, says that "our friends were not unearthly beautiful, nor spoke with tongues of gold; our lovers blundered now and again when we most sought perfection. . ." Do you love your friends because they are perfect? You probably love them because they are kind, generous, and fun to be around—sounds like Adrienne Rich was on to something!

The entire industry of advertising operates on the premise that consumers will perceive that they have a need or inadequacy that can be filled with the offered product or service. Eat this and you'll be satisfied! Drive this car and you will automatically attract a new mate! Go to this particular theme park and create happy family memories! Of course, in a fast-paced society, it is helpful to have numerous goods and services available to make life easier, but not to the point of never feeling like you have enough or are enough.

The effects of the media are especially strong if one is vulnerable for some reason, as many are, such as adolescents, women who hope to keep a fragile marriage together, persons in the entertainment industry, or people who are otherwise constantly in the public eye. Celebrity news is full of instances of anorectic spouses or girlfriends, hoping that the perfect weight will bring the attention wanted from the significant other. Actresses have been told by their agent or director that they need to lose ten pounds in order to have a chance at the coveted part. Dancers go without eating in order to look svelte in their roles and not be too heavily weighted while executing the demands of their roles.

This creeping perfectionism, the mask of appearance and image, requires huge expenditures of energy and money. It is, in fact, exhausting. Such effort is good for the gross national product, but is it good for self-esteem? Sometimes, perhaps, yes. If you think that you would be more confident in interviews with a new implant or teeth whitening session, then that is a possible direction toward self-esteem. If one imagines that a full mouth of replaced teeth and veneers are required even before the initial headshots are sent out, this could be perfectionism. The key is whether the aim is real or imaginary, attainable or always out of reach.

Adolescents are especially impressionable, imagining that the perfect case for their iPhone or great pair of boots will enhance their social status or even wrangle an invitation to a cool party. For decades, the tobacco industry preyed on youth, enticing them with interesting characters and jingles, offering the way to the "in" crowd and assured peer acceptance. Of course, the result was otherwise—possibly a shorter life, even the devastation of emphysema.

ALERT

The personal characteristic of never asking for help can be a route to isolation and unhappiness. Those who openly share their struggles and ask friends, family, and professionals for information and support are more connected socially and emotionally, creating a life of better overall health and well-being.

When one is tempted to go to the knockoff clothing store in search of the perfect item to ratchet up one's self-esteem, it might be more beneficial to call a friend, visit an elderly relative, or participate in useful volunteer work. Instead of a diminished bank account, appreciation is the result.

The media sometimes preys on young parents in insidious ways, pushing products and services to ensure that they will have perfect children. The answers to the parents' insecurities are offered in the form of DVDs to increase the child's intelligence, home-schooling programs to teach foreign languages, and every kind of educational learning, martial arts, music lessons, play environments, behavior modification for less-than-perfect children, and even medication, when all else seems to have failed. One probably knows consciously that it is not possible to buy confidence or perfection in whatever form one would desire in a child, but the corporations are uncanny in their ability to tap into that nagging belief that just this one time the right product or service will rectify the situation.

FACT

The Journal of Pediatrics reported a study of infants who watched the popular video series, Baby Einstein, actually regressed in their language development. Disney offered full refunds to those who bought the videos between 2004 and 2009. Apparently, even high quality recorded poetry and music is not a substitute for quality time with parents.

If one seems to be particularly susceptible to the media forces, it can be helpful to take a break from the various avenues that are customarily seen as entertainment. For example, a family could think of marvelous ways to interact without TV for an entire weekend. The overachiever could make a commitment to stay off of the Internet after 7:00 P.M. for a week. The zealous shopper could take a different route home from work, going to the gym instead of looking for perfect clothing.

You may notice as you work to counteract the effects of early programming and the conditioning of society, schools, and churches that your problems tend to recycle. The second spouse may be better than the first, but still there are the echoes of the nagging parents. One might expect personal growth to follow a steady positive trajectory, but it almost never happens that way.

It is tempting to berate oneself as errors and poor choices are repeated over and over again, but these patterns present an opportunity to learn, and eventually to teach others. Think of it as getting a graduate degree in a particularly annoying habit. You will be the expert in learning how not to do that, and you can assist others who have similar struggles.

Moving out of perfectionism is an example of slowly spiraling growth. Improvement may become apparent in one part of life but become slippery in another. Choices of husbands and boyfriends may improve, but a drastic sugar addiction takes over! You stop drowning your woes in sodas and ice cream, but start bouncing checks! It seems the nature of life is that there is always something to work on. The trick is to remain steady in the effort. Focus on the next thing, and the ultimate result will be visible progress.

CHAPTER 3

The Limiting Effects of Perfectionism

Extreme perfectionism is deadly. An extreme perfectionist is unable to determine priorities for a single day. Bills are ignored and mail is unopened because one cannot perfectly measure up to the task of handling life's administration. Suicide is considered rather than a career change. This extreme black-or-white mindset pushes out a wide range of gray options. One never goes out on a date because the wardrobe is lacking. Someone else might not earn a college degree because of the fear of being the wrong age or level of intelligence.

Getting Out of Negative Cycles

One technique for getting out of a negative trend is to stop everything and start over. You can start your day at any time, even if everything that went before was chaotic and distressing. If the day is a shambles because of traffic, unreasonable demands from work, or conflicting household schedules, stop everything and begin the day at that point, even if it is three o'clock in the afternoon. Perhaps, after quietly enjoying a nourishing snack (with the phone turned off), read something inspirational, do a few minutes of yoga, or walk for a while in someone's rose garden. Then, and only then, take the challenges one by one.

Take It to the Journal

Writing has long been known as a highly effective way of teasing out the wrinkles of the mind. If you can sit down with pen and page, the deeper issues will sometimes jump out and surprise you. The human mind has a way of layering information and beliefs so that some are deeply hidden. The act of writing, especially the old-fashioned way with pen and paper, will often allow the buried thought, feeling, or memory to emerge. If you're in a quandary about what to write, ask yourself some questions, such as "What is bothering me today?" "What do I want?" "What am I so angry about?" "What am I afraid of?" Often just getting started with any sentence will bring forth the stream of what needs to flow out. There may be a situation that needs attention. There may be an impossible circumstance that you have to walk away from. There may be deeply held goals, longings, and talents that are crying out for expression.

Spend Time with a Hobby

It may seem cliché to imagine that a hobby could eradicate your negative trend, but actually, it can. The brain can only do one thing at a time, and if you shift gears to something that you completely enjoy, the brain can no longer go along the negative track. It's a physical impossibility. Those thoughts and emotional trends are streams of electrical synapses, and once you get into a groove, the current tends to stay in that groove. It may seem like turning around the *Titanic* to go a different direction, but it certainly is worth it in order to change the tone of the day.

Do you have long-forgotten interests and hobbies that you enjoyed at a different stage of your life? Maybe you enjoy puzzles, the larger and more complicated, the better. Sitting down with the puzzle quiets the mind and allows different, healthier thoughts and emotions to come forth. Do you have a passion for dance? Turn on some music and dance, volunteer at a dance academy, or sign up for a hot salsa class. When your physical body is happy and expressive, it is impossible to feel negative.

ALERT

Watch out for the tendency to be perfectionistic and competitive even in hobbies and recreation. You do not have to be the best archer, golfer, chef, or karaoke diva. The point is to relax and enjoy life in a way that enhances your happiness, even for a few minutes. The pleasure will spill over into other aspects of life that might be challenging.

Increase Your Exercise

Studies show that regular exercise decreases the tendency toward depression. The chemistry of the body is arranged so that using the body, as it is intended, creates a release of dopamine, the happiness drug that is naturally manufactured in your brain. Doing something physical outside in the sun doubles the benefit, as the added melatonin makes you feel good.

The additional exercise may also improve the quality of your sleep, thereby improving the overall quality of your existence. It is difficult to feel negative if you are fit and well-rested, looking forward to the day. You may find that you need to increase the amount of sleep you get each night, perhaps cutting back on overworking or oversocializing.

Improve Your Nutrition

Entire books have been written about healthy nutrition, and you may want to investigate some of them in order to shift from negativity to a life that is more positive. It is quite difficult to change eating habits, as they are deeply set in one's culture and personal history. However, some foods tend to leave one with a heavy, lethargic feeling, more conducive to that creeping dark mood. Think of a family sitting around after Thanksgiving dinner. There's a reason that is not the customary diet every other day of the year.

Other foods make you feel sparkly and alive. It can be fun to browse through an outdoor farmers' market or upscale health food store, trying samples of unusual things. It can be fun to try a different restaurant to see what they offer and how you feel after eating it. You may discover that you love sushi, Mediterranean, vegan, or vegetarian!

Caffeine and sugar tend to create a temporary spike in the mood, making a person feel uplifted, but there may follow a mood crash, requiring more of the uplifting substance. A caffeine or sugar junkie can sometimes gradually diminish the amount of intake without having to endure terrible detox symptoms. It can be difficult to give up the pleasurable rituals around these favorites, but the reward is a lesser tendency to get lost in negative emotions.

And alcohol in moderation is better, of course, than drowning one's woes in drinking. The answer is not in the bottom of the glass.

Perfectionism, Procrastination, Paralysis

These three Ps can absolutely immobilize a person. They are intertwined in a tricky way that can baffle even the most intelligent mind. Imagine your highly capable, creative, and intelligent friend who wants to start a business. First he has to get his finances straightened out. Then he has to check all his social media sites. Then he has to help a friend move. Then he has to change the oil in the car. Then he has to clean out the garage. Each of these actions is completely forward-moving on their own, but the trend is that of a person who is putting off taking even the smallest action toward launching a new business. The result is remorse, self-criticism, and hopelessness.

If you work in one of the arts and tend to immobilize yourself with panic at the beginning of a project, called the blank canvas syndrome, just throw anything on the canvas to get some momentum going. Whatever you do at the beginning can be changed later, and using some energy to get going will bring other ideas to bear on the project. Make friends with those pesky Ps, so they don't stop you in your tracks. You have waited long enough to begin your novel. Open the document and give it a title. You have intended forever to catalog a large bin of family photographs. Take down the bin and start putting the photos in piles according to branch of the family and time period. It will take shape after you make the start.

Another Visit to Fear

Often it is not easy to see the underlying fear that motivates inaction or perfectionism. If one never takes the steps toward a desired goal, then one never has to experience the consequences, whether they are positive or turn out completely wrong. It is easier mentally to keep it in the abstract, the world of fantasy. You may have known people who have a goal that is actually a fantasy, the actual aim of their life that will be fulfilled when certain other circumstances have changed. One can bet that that fantasy will still be in place at the very end of life because it is a protection against the hard knocks that result from actually trying something different.

The underlying fear is often learned. Perhaps one grew up in a home where the children were criticized if they made a mess, brought home poor grades, made too much noise, or had emotional needs when the parents were too tired, preoccupied with their own lives, or simply incapable of being genuinely attentive to needy children. Parents often yell and lash out when they feel unable to meet the requirements of parenting. Those loud voices become deeply imbedded in the brain and may come out when a person wants to try something quite different. Go traveling in Europe with a backpack? "You'll be overcome by bandits!" Take a job in sales with a high income potential? "Sales is not a respectable profession! Stick with something we can be proud of!" Leave a relationship that has long since lost its bloom? "In our family we don't have any divorces! What will we tell the neighbors?!" These old voices haunt a person far into adulthood, especially when there's an inclination to try something new.

Breaking the Logjam

Paralysis results from an extreme amount of perfectionism and procrastination. At this extreme, it can be helpful to get assistance from others, whether a friend, a support group, or someone in the helping professions. For example, a woman experiences the sudden loss of a boyfriend. He died while visiting a relative in a distant state, surprisingly at a young age with no apparent underlying disease. The woman accepts the daily phone call of a friend who asks what she's going to do that day. The unbearable grief becomes a stream instead of a river, and eventually a trickle, because of the daily need to come up with a plan for the day.

Meeting with others who have similar difficulties can alleviate the isolation and self-recrimination involved with paralyzing perfectionism and procrastination. Others have found a way out, providing a hopeful example. Certain techniques are shared. Perhaps one calls a friend to make a verbal commitment to take a particular action.

Another decides to join a professional group that networks at regular intervals in order to learn how to create a website for a new business. Another decides to let go of a volunteer position that has become a hotbed of political backbiting, creating more time and energy for the direction of his or her true calling. These examples of others' actions and reconnection with humanity take away the luring sting of perpetual procrastination.

Willingness and Readiness

It is one thing to realize one's tendency to get lost in habits of perfection-ism, procrastination, and paralysis, but it is quite another to be willing to release those inclinations and embrace something different. This can seem as traumatic as welcoming a brain transplant, but it is the crux of the matter in terms of letting go of the harmful constraints of the three Ps. Imagine small steps that you are willing to take that are different. Imagine yourself free from the grip of unhealthy thinking. Accept that you are a free, fluid, flexible person, and move into that self with grace.

ESSENTIAL

Whenever you can, celebrate small victories in moving through the abyss of perfectionism. Mark each success with a pleasurable outing or a little treat for yourself. It can be private or shared, small or generous. Gold stars may be enough for one person, and another may desire a five-course dinner with a violin trio. The trick is to make it meaningful to you so you deeply feel the reward.

Substituting Other, More Satisfying Behaviors

Many times you can sidestep the crush of perfectionism by taking your inclination in a different direction. If you're inclined to overeat, prepare a delicious, attractively served meal for a friend. If you're apt to overshop, offer your services to a convalescing or elderly friend. Do their shopping instead of buying more of what you don't need. If you are a writer or editor who tends to agonize over your own projects, consider offering your editing skill to a friend who is finishing a novel. The momentum of extending your skills to others moves back into your own work in a positive way.

Pencil It In

If you tend to cram too many things into your planning calendar, try for a month or so writing your commitments in pencil. Erase things as you change your mind or see that you have included too many things in the day. Maybe you change your mind and don't find something as appealing as when you first had the idea. Erase it. That lunch date doesn't seem as purposeful, now that you think about it. Erase it. You will find yourself becoming less perfectionistic and more relaxed about time and how you use it. Always keep in mind that you are at the helm of your life. You're the decision-maker, and you don't need to spend a lot of energy defending your choices. This is definitely a time when action speaks louder than words.

Redirect Your Talents

Do you tend to compulsively clean your house? There are undoubtedly many people in your life who would tremendously value your skill and energy in sprucing up their place. It is much easier to be detached when it's not your own environment. You will probably find it easier to stop. Do you tend to obsessively wander around the Internet, looking up random topics? There are many who would be happy to have your research skill devoted to their travel plans, medical concerns, or possible schools for their son or daughter.

Marshal Your Marvelous Creativity

Everybody is creative in some way, even if we do live in a culture that tends to only notice the stars in various fields, making them the best and minimizing the creativity of the average person. You, dear reader, have marvelous things to contribute in your life. What do you do naturally? Maybe you make a wonderful homemade soup or play a mean riff on an electric guitar.

ESSENTIAL

Control can often be an illusion. It may seem like one has control or would like to have control. Giving up control and all pretense of control over others and outside circumstances brings enormous freedom. Suddenly there is more free time. People are more interesting. Even the sky is a brighter blue and music sounds more enchanting.

Maybe you are the happiest when you're doing the East Coast Swing to the oldies. Do you have a flair for reading stories to children or inventing stories off the cuff? Do you spontaneously interact with strangers using humor? Harness your talent and express it, even if it seems small in scale and not very important. It *is* important because it tempers that monster voice of perfectionism. No one cares what ingredients you add to the soup, as long as it tastes good, and no one cares what exact tone of modulation you use to read a story, because everyone around is enjoying it. That's the aim—joy for yourself and those you serve with your creativity.

The Perils of Black-and-White Thinking

Extremist ideas about others, life's challenges, and oneself can lead down a dangerous road of self-destruction and poor self-esteem. During the Asian economic crisis several years ago, it was heart-breaking to hear of family breadwinners who chose to jump from skyscrapers rather than try to determine a different way to support their families. Similar events occurred during the stock market crash of 1929.

FACT

One of the tenets of Buddhist thought is that suffering is caused by attachment to particular people, places, identities, situations, or even personal constructs. For example, believing that one will only be okay if a particular candidate wins a presidential election is not a good route to happiness. Having a good day only if it doesn't rain could set you up to have a terrible day. Believing that one can be happy only with one particular lover creates a fragile life. Imagine complete freedom from all the tethers that seem like security.

Imagine a situation where a woman overhears her employer talking on the phone about the status of her position. Her mind takes the essence of the conversation and strings it out to the max—she will be fired and have to file for bankruptcy the very next day! An aspiring guitar player masters his craft and does many presentable gigs around a major city, but at the realization that he will never be famous he wants to stop playing. What's the use?

Thinking in black and white disallows perfectionists to see possible options within the gray. There are always other choices, but the perfectionistic mind gyrates back and forth between extremes like a pendulum gone wild. Often the perspective of trusted people can point out the gray possibilities, assuring the friend or family member that all is well if neither the black or white extreme occurs.

What Can You Do Instead?

It helps to settle in with a sobering awareness of the effects of perfectionism. Journaling regularly or frequent conversations with a caring person can keep the results of perfectionism at the forefront of the mind and emotions. This can be painful, but it's not a permanent state of affairs. The awareness is the first step to getting a handle on that difficulty.

FACT

Often the simple act of cutting back on commitments will diminish the effects of perfectionism. Having fewer things to do will relax a person, and there is more time to enjoy them. Perfectionists tend to have an unrealistic view of time and what they can accomplish in a given amount of time. Less could turn out to be more.

Accepting the tendency toward perfectionism does a lot to diminish the yammering self-criticism. Some people tell the internal committee to be quiet for a while. If it's the voice of a critical parent, one can ask her to sit in the car while an important interview is going on. Everyone is flawed in some manner, and the varieties of characteristics add to the flavor of life. You might have a tendency toward perfectionism. You can laugh about it when you are thirty minutes early for an event. Laugh again when you ask your spouse one more time to look for the lint roller and go over your outfit that is already perfect.

Trying new actions after the awareness and acceptance stages will be a good final step to gaining some mastery over the destructive aspects of perfectionism. Perhaps you are strongly motivated to stop correcting your children, as you notice that they have become super sensitive and tend to tune you out. When you're about to criticize them, take a deep breath and wait. In the grand scheme of things, how important is the small thing you were going to bring up? In ten years will it matter? Instead, give your children a hug and tell them you love them.

ESSENTIAL

Putting off things that one enjoys indicates negative self-worth. Now is the best time to do that fun thing! You're absolutely worth it. Take the kids fishing, plan that trip to Paris, take some steps toward a different career, or make a serious commitment to a yoga and Pilates schedule. It can even be something small like seeing a movie you've had your eye on, or getting a pedicure at a fancy salon. You will feel great about yourself.

People who are inclined to work late at the office can designate one day that they absolutely will leave at five o'clock. They can then see how that feels and then add another day of leaving at five o'clock the following week. Those who tend to work on their laptops in bed can decide on a time to shut it down and read a book or chat with the spouse.

It is pleasurable to approach each day with the question, "What can I do today to make myself happy?" This will move a person toward activities that are closer to the heart, truer to the essence of the self. And isn't that the purpose of life—to express joy? Being a joyful presence among others is a powerful catalyst for cultural and societal change. It could begin with you, this very moment.

FACT

Talented inventors and creators, such as Socrates, Leonardo da Vinci, Benjamin Franklin, and Thomas Edison, were fearless in trying new things and solving practical societal problems. One doubts that they worried whether their creations were perfect. They were relentless in their motivation to constantly experiment in new directions.

Those who are considering a career change, but are fearful of not being competent in the new endeavor, can take on a small part-time volunteer effort to see how it feels. Is it satisfying? Is it fun? Perhaps a small freelance opportunity could give the dissatisfied person a taste of the new direction. The perfectionistic person tends to think that she has to have an MBA from Harvard and a long resume of accomplishments in the chosen field before going the new way. It simply is not true. Competence, willingness, and reliability are so much more important than any particular background.

The key is whether one is happy or unhappy with the direction chosen, moment by moment within each day. With a certain amount of objectivity, it is possible to catch oneself in the act of thinking and behaving perfectionistically. That split second pause can be the beginning of a new direction, even within a single day. One can pause and ask, "Is this next thing making me happy?" If not, think of something else. Pause and do nothing for awhile as the mind clears. Something truer to the self will emerge.

Do everything you can to acknowledge and celebrate small successes. It might be enjoyable to mark on a particular calendar the actions taken to overcome perfectionism and procrastination. Small actions count. Speak gently and kindly to yourself and note when you pause instead of launching into perfectionistic thinking or actions. A person doesn't become perfectionistic overnight, and reversing the trend will also take some time.

CHAPTER 4

The Difficulties of Perfectionism

The consequences of perfectionism are devastating to mental conditions, intimate and social relationships, and even one's physical health. The deep belief that one is never good enough counteracts happiness. Those who try to get along with perfectionistic mates or supervisors will attest to the lack of joy in such an endeavor (walking on eggshells or waiting for the next complaint is certainly no fun). And ulcers, high blood pressure, obesity, and diabetes are the dire results of compulsive worry or behavior.

Pressure to Be Perfect

Pressures to be a particular way or do certain things can come from within the person or from others. It takes some ongoing reflection and sensitivity to ignore the internal drive to perfection. It seems so normal, especially if the person has been that way for a lifetime! Bit by bit, however, honest self-inquiry will tease out the particular statements that seem to be running the show.

ALERT

Perfection is not necessarily a positive goal. Leonard Cohen says it this way, "Forget your perfect offering. There is a crack in everything; that's how the light gets in."

Learning to deflect outside criticisms or otherwise harmful forces will also take some practice. If your mother-in-law always has a sharp dig to make during the weekly phone conversation, a short bookend call to a friend before and after will diminish the pressures from your mother-in-law's comments.

It is possible to dramatically decrease one's susceptibility to the pressures of the media or culture at large by simply cutting down on the exposure to these pressures. For example, spending fewer hours on the Internet or watching TV will take some of the heat off. Replacing those hours with activities that are truly enjoyed rebuilds what is lost from too much conditioning by outside forces. If working with needlepoint or bargello while listening to Vivaldi is the ultimate form of relaxation, then that is what should be frequently woven into your schedule. A person's uniqueness often comes out when he or she remembers and actually does what is deeply pleasurable.

It helps to deliberately reframe your mindset regarding the attractiveness of perfection. What exactly will perfectionism accomplish? The love of a cherished someone? Fame and fortune? Actually, it is more than likely that you will be loved if you can laugh at and own your flawed actions and attributes. Comedians realize this and craft many of their jokes around their own foibles. And fame and fortune come as a result of sincere interest and service to others. Although one may work very hard to master the essentials of a profession, being perfect is not usually a part of the equation.

FACT

How many times did Thomas Edison fail in his quest to invent a light bulb? The story goes that he said, "I did not fail 1,000 times. I successfully discovered 1,000 ways not to create a light bulb." How many times did the Wright brothers attempt to fly a plane? Historical accounts range from four to dozens. Creating something important is a developmental process.

Dan Kuiper describes the cycle of perfectionism in his blog, *www.finding fatherslove.com*. Unrealistic expectations of the self inevitably lead to bad results. Blaming oneself for disappointing consequences, such as not making the big sale, getting a date with a coveted person, or winning love of one's parents, leads to procrastination, guilt, diminished confidence, and defensiveness. Productivity is lowered. One forces oneself to repeat the steps of the process, this time with higher standards of performance than they had before, and one is back to where they started, harboring unrealistic expectations of the self, leading to guaranteed negative results.

Investment in Identities

In the United States, there is a deep investment in the connection between identity and career. Very young children are asked what they want to be when they grow up. Almost every casual conversation between new acquaintances contains the question, "What do you do?" A quirky answer in the realm of, "I eat, I sleep, and I talk with my children," will cause puzzlement and discomfort. We are a society of human doings instead of human beings.

If one is deeply invested in a particular type of business or work and the economy shifts, it can become a personal crisis to adapt to something different and new. This process can be akin to a death or divorce, bringing up feelings of grief, hopelessness, and sorrow. A broader, balanced life, with many avenues for self-esteem, can provide a buffer. This buffer can greatly help a person during times of dramatic loss or change.

It can be interesting and informative to sit down with a journal or piece of blank paper and brainstorm answers to the question, "Who am I?" After the first predictable roles flow onto the page—parent, spouse, worker, career person—be open to what might come next. Perhaps you're a warrior, visionary, gatekeeper, whistleblower, joker, peacemaker, diplomat, scavenger, or inventor. Maybe you're a healer, designer, appreciator, gardener, listener, wizard, aerial artist, or keeper of the stories. None of these ideas are bound by gender or age, and they can be interpreted metaphorically rather than literally. You may strongly identify with something that is not usually what you think of as a part of your identity. This could be a direction to explore.

The Power of Choice

Although it doesn't seem like it when one is in the throes of perfectionism gridlock, one always has choices—always. For example, a woman who was threatened by a rapist calmly said to him, "Why would a handsome fellow such as you have to resort to these extreme measures?" They discussed the extremes of his motivation, and he went on his way. In another case, an elderly minister was accosted by a robber in an urban parking lot. The minister asked what the robber needed the money for, and when the man said that he was unable to pay his rent, the white-haired gentleman wrote out a check for two months' rent and gave it to the robber.

Given these examples, one can see that a large part of choice is keeping mental composure. Yes, emergencies happen. Attaining the mental discipline of poise under any circumstance brings freedom from perfectionism. Yes, the circumstances of external life may be chaotic, unpleasant, and fast-changing, but a calm, deliberate person can usually find something sensible to do, even under duress.

A compulsive overeater feels compelled to eat the juicy Danish, simply because it is sitting there on the plate, calling for attention. The usual reflex action is to reach for the Danish and eat it. Another choice would be to pause and ask the question, "Do I want the momentary pleasure of the Danish or a more slender body?" Sometimes the answer will go one way and sometimes another, but it is good to make the choice deliberate rather than automatic.

A college music student preparing for a solo recital is expected to practice four or five hours a day for several months. She receives an invitation to visit someone in another state during spring break and feels that it is an impossible situation. She wants to have the music perfectly prepared for the concert, only a few short months in the future. The perfectionistic choice would be to decline the invitation and practice daily during the spring break. Another choice would be to accept the invitation and study the music visually and mentally while vacationing, sitting down at various pianos that are available during her travels. It takes a relaxed, creative mind to see that there truly are other choices.

Sometimes a person is compulsively perfect in one aspect of life but not in another. A professional designer finds that she concentrates on each aspect of work to an extraordinary degree, but in her hobby of playing wind instruments in various community ensembles, she is relaxed and carefree, even if she is playing a solo. This freedom is the result of giving herself mental and psychological permission to be less than perfect. It is a hobby, so she doesn't feel so pressured to do it exactly right. She is more open to the pleasure of making music with others and enjoying the spirit of community while doing so.

React or Respond?

It seems that other people and outside circumstances are generally beyond your personal control, but it is important to remember that, almost always, you have the ability to respond to situations however you choose. For example, if a less-than-favorite relative calls with a litany of demands, one might react with an argument, only to repeat numerous other arguments that have happened over decades. Or one might respond with a neutral, "That's interesting. I'd never thought of it in quite that way." The other person will be dumbfounded and the argument is over.

Let It Go and Walk Away

Another interesting choice is simply not to engage and go the other direction. For example, if you get irate e-mails from friends or coworkers, hinting that a response is urgent, try just letting the e-mail sit there. No response can be a response. You can choose not to engage with something or someone that is not going to be beneficial to you. Even in political or social movements that you passionately endorse, there are some issues or problems that you can walk away from. You can't fight every battle yourself. Others can pick up the torch and do some of the campaigning.

Perhaps a friend or relative is mired in an impossible life situation. She is bullied at work and at home. It seems that there is no way out of either situation. You would like to be a savior and rectify the situations, but you find yourself tired after each long conversation. Unless you are a professional social worker, it is not up to you to rescue others. You can gather as much pertinent information as you feel inclined to do, give it to the person, and ask her to call you after she has made up her mind. You are available for her to check in with from time to time but unavailable as a daily therapist. Walking away will result in the person seeking out other internal and external resources, possibly resulting in solutions that you would have never considered.

Internal Locus of Control

Those who have a strong sense of motivation originating from within are said to have an internal locus of control. Such strength enables the individual to make choices and decisions based on what is truly inside instead of reacting to demands and stimuli coming from the outside. This sense of control is a big help when coping with perfectionism. If you are comfortable in your own skin, so to speak, advertising, culture, and the demands of other people will be less likely to cause behavior that is not in harmony with your personal values.

ALERT

Seeking approval is the antithesis of an internal locus of control. A person who is constantly thinking of ways to please others is likely a perfectionist imagining what is going to keep that other person in line. This can actually be a subtle form of manipulation and control. It would be best to turn that controlling, pleasing inclination back to the self.

An externally driven life would be the opposite. A life that is governed by style, fashion, the stock market, or the requests of family members (regardless of how outrageous) can possibly bring material comfort, but it is not a path to serenity or freedom from perfectionism.

Extremism in Hobbies or Volunteer Work

The perfectionist can create a nightmare for himself even when the activities are intended to be fun. Joining the gym evolves into becoming the most talented weightlifter in a fifty-mile radius and entering contests to show off the muscles. The weekend gardener enters the rose competition of the local charity and creates high levels of anxiety around whether she will win or not.

The talented elementary school gymnast starts working out after school with a coach, giving up her social life and family gatherings because she wants to enter the Olympics. This is not to say that goals are not important and that high achievements can be quite fulfilling, but is there happiness? Is there joy in the endeavor or agony? Is the person losing sleep and leading an unbalanced life? Sometimes young gymnasts, dancers, and skaters resort to bulimia in order to maintain the weight that is desired for the work. This, of course, is damaging to the body and is an example of perfectionism that is unhealthy in terms of the person's whole life.

In modern Western culture, higher education is highly revered. Those who find success in academia can take it to an extreme, becoming a professional student, earning degree after degree, much to the detriment of their bank account, often resulting in insurmountable student loans. Such an individual makes learning a hobby, which is innocent enough, but as a lifestyle, especially if the scholar is constantly seeking awards, mentions in all the right publications, and more and more honors along with the degrees, perfectionism is seen in all the diplomas.

What Can You Do Instead?

The limits of perfectionism are not a life sentence. They can be deeply imbedded in the personal psyche, but with effort, there is always a way out. One woman found that she could handle her perfectionism by having several creative projects going at once around the house. For her, it felt harmless to have all of these projects relatively unfinished, and she could pick up each one in turn, giving it some attention when she felt in the mood. These small projects gave her a way of balancing the demands of her business, and she didn't feel the need to make each hobby into another business.

It's a Wrap

In her book, *Refuse to Choose*, Barbara Sher suggests that people who feel the unreasonable need to complete each creative endeavor should wrap the project up in an incomplete form and label the project, including information about what has been completed and what could be done next. In this way, the individual can have many interests and approach life in a relaxed, exploratory way without feeling the perfectionistic drive to complete each and every project to the maximum potential. This frees the individual to choose other interests or to focus on those that are most satisfying.

Lower Your Expectations

It can be fun to try some things with no intention of reaching a mastery level. Maybe you have always been curious about Sufi dancing or modern dance. Seek out a group to explore those pursuits. Many people undertake learning a foreign language as adults with no aspiration of becoming fluent. They only have the goal of being able to communicate pleasantries with people they meet in their travels or neighbors who might be from other countries. Maybe there is a neighborhood French pastry shop with a cashier who would exchange a few words of French with you as you purchase your croissant. Such small, imperfect explorations can bring enormous pleasure into life. Others enjoy seeing people try things and screwing up. Everyone laughs at a bit of clownish self-deprecation.

Indulge the Senses

When you can, indulge in sensory luxury and pleasure. If you think you can't afford top-of-the-line indulgences, seek out free or nearly free experiences. Spend some time at the perfume counter in your favorite department store to see what is available. Enjoy a makeup consultation. Sometimes massage training programs are looking for subjects for the students to practice on. They need to accumulate hours toward accreditation and are happy to give you an almost professional massage, probably at no cost.

Mother Nature

Almost always, time in nature will relax a person and bring a new perspective. A day trip to an outdoor nature preserve brings new insight and focus. Walking on pine needles brings different sensations and thoughts compared to walking on a concrete sidewalk. Riding a horse creates a feeling of unity with other life forms, quite different from the experience of driving a car on the freeway. Observing wild deer in the redwoods brings awe and peace of mind.

New Friends

Even befriending people outside your age range can be fun and enlightening. Maybe there is a nearby seven-year-old who would like to tell you about her day at school and her American Girl collection. Maybe there is a ninety-year-old who has incredible stories to tell about World War II or the Great Depression. Such friendships are enormously enriching and take the focus off the inclination to be perfect. All that is required is to listen and be present for the other person, your new friend.

The Internet holds many possibilities for forums on various topics. It is easy to connect with people all over the world on any topic that is of mutual interest. One can develop real friendships in cyberspace, greatly enriching life for all involved. Many people have e-mail friendships that have been ongoing for years, sometimes resulting in travels and in-person visits.

Flex Your Decision-Making Muscle

Stop yourself when you see that you're second-guessing decisions you have already made—a college degree, choice of spouse, career path. Energy is wasted by going over these life choices.

Perfectionists agonize over decisions, whether small or large. What to prepare for dinner, which gift to get for a secretary. What is behind this anguish? The fear of failure. The wrong choice could jeopardize those important relationships, creating an insurmountable loss. A perfectionist's tendency toward insecurity creates self-doubt.

All you can do is bring everything you know to the situation and give it your very best guess. At some other time in the future, a new decision might be in order if new factors come to light. Alice Domar, author of the book, *Be Happy Without Being Perfect*, also suggests the following:

- Tell yourself that most of your decisions are good.
- Consider the pros and cons of any possible direction.
- Realize that what is right for others may not be right for you.
- You are in the best position to look out for your best interests.
- Changing old traditions can be fun.
- Set aside bias and discrimination toward others.
- Stop approval-seeking in its tracks.
- Adapt to unexpected circumstances.
- Forget about the Joneses and suit yourself.

ESSENTIAL

Accept the fact that every decision means the loss of possibility. This is the nature of life. Focusing on regret slows down the decision-making process. One can embrace the unknown and be accepting of good enough progress. Try to relax while making a decision, as anxiety gets in the way. In the grand scheme of things, many decisions are not especially important, such as which clothes to wear or what to order at the restaurant. Have you ever eaten with people who ask everyone in the group what they are going to have and then grill the long-suffering waiter about every offered dish? Try to spare your companions that waste of time.

Sometimes people who grow up with rigid, controlling parents marry someone who likes to make all the decisions in the family. If this is the case in your life, start asserting yourself in small ways, perhaps voicing a preference for a particular movie. Then progress beyond baby steps to choosing a vacation destination. Flexing the decision-making muscle makes it stronger, and those in your world will learn to respect it.

Sometimes it is impossible to know which one is actually preferred. In this case, there is nothing wrong with the old method of eeny, meeny, miny, mo. It could be that the result of this time-honored technique will show you that you really want the other one!

CHAPTER 5

The Concept of the Adult Child

The concept of the adult child arose in the 1980s with the work of John Bradshaw, Claudia Black, Robin Norwood, and Susan Forward. These self-help writers made Virginia Satir's work on family systems accessible to mass audiences, essentially becoming a part of the personal growth culture of the 1980s and early 1990s. Satir's work was based on that of Murray Bowen, the first researcher who observed that the difficulties of one family member dramatically impacted everyone in the family.

Effects of Alcoholism and Other Family Dysfunction

Entire books and university specialty programs, not to mention twelve-step programs and other self-help support groups, have arisen because of the effects of alcoholism on the family. Resources are listed in the Appendix if you would like to delve more deeply into this topic.

ALERT

Adult children of alcoholics tend to choose mates who are emotionally unavailable, as that was the tone in the childhood home. One becomes distressed that the addicted partner is not really tending to the relationship and tries harder and harder to win the person with increasingly perfect behavior.

It has only been as recent as the latter half of the twentieth century that professionals became aware that having an alcoholic, or some other dysfunction in the family, tremendously impacted the family as a whole. Prior to that time, difficult family members were more or less shrugged off as "the town drunk," "the gambler," or "the womanizer." However with the work of pioneers such as Virginia Satir and Murray Bowen, it has become common knowledge that dysfunction or substance abuse stresses the entire family, creating all sorts of compensating behaviors.

FACT

In one of his studies, Murray Bowen found that when a hospitalized schizophrenic daughter showed improvement and seemed able to start living a normal life, the mother became very uncomfortable and wanted the young woman to remain sick and hospitalized. This was the beginning of Bowen's insight that sickness is sometimes purposeful, and others adjust to it in ways that meets their own needs.

Growing up with alcoholism is far from relaxing, and sometimes the only result is a determination to survive. For example, a woman who grew up with alcoholic parents said that she would have been fine if she had been instantly self-supporting, right out of the womb. Children in such circumstances often take on adult responsibilities—cooking and doing housework for the family, caring for younger children, or even physically caring for their parents when they are drunk. Some adult children, especially in rural parts of the United States, have memories of driving the family car without a driver's license, as young as ten years old, going from bar to bar in a small town, looking for the errant parent.

The Paradox of Adult Children

The concept of adult children arose as professionals began to discover that adults who survived a very difficult family life in which there was alcohol, other substance abuse, incest, gambling, workaholism, excessive debt, pornography, religious addiction, or sex addiction tended to retain certain characteristics as grown adults. The Adult Children of Alcoholics, a twelve-step program that addresses these difficulties, lists the following characteristics:

- Fear of people and authority figures
- Approval seekers
- Frightened by angry people
- Become alcoholic or marry someone alcoholic or otherwise compulsive
- Overdeveloped sense of responsibility
- Feel guilty when standing up for oneself
- Addicted to excitement
- Confuse love with pity
- Repress feelings
- Low self-esteem
- Terrified of abandonment
- Have alcoholic characteristics, even without drinking
- Reactors rather than actors (having a knee-jerk reaction rather than a thoughtful response; being passive in life rather than action-oriented)

Adult children tend to be stuck in their emotional development, often recreating the original family dynamic in their personal lives or in the workplace. The unreasonable, demanding supervisor may be a repeat of an authority figure in childhood who was virtually unpleasable. The spouse may turn out to be an eerie twin of a narcissistic mother.

FACT

Adult children of alcoholics often have an overdeveloped sense of responsibility. They tend to take care of tasks that others do not want to do, look after family details, and carry out plans as promised. They are excellent workers. It is important to be aware of this trait, especially if it is excessive to the point of exhaustion. One has to be alert for those who might take advantage.

The emotions felt during conflict are often as strong as those of a child, creating a fearful, uneasy, restricted lifestyle. It is often a challenge to move out of such an uncomfortable state because it feels normal. This is the norm for a person who grew up in a tenuous, quickly shifting environment.

Adult children are often stuck in isolation, torn between silent despair and outward rebellion. Often lifelong indecision is a part of the picture, as no one ever taught the person how to intelligently make decisions. It is quite difficult to face the reality of childhood neglect and abuse. It is easier to hide in denial and exist in isolation and fantasy.

Adult children often do not have a strong sense of what is normal. The norm in the addicted household was skewed, but an intelligent, adaptive child will become adjusted to that and carry the off-center norm into his or her adult life. Sometimes one guesses what is normal from TV or movies. "That family seems to do things this way, so maybe I'll try that." Observant children learn from friends' families about how other people do things and try a little here and there. Many adult children have a sense that they are acting out a part in life, somewhat on the sidelines. It all seems like being an actor or actress because there was no solid grounding in the family foundation. To a certain extent, the technique of "acting as if" is a way to move into different areas of confidence and competence, but it can be grueling for the person who had no solid mentoring at all during the younger years. It becomes a full-time job to learn how to be a grownup.

Fine-Tuned Sensitivity

Children growing up in an alcoholic or otherwise dysfunctional home develop a fine-tuned sensitivity to the moods and actions of everyone in the household. They are little barometers, able to determine by a gesture when violence might erupt. They can tell by the tone of voice over the phone whether the parent has been drinking or not. If so, that might be a night that the children will prepare their own dinner, even if it is only a bowl of cereal. Individuals with this kind of background can become quite empathetic and skilled at negotiation as adults, if the emotional damage has been repaired through therapy or other focused work. It is not a negative trait to be keenly attuned to the nuances of other people.

Adult Children and Perfectionism

Children who survive a troubled family carry a deep fantasy that somehow they can correct the problem. If they only can achieve enough, be pretty enough, get a perfect batting record in baseball, or clean the house well enough, the family will become whole, loving, and well. One can see that this deeply imbedded drive would lead to perfectionism. The theme of trying over and over again to make it right for significant others becomes a hidden mantra of life, usually with disappointing results, as the original (and possibly current difficulties) are out of the control of the individual.

Birth Order

If you combine birth order, or how a person turns out according to family position, with the adult child/alcoholic family dynamic, one gets a very interesting pot of stew! Generally, oldest children turn out to be high achievers, good at leadership, and comfortable around adults of all kinds, as their first world as a child was that of adults.

First-Born Children

Oldest children in troubled families can sometimes turn out to be the most injured, as likely the parents were quite young and oblivious to their obsessive difficulties. In this case, the oldest adult child can be withdrawn from life and eventually work out a way to just get by without having to participate very much. He may retire at a young age or find a way for someone else to support him. He may feel troubled and ill at ease in social situations, feeling that he does not fit in anywhere. Much of his existence may be endured in isolation, even within a family.

Middle Children

Middle children are sometimes lost in the shuffle, as they never were top banana. The attention is usually on the older one, and later, the younger ones. Middle children learn to negotiate, play both sides of a situation, adapt, and accommodate. In a troubled, dysfunctional family, middle children can become martyrs, more or less selling their soul to the most difficult family member, trying for decades to make everything okay for that person.

FACT

Being a middle child does not always mean that a person is lost in the shuffle. Some famous middle children include people such as Charles Darwin, the Dalai Lama, John F. Kennedy, Abraham Lincoln, Ernest Hemingway, Warren Buffett, and Bill Gates. Middle children can also sometimes develop the skills of leadership and peacemaking.

This role can persist for a lifetime, and sometimes the individual sacrifices life goals and personal happiness in the futile effort to bring healing to the sick family member. The middle adult child hopes that one more birthday party or family celebration will at last make the difficult parent happy. One can squander time and money in the impossible quest, hoping that the effort will have a perfect result.

ESSENTIAL

Many adult children find that their core emotions are shame, guilt, self-hate, and a pervasive feeling of failure. These feelings must be faced, felt, and grieved before the adult child can find maturity and freedom.

Youngest Children

The youngest child is often a bit more carefree, as the parents' dysfunction may have matured and dissipated somewhat through the years. The youngest child has older siblings to help take care of her, and in some ways, take the heat off. She might be indulged and catered to, and in adult years can be charming and clownish. However, in youngest adult children from dysfunctional families there can be a gnawing personal emptiness, as if one never quite knew what was going on. She may marry inappropriately and not understand why she is unhappy.

She may be such an inveterate people pleaser that she has never truly explored her own interests, falling into jobs and pursuits that are lukewarm at best. She tries to be the perfect hostess, sibling, or daughter, but has a nagging feeling that she has missed the mark. The result can be a retreat into depression.

FACT

The experience of isolation is commonly felt in adult children. Such individuals learn that other people are not trustworthy and have a hard time developing emotionally intimate relationships, even personal friendships. This situation is exacerbated by the fact that the isolation is unrecognized. It is assumed that everyone else feels the same way.

The Only Child

The only child will have many of the same characteristics as the first-born child, turning out to be a rather adultlike, responsible high-achiever at a young age. However, if there is alcohol abuse or other severe family problems, the only child may find herself in an intense pressure cooker, unwittingly taking on the emotional work of maintaining the family equilibrium. Sometimes, troubled parents look to the child for love and solace, and the child has no choice but to deliver. Such an individual really has no opportunity to enjoy childhood, as there are jobs to do from the very early years onward.

Beware of the Internalized Critical Parent

Much of the drive toward perfectionism is an attempt to please the deeply imbedded voices of the authority figures from childhood. For example, a mother may have nagged about wearing muddy boots in the house or keeping one's clothes clean, even while playing in the sand box. A father may have shouted, "I'm not made of money!" when the child asked for lunch money, making him feel guilty for even the most basic of human needs. When a child is dependent upon dysfunctional people for survival, what they say is taken as truth. Those irrational criticisms can become an almost permanent part of a person's psyche, unless one takes the time to unravel and face them.

QUESTION

What is the origin of the term "critical parent"?
Eric Berne, the originator of transactional analysis theory, was one of the first to use this term. He described the characteristics of this internal voice as judgmental, punitive, patronizing, and posturing. The points mentioned are often either/or with no safe middle ground.

It takes effort to tease out those voices, as they seem real, true, and factual. Yes, money does not grow on trees, but does this mean that it is normal to be wracked with economic insecurity in even the best of times? Years of admonishments to "clean your plate because there are starving children in Ethiopia" makes it seem like a federal offense to leave unwanted food, perhaps leading to unnecessary overeating.

Superhero Parents

Adult children have an especially difficult time making their own way if their parents are famous. Would you want to trade places with Lisa Marie Presley, Chaz Bono, Sean Lennon, Ziggy Marley, Chelsea Clinton, or any of the Kennedys? When the parent has been perfect in some aspect of life, such as an extremely gifted achiever that has become a household name, the legacy wreaks with possibilities for the development of a perfectionistic child.

It is likely that to rise to those heights of recognition, the adult was, at times, preoccupied with his endeavors, perhaps neglecting the child's needs. The child may have had some dim awareness that the father was famous and known outside the home, but he may just want some quiet time with his daddy to play a game of Scrabble or share a sandwich. The lingering unmet needs combined with the impossibly long list of accomplishments and credits to the famous parent means that the young adult will always fall short, always. This is a difficult family history to overcome. The adult child is sometimes doomed to live in the shadow of the parent, even if there might be financial comfort. However, it is human to wish for a separate identity, one that is not defined in terms of someone else, even if that person is deeply loved. Some of these types of adult children move to a different country and go into a different type of work. Stella McCartney's fashion success is an example of this way of creating an individual life of her own, in spite of the renown of her father.

Arrested Development

Persons who come from troubled families often have difficulty maturing emotionally. It's no one's fault really. It is just the consequence of a family environment that focused on the needs of the addicted person to the detriment of other family members. The result is that adult children have the task of growing up when their chronological age would seem to indicate that they should already be grown up.

ESSENTIAL

Persons who become addicts, whether with a substance or a behavior, often stop growing emotionally at the point that the addiction began. For example, if a drinker started in high school, he will retain the emotional maturity of a teenager throughout his drinking years. If he chooses sobriety, he can start the maturing process from the adolescent level forward. This aspect of being stunted by any obsessive behavior can cause numerous relationship and life challenges.

If one is stuck in the past, dwelling on injustices and nursing resentments, it can be similar to imagining that the wake behind the boat is driving the boat. An impossibility! The wake follows the boat, but it doesn't propel the boat. The same is the case with various emotional rough spots having to do with personal history. It is useful to learn about each aspect, then take action to improve the situation.

Concept of the Inner Child

The idea of a buried inner child arose in the therapeutic community and in the popular culture in the 1980s. Although professionals before that time had a sense that parts of a self could be split off, especially when injured, the term "inner child" provided a way for people to talk about the idea of a younger self, one who was vulnerable, shattered, and scared.

FACT

Charles L. Whitfield, MD, was one of the first to coin the term "inner child." His book *Healing the Child Within* has become a classic in the field of psychology, especially within the specialties of recovery from substance abuse and other addictions.

Reparenting Oneself

Many people embrace the idea of reparenting oneself if the home background is one of emotional deprivation or even abuse. John Bradshaw's book, *Homecoming*, includes a very useful chart at the end of each stage of life with suggested activities for repairing the damage done at that particular age. For example, a person who experienced horrible deficits at the preschool age may enjoy simple walks outdoors, looking at plants and animals and naming them. No goal implied, just the fun of looking at interesting things.

A person who experienced deprivation and painful experiences during the elementary school age may enjoy mastering new skills, as developmentally that is what occurs in a healthy family. One might enjoy getting a new bicycle and riding along a boardwalk. It might be satisfying to learn inline skating or to try a part in community theater. Keeping the cautionary note in mind, it is not a goal to be perfect with these new pleasures but to fill in the missing aspects of child development that occurred because of family dysfunction.

Openness to love will be a part of the reparenting process. Love may, at first, feel dangerous, as in the dysfunctional home people lied about love, or their actions did not match the words. An irate parent may have beaten the child, saying, "I'm only doing this because I love you." However, courageously embracing love will open the doors to freedom, warmth, and wonders of the world outside the self-imposed walls of self-hate. Trust starts to build and a social web of support gradually forms. The warm affection that adult children feel for each other heals the old inner pain. These new friendships provide a framework where individuals mirror for one another the value and self-worth that was absent in the childhood home.

Adult children often enter adult life with little or no social skills. They need to learn the basics—how to introduce people to each other, how to make small talk at a gathering, how to make and receive phone calls, how to ask questions and listen to the answers. Situations with strong, safe parameters sometimes become a practice ground for social skills that eventually will become useful in the larger life outside the therapy session or support groups. Adult children need help in determining who is safe for a friend and who might not be.

Gratitude

When one embarks on looking at so much past history and repairing the psychological damage, it is tempting to simply be angry or depressed. The situation is unfair, and it is a lot of work to undergo a major overhaul of the human personality. Many people stay rageful or depressed throughout much of their lifetimes. However, this represents a loss in human potential and opportunities for a good life and deep happiness, regardless of the past.

ESSENTIAL

A useful tool for healing from the adult child syndrome is to write a daily gratitude list. It helps to shape perception so that, gradually, one starts to see all the incredible good in life, instead of all the problems. The list can include simple things, such as good weather, a full refrigerator, or a bright blue sky. This daily habit is useful for developing ongoing peace of mind.

A focus on gratitude pulls the person back into the present time and forces awareness. Some people make a daily grateful list as a part of their morning journaling. Such things as food, clothing, and shelter; cherished friends and family members, regardless of how quirky; good health; good weather; and opportunities for creative expression could fall on the list. It will be unique to each person and certainly change from day to day and year to year.

Impatience with Children

It is highly likely that the adult child will find it difficult to let her own child be a child. In the troubled family home, there was no room for the normal learning curve for life's necessary tasks. One had to instantly know how to do things, without asking for or receiving help and encouragement. It is a miracle that children can survive such a harsh environment, but often they do accommodate, sometimes with the help of teachers or other adults in the extended family.

Small children need a lot of time and repetition in order to learn the tasks of getting along in life. They need to learn how to tie their shoes, button and unbutton their clothing, put on rain boots, speak courteously to others, manage simple cooking tasks in the kitchen, and take care of their belongings. An adult child who becomes a parent may need help from older, mentor-type friends, as he or she does not have any internalized role model. The built-in knee-jerk reaction is one of impatience and intolerance for a child who is struggling to master something new. It takes a great deal of concentration to break the chain of the negative legacy, but it is worth it to raise children who do not become perfectionistic.

What Can You Do Instead?

The quagmire of adult childhood is not a place to live forever, merely an important place to visit on the journey of self-discovery. It might be tempting to retreat into the world of psych hospitals and social services, but, ultimately, this does not lead to a satisfying life.

ALERT

Watch for procrastination in work and recreational pursuits, even in managing money. Sometimes putting things off forever is a way to forestall the hidden voices of disapproval for not doing the task perfectly enough. If it's not done, ever, it can remain in the fantasy world of being perfect sometime in the future.

All kinds of resources are available to help the sincere person who wants to create a good life, regardless of past injuries. There are twelve-step programs to help with any addiction, many of which offer telephone meetings by conference calls. Such programs are virtually free, only asking for voluntary donations when the participant is able. The loving mentoring of a successfully recovering sponsor can offer consistency and gentle support.

Therapy can work wonders in moving through the feelings of a frustrated child. It is most helpful if the therapist has some understanding of the dynamics of alcoholism or other severe family dysfunction. During an initial consultation, it is permissible to ask questions about a counselor's experience with alcohol, domestic violence, incest, substance abuse, or whatever might be needed. Sometimes referrals from friends can reap good benefits with a therapist that might be compatible. For an adult child, this relationship could turn out to become his or her first trusting, intimate relationship.

For a time, it could be advisable to decrease work responsibilities, as the reparation work of adult children is an unpaid job in and of itself. Strong emotions will spill forward, and it might be difficult to concentrate on a full-time career while working on intense emotional issues. Some clients shift to part time or downsize their lives and take an easier job for a time. The actual work is looking into the subterranean regions of the psyche for a few months or years, and the day job supports that work. Now that is being a grownup!

ESSENTIAL

As one moves through the process of healing from childhood deprivation, it is helpful to know the now classic stages of grief. Watch for the stages of shock and denial, pain and guilt, anger and bargaining, depression and loneliness, reconstruction and integration, and, finally, hope and acceptance.

One has to be courageous about doing grief work. Much of what was lost in the process of becoming an adult child was the rightful experience of being a cherished child. As the layers are peeled away, one can be astonished at the volume of tears. This is a phase of thawing out. Strong emotions were repressed for years, even decades, as survival was the main goal. As life's circumstances become more secure, it is safe to feel those old emotions. It helps to have the companionship of people who understand and do not judge.

From time to time, take a break and notice beauty in your surroundings. Pull yourself into today, letting your mind rest from the intense work of examining the effects of growing up in a challenged family. A walk in a botanical garden or spending a holiday weekend in a woodland retreat will do wonders to heal your sensibilities. Take in cultural events in your community, including museums and festivals, and enjoy the interesting diversity of life. A stroll through a farmers' market is a feast for all the senses, especially if local musicians add their talents to the celebratory event of shopping for fresh foods. Appealing to your senses helps the injured, deprived aspects of one's background to heal.

An important element of adult child healing is to emotionally separate from the parents and even other family members. This does not mean to stop relating and loving them. It means that eventually one will be able to detach, break some of the umbilical cords, and develop a separate life with interests unique to the individual. There may be guilt and longing during the earlier phases of this work, but truer interests come to the forefront, replacing the perfectionistic tendencies to try to do everything correctly to remedy the problems of the family. This thankless task can be set aside, once and for all, and one finds the perfectionism receding.

Giving Up Addictions

In general, adult children find that they have used various addictive substances and behavior to mask intense feelings of sorrow, panic, and fear. Often these feelings are repressed, as they are too scary to face. Using legal substances, such as alcohol, sugar, nicotine, and caffeine, dulls the emotional pain, and survival is possible. Some adult children space out with various defenses of the mind. Perfectionism can be such a defense. Other ways might be projecting or rationalization, such as "It really wasn't that bad. I wasn't beaten every day."

ALERT

Suicide is a danger for adult children of alcoholics and other families with dysfunction. The combination of isolation, exhaustion from keeping defenses in place, and propensity to addictions of substance and behavior are cause for alert. The range of choices can seem quite narrow to an adult child. The world can seem like a dangerous and hostile place.

Some adult children become addicted to excitement. They use high levels of feeling to keep deeper fears at bay. Excitement could come from high-risk activities, such as adventure sports or racecar driving. It could come from gambling. It could come from choosing mates who are indulging in dangerous activities—substance abuse, crime, and other chaotic behavior. The adult child then becomes addicted to the other person.

At times the adult child may force the body to shut down and physically block out normal sensation. The mind can train the body to not feel normal pain. Intuition is lost, and a sort of physical armor makes it possible to exist in the world. The person may be overweight or just exhibit a stiff posture and gait.

Emotional sobriety—the creation of an inner and outer life characterized by serenity, poise, maturity, and acceptance—is a worthy goal for the adult child. Of course, some days can always seem better than others, but after the past is examined and released, even the worst of days are not as bad as the terror and violence of the childhood home. The individual learns to distinguish what is past and what is present and to become aware of personal triggers that send him or her zooming into past emotions. It might be the sound of a slammed door or a particular postural stance of a feared authority figure. Over time, the intensity of the triggers will lessen, becoming only the whisper of a memory. The current, present life moves more to the forefront as the old emotions recede.

Some adult children find that holidays have to be carefully managed. One adult child learned to hate Easter because her father gave up alcohol for Lent and then went on a huge bender on Easter day. Another associated Christmas with the violence of her alcoholic brother. One learns to make alternative plans—quiet, enjoyable times with safe, sane people. Associations with blood relatives may still be a part of holidays but in measured amounts. Many adult children insist on having their own transportation to and from family events and a stay in a hotel room rather than with a relative.

CHAPTER 6

The Relationship of Perfectionism to Obsessive-Compulsive Personality Disorder

Obsessive-Compulsive Personality Disorder (OCPD) is closely linked with perfectionism. The person suffering with this mindset seems to have a built-in "checker" that does not quit. One gets stuck on repetitive thoughts and behaviors that are difficult to halt, and then becomes fearful that if certain behaviors are not accomplished, something terrible will happen. Examples of OCPD thoughts and behaviors can include things like avoiding sharp corners on a table or repeatedly straightening pictures that are a millimeter off.

What Is Obsessive-Compulsive Personality Disorder?

Obsessive-compulsive personality disorder is characterized by a preoccupation with orderliness, perfectionism, and mental and interpersonal control. This disorder, which begins in early adult years, leaves little room for openness, flexibility, or satisfying efficiency in behaviors. Roots for the disorder are often found in some type of addiction in the childhood home. The child learned to try to be perfect to make the problem go away.

Characteristics of OCPD

People with this disorder create and follow extensive rules, attend to details and procedures, and compile lists and schedules that are beyond what the average person would consider, sometimes forgetting the original purpose of the act. Projects are often left unfinished because they cannot be perfect. Workers with this obsessive disorder may turn down invitations for a vacation because they believe they cannot take time away from their projects.

Hobbies and leisure pursuits are viewed as tasks instead of activities to enjoy. What should be seen as fun is overlaid with rules and perfectionistic procedures. It is difficult for the individual with obsessive-compulsive personality disorder to have fun.

Behaviors

Individuals with OCPD are overly critical of themselves and merciless in dealing with others. They have extremely high standards for themselves and other people. Humanitarian thinking does not enter into dealings with others—only rules and the correct procedures. Even if a friend or stranger needs help, the individual with obsessive-compulsive personality disorder will not offer it if it is against any rule.

Such rigidity translates to moral rules and values, with the individual seeing it as their duty to follow rules and help others to do so.

ALERT

If you tend toward obsessive-compulsive behavior, become aware of triggers that provoke obsessive-compulsive episodes. Try to mentally step back, pause, breathe, note the high emotions and rapid thinking, but sit still with it. Perhaps take a walk or a hot bubble bath. Let the aftermath of the trigger move through you with no action on your part. It will pass.

For example, if someone wants to borrow money for a hamburger, a person with OCPD would not loan any money because debt is harmful, and he or she would not think of the nutritional needs of the person.

No Arguing

Individuals with this disorder see themselves as right and feel that their way is the only way to do something. They steadfastly insist on their own views and do not delegate well to others, thinking that they are the only one who can do a good job. They are rarely open to the ideas of others. It is difficult for them to listen to others with genuine interest.

Decisions can be painstaking and very slow, sometimes resulting in nothing getting done. Perfectionism and procrastination are prevalent. Certain authority figures are given undue respect, and others not respected are ignored or resisted. This type of individual is not affectionate and does not easily give compliments. He has difficulty expressing feelings and may not even know what they are.

Resulting Difficulties

Persons with OCPD have trouble letting go of things because they believe they might need them in the future. This can run to the extreme of things seeming to take over a house with no room for a person to actually live. This type of individual may not want to be in intimate relationships with others because he does not understand and cannot negotiate the emotional terrain of closeness.

Obsessive-Compulsive Personality Disorder in the Family

The person with OCPD can be quite challenging to live with, as he obsessively pursues perfection. They want a perfect image of themselves and need everyone and everything around them to be well-ordered. Of course, this almost never happens, and the nearby family members suffer with the forcefulness of the OCPD person's aims.

People with OCPD can appear detached, emotionally cold, and machine-like, and they can be described as control freaks. However, they do have empathy for others. They can be deeply compassionate, especially toward others who do not see the need for control of the chaos around them.

ALERT

Watch for unconscious sabotage in yourself and others. Obsessive-compulsive persons may periodically derail something that is going perfectly well because of the need for chaos. It may be difficult to enjoy an ordinary day.

People with OCPD do form lasting personal relationships, although sometimes with challenges. Women with obsessive-compulsive personality disorder are more likely to seek help than are men.

You Can Choose Your Friends, But Not Family

Family relationships are usually not chosen, as one is born into a home with perhaps disordered parents and siblings who were already on the scene. In these relationships, one usually cannot just leave because it is unsatisfactory. A certain amount of accommodation has to occur with whoever is there, and only later during the adult years can one make independent choices regarding who is to be in one's household.

Growing up with OCPD family members can skew a child's perception of what is normal and acceptable. One can be inclined to make poor choices in life mates or career for lack of appropriate role modeling. Trust and self-esteem may suffer. If the family member with OCPD is a child, other siblings may resent the focus on that child and feel neglected. Parents of such a challenged child may become depleted, forgetting to take time out for themselves and to give quality time to the other children.

Case Study

David, a single man in his midforties, was interviewed for this book. He admits to being perfectionistic. He commented that he was fearful that he would not say completely accurate things about his condition and that a reader of the book might be somehow harmed if he didn't say things perfectly. It's going to be in print, and he would feel guilty if anything were misleading. Also, he related that he spent quite a bit of time deciding where to park his car so the degree of sunlight or shade would not harm his iPhone.

David's father was an engineer of German heritage, a recovered alcoholic who was particular in his life and work but not compulsively perfectionistic. He usually had a right way to do things.

His mother, who is still living, has had times of drinking and times of sobriety, as well as times of emotional stress and other times of what could be termed "emotional sobriety." His mother was very perfectionistic about clothing and about protecting a good image. Appearances were paramount for her and other members of the family.

David recalled that if he was not picked up at school at 3:00 P.M., his mother was probably going into a drinking bout and his father would come at around 5:00 P.M. The family shifted into a different routine for the duration of the mother's binge.

He was embarrassed by his mother's emotional outbursts and tried to create a composed, moderate emotional temperament for himself. The family home atmosphere was a mixture of loving, fun times and angry times surrounding his mother's drinking. His parents divorced when David was fifteen. He sought attention through negative actions up until about eighteen years of age and shifted into getting positive attention as a young adult.

David commented that he believes there are genetic components to perfectionism and also learned components. His mother's father was an engineer who built radio stations. He was precise and careful in his work, but always ended the day at 6:00 P.M. He drank an occasional beer, but there was no drinking to excess. David's grandmother, who is still living at ninety-four, was one of ten children. Her father drank, but stopped of his own accord, and one sibling became a drinker but eventually found sobriety.

David's obsessive-compulsive behaviors started during his teen years when he became excessively interested in hygiene. He did not want to contaminate various objects, such as his guitar. He began repeated hand washings during those years. There was always an undue concern for the care of clothing and material things, and he worked out excessively, wanting his body to be perfect. Any asymmetry of the pectoral muscles was disturbing to him. During his younger years, he had a sense that he wanted to master his own life, to be great at something.

When David was a young adult, he became obsessed with his eyesight. For twelve years he wanted desperately to have perfect eyesight and developed a repetitive habit of taking off his glasses and putting them back on. He read numerous books on healing vision and tried various methods of eye exercises. Finally a friend did an intervention and helped him to accept imperfect vision.

Perfectionism and obsessive behaviors continue to be a part of David's current life, although in a more moderate fashion. He uses his attention to detail in a positive way in his work, checking contracts until they are exactly right. His company has a good record because of his attention to detail. David is also a musician, sometimes doing hundreds of takes on a song. He has learned to practice a song twenty or thirty times and than let it go, revisiting it on another day, and miraculously it sounds fine! Good enough is acceptable.

David is still concerned with complete accuracy in his speech. He wants everything to be communicated in a perfect way so that nothing is misunderstood. He becomes anxious about any error in articulation or word choice. He ruminates over the ramifications of being misunderstood and causing harm in someone's life.

He has had ongoing bodily concerns, worrying about things that could go wrong and sometimes do go wrong. He is passionate about sharing his experience with others who might unnecessarily suffer with similar anguish, going in mental circles with obsessive thoughts.

He wonders if perfectionism is a way to keep the lid on feelings that are too difficult to face, and has a sense that changes in behavior can lead to moderation of uncomfortable emotions and thoughts.

Obsessive-Compulsive Personality Disorder in Yourself

A person with OCPD is not a relaxed, peaceful person. She believes that she is correct and has great difficulty allowing others to do things, as they might do something wrong. She is preoccupied with rules, lists, and accurate ways of performing tasks. She is not a generous soul, tending toward miserliness, and she tends to keep material things, even when they are no longer useful. She is worried and fearful much of the time.

Is This You?

One lives with secrecy, hoping that one's constructed self looks acceptable to the outer world. One has to work to maintain cursory relations with the store clerks, mail carrier, and tellers at the bank. Can they imagine the underlying fears, the constant anxiety? It seems to be written on the forehead.

FACT

Panic attacks can be a part of the obsessive-compulsive constellation. Brief, intense episodes of fear and terror are accompanied by physical symptoms of sweating, tremors, and accelerated heart rate.

Do you find yourself being obsessed with hygiene? Are you checking your receding hairline every day? Do you push others to adhere to your standards of perfection? Do you become mistrusting of others when you see that they do not adhere to your rules or standards?

There is usually an undercurrent of evaluation going at all times, a mental monologue about how one is doing in comparison to others and how others are doing in reference to one's internal standards and rules. The monologue isn't verbalized out loud, but it can be a time-consuming mental preoccupation, a deep habit that leaves one exhausted.

Conversational Style

You may find your conversations peppered with many "always" and "nevers." "Should" appears frequently in your dialogue with others. You quite painfully discover that you alienate others when you coldly cut them off as you decide they do not measure up to what you had in mind at an earlier stage in the relationship. You find yourself manipulating others, distorting information in order to get your way in an effort to feel secure and in control.

You may be angry a lot of the time with a pervasive feeling that you have been wronged, invalidated, and abused. Others do not seem to share this view of your situation, causing further anger. This anger can give your voice an edge that puts people off.

ALERT

Watch out for mood swings that have nothing to do with external circumstances. Efforts to moderate the world within do wonders for a more orderly, serene existence in the outer realm.

Relationships

You find that you withdraw from relationships when you expect to be hurt or rejected. The other person senses your withdrawal and criticizes. It seems you can't win in your efforts to be close to another.

You find that you describe much of your experience as a catastrophe and that others do not share your view. It is annoying when they do not share your sense of the importance of the situation. You participate in endless circular arguments about these things and endure enormous frustration when the other person will not come around to your point of view.

Others have told you that your early experiences, or current situation, were enough to cause serious difficulty, even posttraumatic stress disorder, but you continue to deny that anything really awful happened.

But It Seems So Important!

Individuals with OCPD have a sense of entitlement that is often inappropriate for the given circumstances. They want favorable treatment and living conditions at all times, even if unwarranted or unearned. Reason does not help, as the OCPD person feels she absolutely must have the corner office, the paid parking, and the expense account, regardless of the department budget. It seems like a personal right.

Material items that are valued can turn into hoarding, and no amount of arguing or persuasion can help the obsessive person see that the situation has deteriorated to one of cancelled house insurance, police visits to determine the health of animals and people living with you, and arguments about what is and is not a fire hazard. It's as if a lens has clouded the perception of the individual, making each item a treasure instead of fodder for the local landfill.

Urgency/Emergency

A person with OCPD describes every event as a histrionic catastrophe. It is difficult to have an ordinary, calm conversation with such an individual, as she keeps pulling the conversation back to the disastrous nature of the event, trying to pull in the emotional engagement of the other person. They overreact to bad news or disappointments, often failing to see underlying difficulties that contributed to the deterioration of the situation. Much of this effort is an attempt to draw attention to the self, as if they are starved and this is the only way to be fulfilled. It can be tiring for those who attempt to befriend such a person.

People with OCPD may bait others into viewing a situation according to their opinion or best interests. Such conversations will have little reciprocal give and take, and the other person may walk away feeling as if she has been hit by a hurricane. The agenda for the exchange was not laid out at the beginning but covertly sneaked in after the conversation had begun. Because of these many interpersonal difficulties, it is a challenge for the obsessive-compulsive individual to form and maintain friendships.

What Can You Do Instead?

Be alert for a no-win scenario when you are involved with someone with OCPD. Only two unattractive options are considered, with considerable force to choose one or the other. With help, you can possibly see other choices, even if they are quite different from what could have been imagined by the obsessive-compulsive disordered person.

Resist Objectifying Others

With effort, other people can be seen as true individuals rather than objects. And it is not necessary to hold others to criteria that they have not agreed upon. This pressure causes others to become angry, and they may leave the situation, resulting in continued loneliness.

Try direct requests rather than resorting to passive-aggressive manipulations. Most intelligent people are insulted by such tactics. If there is a situation where you are feeling pressured by guilt or some other less than upfront method, catch it in the bud and decide whether it is something that is of interest to you. A lengthy discussion is not necessary, just a direct statement or request about what you would like to see occur.

Be alert to projection, the act of attributing traits, motivations, or assumptions to another person when they are actually believed or felt within the originating individual. For example, a jealous boyfriend shouts at his girlfriend, "You knew you should not have worn that sexy dress to the party! It caught every guy's attention in the room and made me look like a fool!" The woman had no such intention. She simply selected an attractive dress to wear to a party. Let the other person be a real person with his or her own characteristics and beliefs, not what might have been projected upon him or her.

Resist Miserliness

Do your best to keep unnecessary material objects to a minimum in your home and office. Although it may seem dangerous to get rid of things that you might need in the future, it's quite possible that, when that future moment arrives, you will have what you need.

Make an effort to be a little more financially generous with yourself and others. Miserliness can be a type of hoarding, a behavior and attitude that makes close relationships with others difficult. Try to imagine that life is always going to be generous to you, and no matter what, you will be able to provide for yourself and those close to you.

Aim for acceptance in terms of values, morals, ethnicity, and lifestyle cherished by others. Perhaps others really know what is best for themselves, and you become a more attractive person when you are not molding and judging others, however silently within yourself.

FACT

Selective memory is a habit of retrieving only part of a relevant situation that substantiates a bias or a particular point of view. Such behavior causes arguments and is detrimental to loving relationships. No one likes to have a particular reality dictated to them.

Be Gentle and Kind—Toward Yourself!

Carve out time for leisure and important relationships, even when you have a lot of work to do. It could be that some relaxation will enhance your enjoyment of your career and lessen the overemphasis on impossibly perfect details.

Make an agreement with yourself to work on a task for a finite length of time. However it turns out at that point is good enough, even if it's not perfect. Perhaps hand it off to a coworker at that point for a few finishing touches. This will enable you to complete work without getting stuck in the paralysis of perfection. You can breathe easier and enjoy a more relaxed life.

Continue Therapy

David, the subject of the case study, continues to check in with a therapist who knows him well. There are few crises in his life these days, but he appreciates the support of someone who has been with him on his journey to overcome compulsive perfectionism.

ALERT

Perfection is not all that it is cracked up to be. Winston Churchill said it this way, "The human story does not always unfold like a mathematical calculation on the principle that two and two make four. Sometimes in life they make five or minus three; and sometimes the blackboard topples down in the middle of the sum and leaves the class in disorder and the pedagogue with a black eye." These types of incidents bring welcome comic relief.

CHAPTER 7

The Relationship of Perfectionism to Overeating and Other Eating Disorders

Researcher and writer Alice Domar noted in her book, *Be Happy Without Being Perfect*, that there are approximately 11 million people in the United States with the disorders of anorexia nervosa or bulimia nervosa. As a people, Americans are approaching the 50 percent mark in terms of obesity. Perfectionism plays a part in these tendencies. A study at the University of North Carolina at Chapel Hill identified obsessionality (the psychology term for perfectionism) as a behavior trait of overweight people. Many persons suffering from eating disorders have perfectionistic tendencies in terms of diet, exercise, body image, and weight.

Overeating in the Family

Certain variables in the family home can set up a propensity toward overeating at some point in adult life. Was there a tone of insecurity at home when you were young? One woman in a weight-control journaling group remembered that her alcoholic mother would sometimes fix dinner for her and sometimes not. On the afternoons she was passed out on the couch, the little girl would eat whatever she could find in the cupboards. This set up a dynamic of insecurity around food that was still present in her adult years. Nervously, she planned each meal and snack as if it might disappear.

Influences of the Mother

According to Domar, mothers who are perfectionistic and insecure have a detrimental effect on their daughters' body image. Such a mother may not feel attractive. She is never satisfied with herself or others, puts others down, never admits when she is wrong, is afraid of making mistakes, and is preoccupied with her weight and appearance.

ESSENTIAL

An interesting journal topic to explore is kitchen memories. Descriptions of those childhood scenes can sometimes unearth a surprising variety of memories and emotions. Who was there? Who did the cooking? What was the emotional tone? What are the fragrances? How do these almost forgotten associations influence you now?

This type of mother teaches insecurity to her daughters, increasing their risk for eating disorders. Mothers influence daughters' eating habits, body image, interest in physical activity, and level of self-esteem.

Scarcity Mentality

Were any of your relatives dramatically affected by the Great Depression or otherwise inclined to be excessively frugal? Scarcity around food or money can lend itself to overeating. If one is taught to waste not, want not, it ends up going to the waist. Overeating can be generational. If your parents were taught by their parents that food was hard to come by, those attitudes were part of the family legacy, which affects your shopping and food consumption today.

Incest

Were there conditions of incest in the home? In those types of families, layers of body fat can provide a protection against unwanted advances. Relationships are not a possibility because one does not feel attractive enough.

FACT

Research shows a relationship between incest and overeating. One may tend to bury unwanted memories and truths with the sedating aspects of food, or one may be tremendously dissatisfied with the physical body because it was misused by others. Or, if the child or youth felt physical pleasure during the unwanted act, there may be feelings of betrayal by the body, and often tremendous anger, which is numbed by consuming food.

Sex is not necessarily enjoyed if it was experienced under conditions of force at too young of an age for there to be mutual consent. Often persons with incest issues don't remember the incidents until they lose weight, as the memories are pushed underground. As the person gathers strength in the direction of having a positive body image, the psychological strength comes forward to handle the emotions of incest recovery work.

Anorexia and Control

Perfectionism in relation to eating disorders can become apparent in teenagers with anorexia when their behavior is about control. If the family environment is such that the family is constantly harping on the youngster, the one thing the child can control is what to eat and not eat. It can be the only out for a teenager who is controlled in every other aspect of life, sometimes bringing attention that is deeply desired, even if more negative than positive.

FACT

Anxiety can be a trigger for emotional eating, and food becomes a sedative rather than a source of nourishment. Reducing anxiety will reduce such triggered eating.

Criticism from other relatives dramatically impact a child and teenager. Were there instances in your childhood years when someone made comments about your weight? Were you measured, touched, or criticized in a bodily sense? This can set up hypersensitivity to weight-related topics in your adult years. One expects criticism, so it becomes internalized as a self-fulfilling prophecy.

Parental Example

Was food used as an abused substance by any of your parents, step-parents, or grandparents? A child who sees others binge learns that this is an acceptable way to pass time and endure difficult emotions. If weekend mornings included frosted doughnuts without fail and entertainment was eating in front of the TV, the die is cast in terms of the role of overeating for the children in the family.

What's Your Eating Style?

The following questions were developed by the National Eating Disorders Association to help people determine whether or not they have a problem with eating. An answer of "yes" to more than two could indicate the need for professional help in this area.

1. Do you prefer eating alone?
2. Do you constantly calculate calories?
3. Do you weigh yourself often?
4. Do you exercise because you have to, not because you want to?
5. Are you afraid of gaining weight?
6. Do you ever feel out of control when you are eating?

7. Do your eating patterns include extremes of dieting, food preferences, rituals, or secretive binging?
8. Has control over food become one of your primary concerns?
9. Do you feel guilty, disgusted, or ashamed after eating?
10. Do you worry about the size or shape of your body?
11. Do you feel as if your value is based on how you look and what you weigh?
12. Is it an emergency if you gain or lose a few pounds?

ALERT

Most people think that the biggest cause of death among persons with mental illness is suicide, but, in fact, more people die from eating disorders than other psychiatric illnesses. Exact figures are elusive because some die from associated disease, such as diabetes. One source estimates that 350,000 Americans die from eating disorders each year.

Numerous studies show a relationship between perfectionism and eating disorders. The person needs to feel perfect, and it comes out in exercise and eating patterns. Eating disorders are far more common than one would realize, and many are hidden, even from family and friends.

Usually the difficulty arises during the adolescent years, taking the form of starving, exercising excessively, forced vomiting, or purging with laxatives, enemas, or diuretics. Many people with eating difficulties look quite normal.

FACT

Victorian social thinking and art critic John Ruskin said, "All things are literally better, lovelier, and more beloved for the imperfections which have been divinely appointed."

How do you talk to yourself about your body and weight? Perfectionistic people may indulge in negative self-talk that could include the following statements.

- My thighs are too fat.
- My belly is too large.
- My weight is too high.
- I'm out of shape.
- My hair looks awful.
- I look ten years older than my actual age.
- My friends look better than I do.
- I'm disappointed in my body.
- I should be on a diet.
- I should have a higher sex drive.
- I am a pig.
- I am a failure, a disgusting mess.

Substitute a More Pleasurable Activity

Food is such a primitive pleasure that it may seem like a challenge to think of other things that could be as rewarding. It may take some time to trade food rewards for other rewards. It sometimes helps to think of other sensory rewards. Often participating in something highly creative will bring as much pleasure as favorite foods.

Black-and-White Extremes with Food

Do you find yourself going on an occasional or frequent fling of binging because you ruined the day with one extra snack? You may have added a pastry to your midmorning coffee break and find yourself bulldozing through the rest of the day with pizza, candy, cookies, chips, and a nighttime snack of ice cream out of the carton. The day was shot anyway and you can always start again tomorrow. Literally, this is true, but it is also possible to stop the trend after the first unneeded snack without going to the extremes of indulgence. Distorted thinking is behind such actions.

FACT

Magical thinking and fantasy can sometimes be a part of perfectionism and weight difficulties. "When I'm down to my perfect weight, I'll find the perfect mate." "After I've lost my extra twenty pounds, I will look for a more satisfying job." "Getting down to the weight I had as a newlywed will solve all my marriage problems." One knows subconsciously that these things are not true, but the emotions are too difficult to face. The result is inaction and stagnating in the status quo.

One can also find distorted thinking in regard to exercise. There is a hesitation to exercise for only ten minutes, as everyone knows that one has to exercise thirty minutes three times a week to have any effect. Any exercise is always better than none, and some studies reveal that short exercise sessions spaced throughout the day are quite effective in lowering blood pressure.

Set Some Realistic Goals

It probably is not possible to attain the appearance and weight you had in high school. A size four is not the answer to happiness. Sometimes it works well to set weight-loss goals in increments. A pound a week is usually manageable. One can reach a plateau, become comfortable with it, and then set a new goal.

Some people are less perfectionistic about weight loss if they stay off the scale and focus on forming different habits, especially with exercise. One can decide to use the stairs rather than the elevator and park at the edge of the parking lot instead of close to the office door.

Some individuals find that focusing on one health change at a time brings good long-term results. A person might decide not to eat while watching television, or to perhaps drink coffee black instead of with sugar and cream. It might be fun to take over the dog-walking responsibilities from the children and enjoy the added exercise. Physical exercise is a wonderful substitute for formerly unhealthy habits because it decreases stress, one of the triggers for excessive snacking.

Learning Some New Sensory Pleasures

If food is the only pleasure or the most significant sensory pleasure in life, it helps to learn others. Then excess food won't be missed so greatly. It can be a slow process, building a larger repertoire of things that are satisfying to the senses. Some of the senses may be dulled, due to years of overeating.

What about Sex?

Perfectionistic people assume that everyone is having mind-blowing sex, as the characters in popular media seem to have that sort of lifestyle. In actuality, the sex drive waxes and wanes throughout different stages of life. It is normal during times of great stress or crisis for the sex drive to be at almost zero. Having a baby, going through a job layoff, or divorce can plummet the libido.

Here are some thoughts for enjoying sex, even if you don't have a perfect body:

- The opposite sex does not need for you to look perfect in order to enjoy sex with you.
- More than likely, you are more critical of your appearance than your partner is.
- Actions are more important than appearance, and if you feel sexy, you will be sexy.
- Sometimes sex isn't perfect, but it still can be enormously enjoyable.
- Self-pleasuring is a good way to learn one's specific preferences for arousal, which then can be communicated to the partner.
- Read books to learn about sexuality, especially if you are in a category that is usually ignored (handicapped, ill, or aging). There are many useful, adaptive suggestions out there.
- Consider therapy if you feel intense shame, guilt, remorse, or fear around sexual activity.

Focus on the Aesthetics

Have you ever had an opportunity to eat while immersed in the rituals of another culture? Often the meals are pleasurable because of the beauty of the process, the dishes and utensils, or the marvelous companionship involved. For example, the Japanese tea ceremony is lengthy and quite beautiful, focusing on the honor of the person served. It is deeply satisfying to be the recipient in the ceremony. Korean people sometimes use communal service dishes, as each individual at the table takes bite-sized pieces with chopsticks. This custom adds to the fellowship of the occasion.

When you eat alone, set yourself a fine table, using attractive dishes, tablecloth, and cloth napkin. Caution yourself against rushing through to the end of the meal. The slower you savor the experience, the less you will be inclined to eat. If you eat alone in a restaurant, you can enjoy the ambiance of the place, the service, and the presence of others dining, even if you are not directly talking with them. Perhaps there is live music to add another layer of sensory delight.

When you cook at home, aim for a variety of colors, temperatures, and textures on your plate. Balance something mild with something a bit spicy. Bright colors are satisfying to the eye. Surprises in texture delight the senses involved in taste, chewing, and swallowing.

ALERT

Different cultures have different temperature and taste rhythms that are customary during a meal. If you're missing that "certain something" to satisfy yourself, it could be a part of that cultural meal rhythm. You can eat your way through a lot of food, trying to find the missing taste or satisfaction. In western European and American dinner culture, a meal usually concludes with a hot drink and something sweet. A cup of hot tea and a dish of sliced fresh fruit might be satisfying.

If a dish is meant to be hot, serve it hot, not lukewarm. Although it is natural to gravitate toward preferred favorites, it can be enjoyable to try something different. Kale chips are flavorful and healthy. Mediterranean figs wrapped in grape leaves are surprisingly delicious. It might be fun to partner with a friend to explore a different ethnic restaurant once a month and then try to prepare similar foods at home.

Pack Your Lunch

If too many business lunches are wrecking your waistline as well as your bank account, it makes sense to plan your food at home and take it to work. The old days of baloney sandwiches and potato chips are long gone. Carry over your new-found enjoyment of the aesthetics and ritual of food to your lunches at your desk. Focus on the same variety of color, texture, and temperature that you enjoy in your own home. Such self-care can provide you with a psychological lift that protects you from hitting the vending machines at 3:00 P.M. Broccoli florets, hummus with pita, and herbal tea nurture the spirit as well as the body.

Focus on Sharing Rather Than Eating

If you love to cook but want to minimize the risk of overeating your creations, it can be very enjoyable to prepare meals or snacks for others. The emphasis is on what they enjoy rather than what you're consuming. Most people love to be catered to in this way, as it recalls associations of being provided for in their mother's or grandmother's kitchen. You can solidify important relationships be preparing good food and serving it.

ESSENTIAL

Cooking as a creative act is marvelous. The cook will enjoy experimenting, and the praise will make the cook feel appreciated. One might develop a specialty of homemade breads, soups, or party cakes. Mistakes are almost always easily fixed. Too much seasoning is rectified by adding more flour or liquid, and the fallen cake layer can be propped up with toothpicks, marshmallows, or stiff frosting.

Others may be interested in learning cooking skills from you. When your kitchen, heart, and talents are open to others, everyone benefits, and the heat is off your perfectionistic tendencies with food and eating. The focus is on learning something new and enjoying the communal pleasures of preparing food together and having a friendly meal.

Explore Your Other Senses

It can be a wonderful adventure to fully indulge senses apart from taste. It might be interesting to get a season ticket to a symphony series or seek out strange music in hole-in-the wall venues. Imagine a stroll in the French Quarter of New Orleans. Although the wonderful food is certainly present, the focus is on the luscious sounds of Louisiana jazz. Be aware of summer music events in park bandstands or farmers' markets, often free.

Consider getting a museum membership so that you can satisfy your eye and intellect with marvelous creations arranged beautifully. A long visit to a museum store can be as fun as a stroll through a gallery, and you might find a journal that will make your self-exploration appealing rather than another chore.

If you have never considered massage as a typical part of your life, at least think about enjoying this type of attention occasionally. It can be interesting to sample the various modalities of bodywork. You might like Trager, Reiki, or heavy duty Swedish. Try a hot stone massage at least once. It can be great to work with a massage therapist who includes rituals from various healing cultures, incorporating fragrances and healing totems.

What Can You Do Instead?

It might be interesting to go on a media diet. Refuse television for a week or so and cut down on magazines. One has to realize that hundreds of people apply for positions in the public eye, and the producers choose the most attractive ones. Even models themselves say that when they see a perfectly airbrushed photo of themselves, they exclaim that they do not really look like that image. It helps to stay away from it for a while, as it is natural to compare oneself to those unrealistic portrayals of the human form.

Writer and researcher Alice Domar offers a checklist to determine whether an individual is preoccupied with an unrealistic body image. See what you think about these statements in connection to what you believe about yourself and your body:

- I am completely aware of what I eat.
- When I interact with a very attractive person, I feel inferior.

- I point out my flaws when I speak with others.
- I don't enjoy shopping because nothing looks good on me.
- People say I exercise too much.
- I don't believe people when they say I am attractive.
- I believe I should have self-control over what I eat.
- The thinner I am, the more I like myself.
- My anxieties about how I look interfere with my enjoyment of sex.
- I don't like seeing pictures of myself.
- I am disappointed with myself when I become sick.

These beliefs are clues to an unrealistic perception of one's physical self. Such attitudes can be corrected with effort. Try to catch yourself making silent, perfectionistic statements to yourself, and offer a loving comment instead.

Balance Solitary Eating with Social Meals

If you discover that most of your temptation to overeat comes when you are alone, remember to include others in your mealtimes. Such social experiences take away the taboo nature of food, as everyone is eating and enjoying themselves. The emphasis is on the conversation rather than the specific foods and how much is eaten. On the other hand, if you have found yourself with a crowd of friends or family members who tend to overeat as entertainment, you might want to pull away from that and eat alone some of the time, find more health-conscious eating buddies, or join the overeaters only for coffee.

What about Meals While Traveling?

What can you do when you travel, visiting family, friends, or a business conference? These occasions require some advance planning. For friends and family, you might offer to prepare some of the meals, so you have some of the decision-making control of what goes into the meal. Offer to shop with family members, and if necessary, fix your own meal apart from those indulging in the ten-cheese burritos. It doesn't hurt to pack along some of your healthy snacks in an airline carry-on tote. Often business conference chefs are quite able to prepare adaptive meals for special preferences—low sodium or fat, gluten free, vegan or vegetarian. Watch out for the temptation to eat whatever is available simply because it is covered by the expense account.

Remember Self-Forgiveness

Perfectionists with eating issues tend to be so very hard on themselves. One little mistake and the day is shot, offering an excuse to eat oneself through the remainder of the day, starting anew tomorrow. Instead, practice self-forgiveness with each infraction, regardless of how small or large. Think in terms of which foods are healthy for your body and which are unhealthy, making your eating decisions accordingly. Consider changing your self-talk, eliminating statements such as, "I was bad today" or "I was good today" in reference to whether you had a candy bar or a handful of baby carrot sticks. The things you eat do not define a person, and certainly no eating action makes an individual bad or good. Such extremism lends itself to many errors and too much self-criticism.

Substitute Exercise for Eating

In recent years exercise has taken so many specific new directions that it seems overwhelming to think of beginning a new physical habit. Pilates seems so challenging, and all of the participants already look perfect and do not even need the class. Yoga might require that you twist yourself into a pretzel while chanting "Om," and the hikers expect you to be able to walk five miles, which, of course, requires a whole different wardrobe of hiking gear.

FACT

A type of exercise that is enjoyed is more likely to be repeated, and ultimately embraced, as a longer-term part of a balanced life. It takes about twenty-one repetitions for a new activity to become a habit.

Such perfectionistic perceptions are apt to stop a person even before the new habit is begun because it seems to be a sheer impossibility. What about choosing something that you actually like to do? Remember some of your childhood pursuits when you did physical things for fun? Maybe you loved the roller rink. See if your local rink has an adult night and try it once. Did you enjoy a swim club? Look for a pool where you can pay as you go without committing yourself to a membership. Perhaps social dance is your forte. This type of event combines exercise with socializing, which is marvelous for your overall well-being.

A simple walk each day requires no special clothing or shoes and raises your mood while lowering your blood pressure. Even an outing of twenty minutes connects you with nature and your neighbors. It can be quite pleasurable to breathe deeply, lengthening the stride, and swinging your arms rhythmically.

Part of the challenge of managing perfectionism as an aspect of an overeating difficulty is that one has to eat in order to survive. It is not an obsessive substance such as alcohol or cigarettes, where one can completely eliminate the culprit and lead a normal life.

Consider Gardening

Working with your hands in the soil can be a soothing antidote for difficulties with eating issues. The elements of nature are calming, and you may attain a sense of peace as your actions increase the health and beauty of your flowers or homegrown herbs.

FACT

Famous transcendentalist Ralph Waldo Emerson said, "When I go into my garden with a spade, and dig a bed, I feel such an exhilaration and health that I discover that I have been defrauding myself all this time in letting others do for me what I should have done with my own hands."

It might be satisfying to cultivate your own vegetable garden, even if you only have a bit of balcony space in a busy urban environment. Raised beds are popular and do not require a lot of ground space, as you can walk around all four edges of the perimeter. Once you have tasted fresh tomatoes directly from the garden, you will wonder how you ever could eat supermarket tomatoes that have been trucked thousands of miles and artificially ripened.

Getting Support

As perfectionism in connection with eating is one of the more difficult obsessions to manage, it is helpful to seek out individuals and groups who can assist you along the way. If you work in an office where everyone heads for the break room and double chocolate brownies during the afternoon coffee break, you may want to find at least one coworker who will agree to keep you company as you forgo the temptations. It is difficult to endure the questions and teasing when one changes a habit. A walking buddy can give you attention as you share your successes and struggles, and someone you could check in with by phone when you are battling with a stressor.

The thriving weight-loss industry provides many choices in individual help and group offerings. It may take some time to investigate the many alternatives to see what feels comfortable in terms of the personal value system and pocketbook. Overeaters Anonymous is free, except for voluntary donations. There is no pressure to contribute. Weight Watchers has been thriving for decades, as its simple program teaches the participants new tastes and portion sizes compatible with a healthy weight.

CHAPTER 8

The Relationship of Perfectionism to Alcoholism

More is known about alcoholism than other addictions. Since the 1930s and the inception of the worldwide program of Alcoholics Anonymous, alcoholics, their friends and family, and professionals in the field of substance abuse continue to learn about the complex nature of what is now termed a disease, not a moral weakness. Alcoholism seems to be a multifaceted affliction, a disease with spiritual, emotional, mental, and physical components. Genetics play a role, as alcoholism moves through generations, more often affecting males. Perfectionism is an aspect of the puzzle of alcoholism.

Perspective of John Bradshaw's Work

John Bradshaw's books and seminars brought a greater understanding of alcoholism into public awareness. *On the Family, Healing the Shame That Binds You*, and *Homecoming* fully explore the far-reaching tentacles of the disease and how these tentacles damage each person in the family in ways that continue through adult life and generationally, unless each person makes the effort to heal. Numerous recovery programs and therapeutic specialties have arisen from this work in the 1980s.

Family Roles

Bradshaw makes it very clear that the presence of an addiction or major dysfunction in a family splinters the group, and each person is likely to take on a role so that the organism can function as a whole, though in a halting, faulty way. Some of the family roles he recognized are as follows:

1. Star or Hero

The Star in the alcoholic family is the high achiever who wins acclaim and some positive attention for the group. She is a straight-A student, known and respected in the community, and is likely multitalented, earning prizes, newspaper accounts, and praise from teachers. She is expected to be perfect because her job is so important.

Alcoholism is often connected with a child trauma. In the case of Bill Wilson, the founder of Alcoholics Anonymous, his parents separated and divorced. He lived with his grandparents while his mother went to medical school. He had little contact with either parent and became obsessed with learning to play the violin.

The family has so many difficulties that it is up to this one person to rectify the situation by creating something positive. If she fails, the family is likely to disintegrate, so there is a lot of pressure inherent in the situation. This role can be akin to that of a sacrificial lamb, as the role does not allow for self-inquiry, fooling around, or simply doing things because they bring joy. It is almost as if the whole purpose of the Star's existence is to make the family okay or to make the alcoholic okay. The personality has been seriously hijacked for other uses.

2. Clown

This role brings comic relief, as everyone in an alcoholic family is stressed, tired, worried, and frightened. The Clown, sometimes the youngest child, is finely attuned to the alcoholic dynamic and knows with perfect timing when to crack a joke or accidentally on purpose fall off a chair in order to dissipate tension and divert attention. Everyone in the family depends on this person to do this job without fail. It seems a pleasant enough role, but limiting in the long run. It is difficult for the family clown to be taken seriously in life. She may want to pursue a demanding profession, but the family minimizes her goals, seeing her only as the fluffy goof-off. This role can be taken into the work environment. The person might be very well liked, but her contributions to the board meeting are often restated by another person, who then takes credit for the idea. The Clown's input is likely to be trivialized both personally and professionally.

3. Rebel

This person in the alcoholic family is similar to the Star, but in a more negative way. Often a son, he draws attention away from the alcoholic problem by getting into trouble himself. He may be truant from school, in trouble with the law, dabble in illegal or legal substances, or involved in crime at a young age. He is perfect in his ability to create a diversion when the family is wound up to the breaking point over the difficulties caused by an alcoholic.

ALERT

Alcoholics sometimes create diversions with accusations and other provoking actions. This is to take the attention away from their drinking. It is wise not to react to such tactics, as the arguments are futile. If one topic isn't successful, the alcoholic will toss out another. It is best not to engage.

The Rebel's job is as important as any other role, and as with the other roles, it is limiting. He has difficulty growing out of the bad boy image, even when the role has been outgrown. He, like other members with a role, is denied the freedom to experiment, to try various ways of living and solving problems in order to meet his needs. Sometimes he drops out of school and is handicapped in choosing a career, turning to crime in adult years.

4. Lost Child

Like the family Hero, the Lost Child is very good. She wouldn't dream of doing anything wrong because she is frightened of losing approval. She is somewhat invisible, as everyone is too busy putting out other brush fires in order to see that she even has any needs. She is average in many ways—appearance, personality, and school achievement. Sometimes she brings attention to herself by becoming sick. This type of diversion is not criticized, as it seems genuinely out of her control. A major illness can momentarily shift the family focus to this Lost Child and give her some needed attention. Sometimes the Lost Child continues being sick in adult life, as illness is perceived at the subconscious level to bring rewards. Persons with chronic illnesses in adult years may find that the role brought attractive goodies in the alcoholic home. If one develops a perfectly horrible illness, there is even more attention.

Codependency

All the family members are codependent with one another. Each one is finely tuned to the other, as needs are anticipated without them being spoken and pressures are exerted to keep everyone in their proper place. Often the partner of the alcoholic is highly codependent, imagining that making circumstances perfect in some way will have an effect on whether or not the person drinks. This type of magical thinking is exhausting and time-consuming, as the codependent spouse works harder, keeps the career going, ensures the children are clean and well-behaved, and presents a good face to the community. The situation is rampant with perfectionism, as none of the actions have the desired effect. One tries harder but can never succeed. Perfectionism is a quite common trait for the spouse of an alcoholic.

Alcoholism in the Family

Alcoholism devastates family relationships. Each individual has deep, unmet needs but does not realize it. Family pressures keep the dirty laundry within the home, and secrets are locked into each person. Older children sometimes take over the cooking, childcare, and management of the household.

Alcoholics are sometimes the type of person who tried very hard to do something but failed. The deep remorse pushes the person toward the bottle. Jim Rubens, author of *OverSuccess: Healing the American Obsession with Wealth, Fame, Power, and Perfection*, found interesting connections between perfect success and addictions of various kinds. Those who lose out, such as chronic gamblers and failures in the work force, turn to smoking and alcohol. Rubens cites figures of one in four Americans who are clinically addicted to a substance or behavior, indeed a high cost to being a part of the rat race of high success.

On the other hand, highly recognized success is no guarantee against the grip of addictions. Those who make it in a visible way can become over-sensitized to perfection and seek an addictive outlet, such as pornography or cocaine. One sees examples of this in highly successful businesspeople or celebrities in the entertainment industry. To the outside viewer, it seems that such a high degree of success would bring enormous security and satisfaction, but sometimes the opposite is true. The material opulence brings forth deeper inner demons, and the tortured person seeks greater addictive experiences, such as hard drugs or dangerous behaviors. Rubens views the American culture's extreme emphasis on perfection and success as a costly social disease.

Denial, Not a River in Egypt

Sometimes called the elephant in the living room, denial is rampant in alcoholic homes. "The alcoholic is not drunk; she is taking a nap." "No, there wasn't a fight last night; you made that up." "I didn't go to your school play because you didn't tell me about it; how could you be so stupid?"

FACT

Alcoholics Anonymous (AA) was founded in Akron, Ohio, in 1935 by Bill Wilson and Dr. Bob Smith. Its structure of Twelve Steps and Twelve Traditions has helped millions of alcoholics to achieve and maintain sobriety and provided a model for numerous other twelve-step programs. The focus of AA is on service to other alcoholics, thus enabling each member to stay sober.

Each individual in the family used denial to protect themselves and each other from the surreal horror of the disease. Otherwise, nobody could function.

Denial is prevalent even among highly intelligent people when alcoholism is very much part of the picture. It can be a protection so that the person can function in life, as the bald truth would be devastating. The spouse may realize on some level that there will ultimately be a divorce but feels unable to accept the idea at the moment. Sometimes, with the help of therapy or recovery groups, the layers of resistance are peeled away, one at a time, generally at the pace that the person can accommodate new understandings.

Isolation

Each person is emotionally isolated, and the family as a whole is isolated from the community at large. The family members are ashamed about the alcoholism and its effects, often blaming themselves for the problem. It is common to see people in an alcoholic family spending large periods of time alone in separate rooms in the house, or in the same room but each plugged in to his own electronic device.

ESSENTIAL

A helpful antidote for isolation is performing a kind action for another person—assist an elderly person at the supermarket, chat with a neighbor about his prized tomatoes, or help with a favorite charitable organization. A library book sale can be a wonderful opportunity to strike up conversations with other book lovers.

Because they don't have the emotional support to help with their burdens, children in alcoholic families suffer socially. They realize that they are different, although may not be able to pinpoint exactly how. They are discouraged from bringing friends home from school, as they never know if the parent will be drunk or not. They are embarrassed by unpredictable violence or inappropriate verbal outbursts. Some clever children in these types of families form close alliances with teachers or parents of their friends, easing some of the discomfort of the alcoholic dynamic.

Distorted Communication

Communication in alcoholic families is badly distorted or nonexistent. Children are punished for speaking up about their wants and needs, so they learn not to have wants and needs. The exception to the pressures against honest talk is that the alcoholic generally has free rein, shouting orders to everyone or plaintively manipulating from the sick bed.

Alcoholism, sometimes termed an obsession of the mind, twists all channels of communication within the family. The alcoholic can be very quick to divert the attention from his wrongdoing, thus persuading others in the family to doubt their perceptions and blame themselves for being mistaken about something. What seems true is untrue, and something else is deemed to be true. This distortion afflicts even the brightest members of the alcoholic family and can take years of effort to untangle. Some people with alcoholic relatives who have died still feel unspoken directives from the grave.

FACT

Stepping Stones, the home of Bill Wilson and Lois Wilson in New York State, is now a museum where visitors can see materials from the early days of AA and Al-Anon, enjoy the simple household furnishings of the influential couple, and visit Bill's writing cabin, where he wrote some of the AA books. Lois Wilson was the founder of Al-Anon, the sister program to AA, which helps friends and families of alcoholics.

Persons in an alcoholic family are quick to accuse each other of wrongdoing, and no one is encouraged to own up to mistakes. Some people become very meek, while others mask their insecurities with bravado. Perfectionism and other addictions become rampant, but nobody speaks of them. All these outlets and compensations are necessary to keep the family functioning. These tendencies increase in intensity as the disease runs its course, becoming progressive with ensuing problems of greater severity.

Compulsivity and Perfectionism

Compulsivity and perfectionism go hand in hand with alcoholism and the effects on other family members. The alcoholic tends to be an all-or-nothing kind of person. If she has a bottle of wine, she is driven to finish it off. Alcoholics are famous for "closing the joint" when they are out enjoying themselves with other drinkers. Those close to the alcoholic become compulsive in other ways. Most of the addictions of substance and behavior find their roots in the presence of alcoholism or some other addiction in the childhood home. Those in the family try to cope with the distress of alcoholism in a variety of ways. They may become people pleasers, workaholics, overachievers, substance abusers, obsessed with fame and attractiveness, or struggle with money issues, such as debt or gambling.

ESSENTIAL

Anxiety drives perfectionism in the members of an alcoholic family. Each individual hopes that she can control the drinker's behavior by doing something perfectly. As this, of course, is never going to happen, the anxiety becomes a deeply ingrained motivator for behavior. Even though the cycle is futile, the individual keeps trying unless outside information and help is sought.

Self-esteem is lacking within each person in the family, although it will be difficult for the alcoholic to admit it. Sometimes basic survival needs are barely met, not to mention the niceties of emotional support and spiritual sustenance. Therapists' and psychiatrists' offices are filled with clients whose difficulties originated in alcoholic homes, as the effects touch every aspect of life far into adult years. As those effects are invisible, it takes tremendous tenacity to trace them.

One person may become a compulsive cleaner, never satisfied until there is not a spot of dust anywhere in the home. Another becomes obsessive-compulsive, washing his hands until they are raw. Another may become a dropout from society, as he could never measure up to the idea of what his parents expected in a son. He languishes in his camper home, randomly reading books, as life passes him by.

Compulsivity and perfectionism are present in persons with the disorders of narcissistic personality disorder and borderline personality disorder, both of which have possible roots in alcoholic or other dysfunctional homes. Narcissists demand that everyone cater to their needs and expectations, requiring that circumstances be perfect in order to feel okay. Borderline personality people have no tolerance for error, in themselves or others, creating a dynamic that is challenging in relationships at work and at home.

ESSENTIAL

Persons who come from alcoholic homes tend to select mates who are unavailable in some way, thus creating the drive to make things right in the family of origin. The workaholic spouse is too busy to spend time together, and the Internet-addicted partner has more important things to do than enjoy a romantic evening. One may develop a pattern of relationships with people who are already married. The neglected one tries very hard to win over the other, repeating the earlier pattern from the childhood home.

Alcoholics perhaps tend toward perfectionism because of low self-esteem themselves. They are quick to judge—especially others. In order to try to feel good about themselves, they want to be the smartest and the best at whatever they do. It is difficult for the alcoholic personality to accept the idea of being an equal among equals or to simply put in a day's ordinary work for an ordinary wage. Often very creative, charismatic people, they expect themselves and others to be at the top of their game at all times. The trait of perfectionism in alcoholics and those who are closely associated with them can be taxing and wearing. The challenge is that the alcoholic perfectionist sees this position as a good thing. She believes that at least one person has to do quality control in the situation.

Are You a Drinker?

Alcoholics Anonymous created a list of Twenty Questions, which is a quick checklist for possible alcoholism. The list, one of the early pieces of AA literature, is as follows:

1. Do you lose time from work due to drinking?
2. Is drinking making your home life unhappy?
3. Do you drink because you are shy with other people?
4. Is your drinking affecting your reputation?
5. Have you ever felt remorse after drinking?

FACT

As of January 2012, there were 114, 070 Alcoholics Anonymous groups worldwide with over 2,133,842 members. The organization is supported by the voluntary donations of members at the meetings.

6. Have you ever gotten into financial difficulties as a result of drinking?
7. Do you turn to lower companions and an inferior environment when drinking?
8. Does your drinking make you careless of your family's welfare?
9. Has your ambition decreased since drinking?
10. Do you crave a drink at a definite time?
11. Do you want a drink the next morning?
12. Does drinking cause you to have difficulty in sleeping?
13. Has your efficiency decreased since drinking?
14. Is drinking jeopardizing your job or business?
15. Do you drink to escape from worries or trouble?
16. Do you drink alone?
17. Have you ever had a complete loss of memory as a result of drinking?
18. Has your physician ever treated you for drinking?
19. Do you drink to build up your self-confidence?
20. Have you ever been to a hospital or institution because of drinking?

This list is often used in hospitals and recovery centers to determine whether the patient is possibly an alcoholic. Generally, within the recovery movement it is presumed the decision of the alcoholic to determine whether or not he is an alcoholic. He is apt to be quite resistant to others labeling him as such, an aspect of the trait of denial. The trait of defiance may become painfully evident with year after year of protest.

Learning Other Ways to Have Fun and Be with Others

After becoming sober, the alcoholic has to learn new ways to enjoy herself. While drinking, the alcohol was necessary to smooth over human interactions, as often the alcoholic is somewhat shy, feeling ill at ease in many social settings. With drink in hand, the person feels instantly charming, clever, and wise. It is quite difficult for alcoholics to give up the social crutch of liquor, as the uncomfortable emotions and lack of social skills have to be faced and overcome.

Those who become sober in the context of a recovery center or AA club will find many alcohol-free events to enjoy, especially around holiday weekends when alcoholics tend to feel vulnerable and at risk for drinking again. Often with the help of a sponsor, a person who mentors the newly sober alcoholic through the Twelve Steps and through life's various challenges, the alcoholic learns to enjoy new activities.

FACT

In the context of safe recovery settings, alcoholics can learn social skills—extending a hand to newcomers, introducing fellow members to each other, and getting together before and after meetings for extra fellowship. The comfort of commonality gives the newly sober individual a bit of courage in speaking to others without alcohol coursing through his or her veins.

Sometimes in the company of fellow sober people, the alcoholic travels, undertakes hobbies, or throws himself into service for the benefit of other new people in sobriety. Some become quite active on the speaker circuit, sharing their recovery stories with others who are just starting their journey.

Sex and Sobriety

Many alcoholics have never had sex without the relaxing effects of alcohol. Inhibitions are set aside with the help of the bottle. Within the context of sobriety, one has to learn new ways of being intimate, learning not to be afraid of strong, complex emotions that emerge in the close presence of another person. Some programs in recovery centers and some meetings with twelve-step programs focus on the challenges of intimacy after the effects of alcoholism, both for the alcoholic and those other members of the family who have been scarred by alcoholic behavior. Some speaker events spotlight the success of a particular couple who is doing well to maintain their relationship within the context of sobriety from alcohol. Others shun sex, finding it too frightening, focusing instead on the daily challenge of staying sober.

Redefinition of Fun

For the person who has only realized pleasure as being drunk and high, it is an enormous culture shock to imagine life without the chaos and commotion surrounding substance abuse. One has to find different friends, as their former buddies are still drunk and high. More time is available for leisure, as one is not preoccupied with getting the next drink and figuring out who is going to pay for it. The alcoholic may have to become accustomed to more subdued levels of pleasure—expressing oneself on the dance floor or going on a sober cruise. The wonders of nature may bring more appeal, as weekend binges are replaced with trips to the beach. Another may become fascinated with books and literacy, seeking out similar friends or online groups for the discussion of ideas found in books.

What Can You Do Instead?

For alcoholics, substituting one thing for another can be tricky, as it could veer into the dangerous thinking of substituting beer for hard drinks, drinking only on weekends, or only drinking at home. These are the attempts of the clever mind to sidestep the progressive nature of the disease. Unlike food as an addictive substance, alcohol has to be completely given up in order to arrest its devastating course. Abstinence means no alcohol. However, those in sobriety discover that there are other ways to enjoy life.

Sports and Fitness

After years of abuse to the body, it can be enjoyable to shift gears and cherish the miracle of the human form. Past enjoyable pursuits can be cultivated again—racquetball, swimming, horseback riding, or hiking. Many types of sports include the social aspects as well, counteracting the alcoholic's tendency to brood alone.

Service to Fellow AA Members

Service is generally a requirement of AA sponsors, but it can be up to the individual to take on more responsibility, possibly serving the fellowship above the group level. When one is a group representative at the state, national, or international level, the obsession with alcohol is redirected toward the good of the organization as a whole and its continued ability to assist others who are at a different stage of recovery.

FACT

Returning to school can be appealing to alcoholics after sobriety. Some find a satisfying niche in programs leading to certification as drug and alcohol counselors. Having "been there," the sober alcoholic can effectively combine service to others and a new, useful career.

There are panels to present in hospitals and institutions, and committees to plan numerous conventions. Whatever perfectionistic inclinations an alcoholic has can be focused on being friendly to every newcomer and offering coffee and snacks to each person who visits a convention hospitality room.

Healthy Relationships

Generally, alcoholics are advised to stay out of romantic relationships until after a year of sobriety. At some point, though, it can be appealing to form and maintain a close, sustained relationship with another person. If one is already in a relationship while achieving sobriety, one can recommit to that person in a healthy way, correcting problems that were a result of the drinking and emotional neglect.

ALERT

Sober alcoholics have to be constantly vigilant for the pattern of putting down one addiction only to pick up another—overeating, gambling, overworking, spending too much time on the Internet, or participating in compulsive relationships. In the early years of AA, the rooms were guaranteed to be filled with smoke, and sweet treats were, and still are, almost always available.

Many alcoholics find that they are most comfortable with a partner who has a similar path, someone from the same recovery program. Others prefer someone who has a commitment to another program, such as Al-Anon, which provides that family member with healthy tools for relating to an alcoholic. Both people in the relationship have to keep their perfectionistic traits in check, as the temptation is always there to criticize the other person. Those difficult characteristics are always easier to see in someone else!

Improvements in Career

Alcoholics are generally quite talented, capable people, and after the detrimental effects of daily drinking are removed, the attention can be shifted to meaningful work. Often there is a great deal of damage to repair—debts to be repaid and apologies to supervisors and clients. Or one might want to retool and move into a different type of work. Sometimes people in sales, for example, find that the temptations of expense accounts and life on the road are too great for a newly sober person. There is a bar in every hotel.

A life closer to home and familiar meetings contributes greater security. Traveling musicians often discover the same thing. The adulation of the concert audience creates a high that can lead to drinking and other excesses of all kinds, but the adulation of the toddler son at home has no such risk. The musician may shift to session work or special events, such as conventions or weddings, trading stability and sobriety for fame.

Often as an alcoholic becomes more emotionally mature, former ego-driven striving gives way to enjoyment of being a part of a group, whether family or the sober fellowship, and eventually the satisfactions of giving service to humanity as a whole, as directed by the Higher Self or the Divine Source, emerges as the main point of one's time on earth. It's never too late for a fresh start or even complete reinvention!

CHAPTER 9

The Relationship of Perfectionism to Other Addictions

Generally speaking, the United States is an addictive society. Numerous addictions are rampant, especially behavioral addictions. You may know highly addictive people without realizing it. Imagine a paralegal preparing yet one more brief before going home at 10:00 P.M., the philandering spouse making a rendezvous on the way home, the gambler losing his apartment because of his inability to use his rent money for its proper purpose, the scholar insisting upon being published in the best journals every year, and the shopper filling the emptiness she feels in her soul with a massive redecorating project while running up all the household department store accounts and credit cards. You probably know someone similar to those scenarios.

Workaholism

Workaholism is a difficult addiction to pin down. It's somewhat like overeating, as a person has to work in order to survive. Most people spend many hours a week and many years devoted to gainful employment. The American culture reveres the ethic of working hard, so it can be somewhat tricky determining if a person has gone over the line of working addictively to the detriment of other aspects of life.

Signs and Symptoms of Workaholism

David Krueger, MD, offers the following list of questions to determine whether or not workaholism is present:

- Is there a set time to end the work day and start the evening or weekend?
- Do phone calls, meetings, and projects erode leisure time?
- Do you have withdrawal symptoms when not working—anxiety or depression?
- Has someone close to you accused you of being a workaholic?
- Do you constantly second-guess decisions and replay conversations?
- Is your identity as a person deeply intertwined with your work? Do you not enjoy yourself when you're doing something not connected with work?
- Do you take work setbacks very personally?
- Do you try to prove your worth to yourself or someone else by working hard?
- Are you working to please someone else or to satisfy your own ideals?
- Is work an escape? From what?

There is nothing inherently wrong with being passionate about one's career, thoroughly enjoying almost every aspect of it. It becomes addictive when one cannot stop, feeling that there is some danger when not working. Workaholism is the inability to relax. Often, workaholics will feel a need to constantly engage with work. Workaholism interferes with satisfying functioning in other areas of life.

ALERT

Perfectionism in the office holds inherent dangers of job dissatisfaction, poor relations with coworkers, procrastination, poor performance reviews, and carrying stress home.

Workaholics may struggle with underlying feelings of inadequacy and poor self-esteem, trying desperately to fill in the gaps of a shaky identity. Workaholics even work while on vacation, doing deals over the cell phone or laptop while sitting next to a beautiful beach in an exotic location.

A workaholic's significant other eventually starts to complain, as the loved one is never truly available. It's as if work is the mistress and the worker is constantly on call, never giving quality attention to friendships, family, or other aspects of life such as community, health, and enjoyable hobbies. Resentment builds up, and at first it seems difficult to criticize the person who is working all the time as there is a tangible result—support of the family. But this comes at what price?

Alice Domar discusses several cognitive distortions of people who are perfectionists in their work. She calls these twisted, unrealistic ideas "auto-thoughts." Some examples are as follows:

1. I can't start the next project until my desk is clean.
2. Everyone else is more competent than I am.
3. If someone criticizes my work, I'm a failure.
4. I can't leave this job because there's nothing else for me out there.
5. My coworkers are stupid.
6. If I had a better boss, my life would be better. I would be happier.
7. If I take personal time off, I won't get a promotion.
8. I shouldn't ask for help.
9. I cannot ever fail.

It's quite likely that what you expect of yourself as a perfectionist is far more than what your manager or supervisor expects of you. Think about whether your time could be spent doing other things if you did "good enough" work and stopped there.

Sex Addiction

Dr. Patrick Carnes brought the field of sex addiction into public awareness in the 1990s with his landmark books *Out of the Shadows*, *The Betrayal Bond*, and later *In the Shadow of the Net*, and *Don't Call It Love*. His work with thousands of patients in clinics in Mississippi and Arizona brought greater understanding about this painful addiction.

What are the signs and symptoms of sex addiction? Following is a brief checklist:

1. Do you spend time thinking about sex when you don't want to?
2. Does paying for sex negatively impact your finances?
3. Do you regret the time and energy spent on sex and romance?
4. Do you buy or rent pornographic videos or magazines? Pay for phone sex?
5. Have you had sex with a prostitute or visited massage parlors for sex?
6. Do you stare at people in public, imagining having sex with them?
7. If married, have you had sex outside your relationship without your partner's knowledge?
8. Does your sexual activity put you at risk for disease, or loss of marriage or your job?
9. Do you feel guilty or depressed following your sexual activities?
10. Do you keep your sexual activities secret from family, friends, and coworkers?

These behaviors and feelings about the behaviors indicate a problem with sexual addiction. The sex addict feels unable to stop or control the behavior, in spite of the emotional, social, physical, or financial costs. They often do not have emotional ties to the partners sought for addictive sexual activity.

FACT

In the United States alone, it is estimated that there are more than 60 million men, women, and children involved in Internet pornography addiction. Pornography use has a dramatic impact on individual lives, families, and society as a whole.

Perfectionism seems to be at the core of most addictions, including sex addiction. The afflicted individual has a drive to seek the perfect experience at all costs, to be perfect in the eyes of the other or oneself, and if he or she does not measure up, there is always the next time. Sex addiction can be a way of compensating for a feeling of failure in other aspects of life. One didn't reach the heights of success imagined at an earlier age, so it is easy to retreat to the sex chat rooms on the Internet.

Gambling

In many ways gambling is a part of the historical fabric of the United States, embedded in the psyche as romantic images in Western saloons of the nineteenth century and backroom poker games in speakeasies during Prohibition. Like the cowboy, the gambler is an icon of masculine skill, with a bit of lure of danger.

The famous Shoshoni Native American woman Sacagawea, who accompanied Lewis and Clark on their great expedition across the country, was won by her first husband, Toussaint Charbonneau, in a gambling game.

As with the other behavioral addictions, when the activity takes over a person's life and one is unable to stop, the line has been crossed from pleasurable fun to problematic addiction. A well-situated attorney may keep his racetrack diversions secret from his wife, and she cannot figure out why they seem to never have any money, even though they both earn good salaries. A wealthy landowner plays the stock market every day, even though the bottom line shows a loss for several years in a row.

Signs of Gambling Addiction

Some signs of gambling addiction include:

1. Inability to stop gambling or cut back, even when losing.
2. Compulsive thinking about gambling.

3. Continued gambling despite loss of marriage, job, and good opportunities.
4. Needing more frequent and larger wagers in order to get the mental rush.
5. Withdrawal symptoms of irritability and depression when not gambling.
6. Using gambling for mood alteration and to attempt to win back losses.
7. Stealing and other fraudulent actions to get money for gambling.
8. Borrowing money in order to continue gambling.
9. Lying to friends and family about the extent of gambling.
10. Mood swings.

Like alcoholics, compulsive gamblers tend to show progression in their struggle with the grip of the addiction. Some suffer life-threatening situations before admitting that they have a problem. Others steadily deteriorate over a long period of time. Sometimes gambling runs in families with the children copying the patterns of gambling parents, or choosing a spouse with a gambling habit. One habitual sports bettor describes the childhood incident where he won $3.75 on a horse in the company of his father and uncle, setting a pattern that extended throughout his adult years.

What Does Research Say?

A study done at the University of Toronto and University of Winnipeg found a strong link between perfectionism and procrastination, with the added correlation of fear of failure. This could provide an explanation why the gambler continues, even with the losses piling up. There seems to be a belief that the next play will overcome all the losses and spare the person from failure. Other issues linked to problem gambling are poor impulse control, hoarding, and high-risk taking.

ESSENTIAL

Research studies show relationships between uses of substances and gambling activity. One shows that the brain activity of a cocaine user is similar to that of a gambler in the midst of gambling. Another shows that persons who smoke or use other substances addictively are more likely to continue gambling.

A Case Study

A middle-aged woman had a successful professional life as a researcher, but she was unable to maintain relationships with men because of her tendency to criticize and correct them. They would leave after a few months. During an outing to a casino with several girlfriends, the woman had her first experience of winning $200 at a slot machine. It seemed like heaven. She loved the trancelike feeling of sitting at the machine, hour after hour. The musical sounds of the machine calmed her perfectionistic thinking.

ALERT

Gambling is not age or gender specific. Some casinos in gambling towns have found that offering senior specialties will bring in large numbers of loyal customers. Loneliness seems to be a factor for isolated seniors, and having a meal and sitting at the machines or poker table becomes a habitual way to spend the afternoon and evening.

It was like a meditation that paid money. As months and years went by, she lost hundreds of dollars, but she also won many perks at the casino, such as a free hotel room and meals. One weekend she lost $2,000, and her stomach ulcer flared up. She was hospitalized and started treatment for chronic gambling. It was found that her perfectionism was the underlying difficulty that led to gambling. She attended Gamblers Anonymous, learned to be less critical of herself and others, eventually married, and was able to stay happily married.

Types of Gambling

There are many types of gambling, and compulsive gamblers generally settle on one that is most satisfying. The choices include casinos, sports betting, horse racing, video gambling, Internet gambling, playing the lottery, and playing the stock market. Often a person will go to extreme lengths in order to participate in his or her favorite form of gambling. Persons living in a rural area may drive hundreds of miles to a casino, even though the lottery is available at the corner convenience store.

Overachieving

In a success-driven society, it is difficult to imagine that achievement could be a negative thing, but for the person driven perfectionistically, overachievement can become a waking nightmare. This type of individual goes to the top at all costs, sometimes to the detriment of health, relationships, and self-respect. It would seem that one could glean a great deal of happiness from achievement, but sometimes the opposite occurs, and the final years of life are spent in isolation and tremendous loneliness.

Fame and Reclusiveness

One can see that high achievement does not necessarily bring happiness in the example of Howard Hughes, who only saw his physician and other paid companions during his final years, even buying the hotel he was living in so that he would not have to move out! Writer-anthropologist Carlos Castaneda was reclusive after his bestseller years, refusing interviews and public appearances, only leaving his house at night, and finally staying in his sickbed, only seeing his physician and long-term women friends. For years the public did not know if he was alive or dead as he studiously manipulated his image in the media, wanting to be seen in a positive light no matter what. He did not allow himself to be human.

Unrealistic Expectations

According to author Jim Rubens, younger Americans have become more and more self-entitled. They feel that they are very special and able to achieve whatever they imagine. The percentage of students who rank high on scales for narcissistic personality disorder has risen in recent decades, and if these students embrace the American value of meritocracy, they fully expect to be at the top of whatever field is chosen. This can be a brutal illusion, as there is only room for so many high achievers at the top of each profession. The illusion that everything is accessible is a unique part of the American culture that can bring a lot of pain and disillusionment.

Family History

The drive to achieve at all costs can sometimes be rooted in the family history. Something in the dynamic of the childhood home drives the person to keep repeating the effort to win, to please someone important, or to definitely make a mark. It often takes some psychological archeology to find the underpinnings of perfectionism in the high achiever. It is tricky because on the outside it seems a positive thing, resulting in a stellar resume that impresses everyone.

The Pressure to Succeed

American childhood is no longer a time of leisure and exploration. Time is strictly scheduled, especially for families in which both parents have full time jobs. Wealthy couples spend large amounts of money on special training and coaching for their children, as they have them already placed on a prestigious career track. There is enormous pressure to perform, and time dawdling in a creek or abandoned quarry is not a part of today's childhood.

ALERT

Parents are likely to have so little free time to spend with children that aspects of parenting are delegated. An enterprising person in New York, Aresh Mohit, has a thriving business teaching children how to ride a bicycle!

Millions of children compete in the National Spelling Bee. One father of a child who placed ninth in the competition paid 1,000 people to pray for his son. This was in addition to spending years with the boy, helping him to memorize root words in three languages. The 2002 documentary film, *Spellbound*, directed by Jeffrey Blitz, tells the story of the competition.

On the other end of the achievement scale, the top companies only recruit MBAs from Harvard, MIT, Stanford, Dartmouth, and other Ivy League schools. The most brilliant, charismatic candidates are chosen, and they are expected to work eighty-hour weeks. It seems that from preschool through the adult years, the pressure is on. Only perfection can prevail in this cultural mindset.

Overspending

Somewhat similar to gambling, the compulsion to shop combines perfectionistic tendencies with money. The answer to life's problems is found in the next department store or car dealership. It seems very rational and real to the shopper that the purchase will finally make the person happy. Interacting with clerks, cashiers, and salespeople eases loneliness and isolation, and there is a bit of power felt during the transaction of handing over a credit card or cash. Some compulsive shoppers prefer shopping over the Internet out of secrecy and shame.

Compulsive Debt

Often high levels of debt accrue when a person struggles with compulsivity about money. Some money addicts go in the complete opposite direction and are miserly in their dealings with money—not earning enough to take care of themselves and having great difficulty spending money on themselves, ignoring needs for medical or dental care, and not saving for retirement or other legitimate purposes.

Signs of Compulsive Debting

Debtors Anonymous, a twelve-step fellowship based on the model of Alcoholics Anonymous, offers the following checklist to determine whether or not a person is in trouble with money:

- Not knowing monthly balances, monthly expenses, interest fees, or contractual obligations.
- Borrowing items from others and not returning them.
- Poor savings habits, not being prepared for taxes and insurance payments.
- Compulsive shopping, leaving price tags on items and returning them later.
- Difficulty meeting one's basic financial needs.
- Feeling especially grownup when using a credit card.
- Bouncing checks, living in chaos and drama around money.
- Living on the edge, paycheck to paycheck, taking insurance risks.
- Embarrassed when discussing money.

- Using time inefficiently, taking jobs under one's education level.
- Unwilling to value oneself, living in self-imposed deprivation.
- Hope that someone will save the day, pick of the pieces of serious financial trouble.

Persons that have compulsive issues with money sometimes discover them after other addictions have been managed, finding that the core insecurities under other difficulties had to do with money.

Case Studies

According to Jim Rubens, author of *OverSuccess: Healing the American Obsession with Wealth, Fame, Power, and Perfection*, overspending is no laughing matter. He recounts the situation of Elizabeth Roch, a worker in an accounting firm, who was fired for embezzling $241,061 to support her shopping habit. A male addicted to shopping bought 2,000 wrenches. Uno Kim, a gambling addict now in jail, entered the home of two elderly people in New Hampshire, killed them, robbed them of $36,000 in cash, and drove to the Mohegan Sun casino.

What Can You Do Instead?

It is possible to moderate each of the behavioral addictions. In order to lead a more balanced life, consider the following suggestions.

But I'm Working!

Create a transition time at the end of each day. Think of it as a period at the end of a sentence. Close the computer, close the files, and turn off the cell phone. The work will still be there tomorrow.

Set a clear time that you will stop working, and honor your commitment to yourself. Remember that the mind works best if it has time for play or just goof off. Most creative ideas emerge when a person is relaxed. Shift that intense focus to your loved ones and reap the benefits of their presence. Learn to not take things personally, especially criticisms of something at work. What is said is only that person's opinion. It's not about you as an individual.

A recent study done by researchers at Harvard University and the University of Arizona found that men worry about three things every day—money, their job, and their family. Women worry about much more—money, their job, immediate family, extended family, friends, appearance of their home, etc. Women are spread much thinner.

Strive for a more reflective life. One does not have to go, go, go in order to be important in life. And watch for the tendency to talk about work excessively. Set down that burden and ask others how they are doing. What was eventful in their day? Personal relationships will rekindle with this type of attention.

On the job, take the advice of one supervisor who gently encouraged a perfectionistic employee, "Let it go. It's already quite good enough."

Don't lose sight of the big picture. It is not a catastrophe if your spouse neglects to write down one item in the check register.

Place a sign on your computer or work area that says, "Done is better than good." This will move you to completion on those days you're nitpicking over small details.

Instead of Addictive Sex

Therapy and support groups help enormously once the addiction is recognized. Any efforts toward building self-esteem will lessen the desire for the quick fix. Spending quality time with loved ones helps to build an inner reservoir of true caring, ultimately more satisfying than the fleeting pleasures of addictive sexual activity.

Taking time to learn about healthy sexuality lessens the inclination toward addiction. Twelve-step programs are available to help individuals with sex addiction, some offering meetings over the phone with conference calls.

It generally takes a significant event for a sex addict to admit that there is a problem—arrest, loss of a job or marriage—but when that occurs, the denial starts to lift, enabling the individual to face and remedy the problem.

Couples therapy can be beneficial if great care is taken to properly disclose information that impacts each of the individuals. The partner may elect to undergo individual therapy or a support group for partners of sex addicts.

Instead of Compulsive Gambling

Recovery programs specifically for gambling are relatively new. For example, one recovery center in Reno, Nevada, had, in recent years, several dozen beds for people overcoming drug and alcohol addictions, but only two beds for persons struggling with gambling. If formal intervention or therapy is undertaken, it generally is on an outpatient basis, often in conjunction with other addictions, especially to substances. Therapists with specialties in gambling are relatively scarce, and it would be good to ask many questions before undertaking extensive therapy with a counselor, learning first of the person's experience with chronic gambling.

FACT

Thought distortion is a part of the gambling dynamic. Otherwise highly intelligent and rational people develop systems that they believe will help them to win, such as counting wins per plays, switching machines and tables, or going with a seemingly intuitive hunch that it is going to be a winning night. Guidance and practice is needed to face and change such distorted thinking if it is deeply imbedded in the psyche.

As with the other addictions, replacing the activity with other pleasurable pursuits sometimes causes the gambling to recede. Physical exercise is especially good because it creates endorphins, the positive high that the brain interprets as satisfying as gambling.

Weekly support groups, whether twelve step or otherwise, help counteract the isolation and shame that surround the gambler's self-image. Friendships form, and the gambler has someone to check in with when lonely, agitated, and feeling on the brink of hitting the slots just one more time.

Gamblers often need help in structuring time, as during the gambling days and nights, long hours were spent in the casino or other gambling venue. An altered state of consciousness ensues and the concept of a normal day is eventually completely lost. Time management guidance—what to do with those days and nights—can ease withdrawal. Some gamblers become avid volunteers, doing service in community endeavors. Others go back to school and become addiction counselors, sometimes with a specialty in gambling addiction. It helps greatly to have one or more people who understand the details of the gamblers routine and triggers that may set off relapses. Such a trusting relationship can make the difference between a gambler who recovers and one who does not.

Moderation for Overachievers

Martha Beck, in her book, *The Joy Diet*, has interesting ideas for taming the person who strives too much. Some of her suggestions are as follows:

1. Spend a few minutes each day doing nothing. Be lazy; embrace your dark side, or what Beck calls "the lying scumbag." Love all parts of yourself.
2. Insist on fifteen minutes of privacy each day. Hang a sign on your door that says you are not to be disturbed. Get acquainted with your emotions and bodily sensations.
3. Find a place in nature and observe the natural elements. Let yourself relax.

ESSENTIAL

Lao Tzu, the father of Taoism, wrote about inner quietness in this poetic way: "We shape clay into a pot, but it is the emptiness inside that holds whatever we want."

4. Feast your senses on beautiful and luscious things. Take your time and be certain that each sensory feast is something you genuinely like.
5. Be very honest in your relationships. Ask yourself what you want in the relationship and if there are important things you are withholding from the other person.
6. Seek out opportunities to laugh. This could mean attending comedy clubs, browsing the humor section in the bookstore, or hanging out with your weirdest friend for a while.
7. Give yourself time to play and ask yourself honest questions about how your play relates with your work. Are they compatible? Are you doing what you want to do?

Writer Toni Raiten-D'Antonio offers wonderful suggestions for moderation in her book *The Velveteen Principles for Women*. Those who tend to overachieve can find solace in the following ideas:

1. Real people are ethical.
2. Real people are sexual.
3. Real people are generous and empathetic.
4. Real people are flexible, staying away from absolutes.
5. Real people face their emotions, even the dark unpleasant ones.
6. Real people are honest with themselves and others.
7. Real people know their mission in life and live it to the best of their abilities.

The overachiever with a perfectionistic drive can tone it down, with practice. It sometimes takes many attempts to change old habits, many of which have been refined for decades.

But There's a Sale This Weekend!

Perfectionists with money difficulties can turn their lives around with the help of others on the same path or a therapist who understands the core issue of anxiety around money. Some find that cutting up all the credit cards is a good start. Doing everything possible to live within one's means, however simple, will bring peace of mind. Keeping track of expenses and expenditures will bring clarity, and necessary adjustments become apparent. Lifelong dependencies on others can evolve into true self-sufficiency. Some find that they are interested in developing a new career or starting a business for themselves, something more enjoyable than the stressful work that led to unfortunate perfectionism.

Spiritual activities such as prayer, meditation, and meeting with like-minded friends help the stressed-out consumer feel more connected to a larger source, as if perhaps the weight of the world does not necessarily rest on one's shoulders after all.

CHAPTER 10

The Relationship of Perfectionism to Mental Illness

The early twenty-first century is a favorable time for those who struggle with mental illness or who find mental illness in their families. During even the not-too-distant past, there was considerable prejudice and misinformation about mental illness. Problems were hidden or spoken of in hushed tones, as if there were something shameful about emotional difficulties. Families accommodated difficult behavior as best they could, as help was not readily available. In these unfortunate situations, everyone in the family suffered.

Mental Illness in the Family

It is unknown whether there is a cause-and-effect relationship between mental illness and perfectionism or vice versa. What has been shown is that there is an overlap between the trait of perfectionism and such disorders as depression, anxiety, obsessive-compulsive disorder, and insomnia. Perfectionism is also linked with sexual dysfunction and relationship problems. Regardless of the exact cause, one mentally ill family member affects the entire family. Those tendrils of effects reach into every aspect of adult life, like the tenacious tentacles of an octopus.

Origins in the Childhood Home

Extremes of perfectionism seem to find their roots with parents who were critical and punitive. The child tries very hard to measure up, but the high standard demanded seems to be a moving target. The child wants so very much to please the authority figures, but it almost never happens. The seed of perfectionism is planted and grows out of control in the adult years.

Case Study

In 2009, the *Boston Globe* printed an article about a child, aged twelve, who had to stop doing homework with a pencil because he was tempted to erase whole lines of writing on his paper that were not perfect. Staff writer, Carey Goldberg, noted that he worked on individual letters, erasing over and over again until the paper was worn through. In a like manner, on tests, he would get stuck and spend an inordinate amount of time erasing marks that did not seem perfect. The child is now grown, working as a research coordinator, after receiving help to find the dividing line between high standards and mental distress. He is able to negotiate that terrain somewhat better for himself now. He was diagnosed with obsessive-compulsive disorder. His perfectionism caused him and his family great distress as he was growing up.

Identity and Mate Selection

Persons who grow up with a mentally ill parent have difficulty creating a well-balanced life for themselves, as that first important example becomes deeply imbedded in the psyche. If the mother struggles with narcissistic personality disorder, sons are likely to choose a mate with some kind of grave difficulty, and daughters will have a struggle creating a strong, solid life for themselves, as the illness seems intertwined with being female. They may understand rationally that the mother is a separate individual and there are possibly other ways of being, but emotionally it is as if the imprint sets a default mode, the place the daughter returns to during times of duress.

ESSENTIAL

Fragrance and tone of voice are powerful attractors. Be aware if you find the fragrances—alcohol, tobacco, a particular perfume or aftershave—of someone from the past who was problematic appealing. Do you gravitate to someone with a New York accent or a Southern drawl? Take note, remember those first associations, and decide if they really apply in the present time. It will be difficult, but you can reteach your olfactory and sound radar.

When there is any kind of mental illness in a parent, the children tend to choose partners with some kind of challenge, as it feels normal because of the childhood dynamic. There may be a perfectionistic drive to "help" the spouse or even to fix or cure them. This can lead to a lifetime of exhaustion and frustration. Usually helping the other person makes the helper weak and dependent, although at first she may seem appreciative.

Are You Mentally Ill?

Mental illness is a broad topic. It is often difficult to see problem traits within oneself. However the website *www.outofthefog.net* offers a list of traits that are helpful when observing others and even oneself. Some of the behavioral characteristics of mental illness noted are as follows:

1. Putting others down, constantly picking fights
2. Manufacturing chaos and catastrophes
3. Cruelty to animals
4. Dependency and depression

5. Stealing at home, taking things without permission
6. Emotional abuse and emotional blackmail; gaslighting

ALERT

Gaslighting is a term used to describe the behavior of systematically persuading another person to mistrust her perceptions. The word comes from the 1944 MGM movie, *Gaslight*, in which the female lead is made to feel crazy because the lights flicker and lower each day. Her husband says they do not.

7. Enmeshment and engulfment with others in the family (The person who is the target of someone else's enmeshment or engulfment may, at first, feel flattered. He calls several times a day and is interested in every nuance of your feelings and details of your day. Eventually the situation becomes cloying and you feel strangled, willing to do anything for some space and a breath of fresh air.)
8. Emptiness, feeling worthless
9. Frivolous litigation (suing people for sheer drama)
10. Hoovering (A term coming from a popular brand of vacuum cleaner, indicating a trait in which the person with the disorder temporarily improves her behavior and her significant other gets sucked back into a hopeful state regarding the relationship.)

Of course, a simple checklist is not enough to determine whether a person is mentally ill, but it can serve as a guide to prompt further investigation by professionals in the field, gathering a body of information over time. Mental illness is not an all or nothing situation. Conditions can occur along a continuum, with the individual exhibiting greater symptoms one day or one year and less at other times.

Just Act Normal

There is much to be said for the old adage of "acting as if." For example, if a person is extremely frightened of job interviews, one can act as if she is completely confident, able to have a pleasant conversation with the interviewer, fully expecting that she might get an offer because she believes that she has a lot to give to the employer. Often mentally ill persons are quite intelligent and have gathered a vast storehouse of information about what is normal from watching television and movies, noting what average people seem to say and do in a wide array of life situations. One can draw upon that knowledge and essentially become normal by acting in those learned ways.

It can be helpful to bookend calls to supportive friends when trying something new that seems especially daunting. Call or text the friend and tell him what you are about to do. Perform the new action, and then make a second call to the friend, telling him how it went. Bookending is a marvelous way to bolster confidence when embarking on new habits and behaviors.

ALERT

Presentation and confidence carry the day. In the film *Catch Me If You Can*, the main character, based on a true individual, was able to wend his way through many high-profile occupations without credentials, simply by procuring appropriate uniforms and learning the jargon of the profession.

Some challenged individuals find that pretending to be an actor or actress serves them well in challenging situations. For example, if a young man has tremendous fear of authority figures, especially the police because his abusive father was a law enforcement officer, when he is pulled over on the freeway, he can take a deep breath, imagine he's an actor playing a part in a film, and calmly answer the officer's questions.

Rethinking Relationship Choices

Selecting appropriate partners can be a landmine of difficulty for mentally ill persons. On the one hand, there is the deeply imbedded role model from the family of origin, which may have been less than ideal, and at the other extreme, one swears to find the perfect mate in order to overcome the past history. One can read all the self-help books and engage in years of therapy and still have trouble finding a suitable life partner. Couples therapy can offer wonderful support; it's like having a coach for your relationship.

Trial and Error

If one can view the dating game as an endeavor of trial and error, it can be somewhat fun. Each person and each relationship will have pros and cons, and it all is ultimately a learning process. It is not necessary to find the perfect spouse the first time out of the gate, especially if there is the handicap of a problematic background. One gentleman goes so far as to describe his first marriage as his "warm-up marriage," where he was somewhat learning the ropes, taking that knowledge into the next relationship.

Often one goes through various relationships working out the challenges of interacting with a partner who surprisingly seems just like the mother or father. It can be even humorous when the husband has traits identical to the mother, or the wife turns out to be the evil twin of an abusive father. Ultimately, tremendous healing can come from such discoveries. Don't view these experiences as failures. They are stepping stones to further knowledge about the self.

ESSENTIAL

Don't be too hard on yourself if a marriage or significant relationship ends. Keep in mind that the institution of marriage was designed centuries past when people hardly ever lived beyond forty years old. It is illogical to imagine that a partner selected at age eighteen will still be compatible at age fifty or sixty, although many couples do manage to negotiate many stages of individual and relationship change and growth.

There are bound to be wounds and a grieving period if a relationship does not work out as planned, but it does not have to immobilize a person for extended lengths of time. Sometimes there are buried feelings of abandonment left because of unresolved needs from the childhood home, and these can erupt when a relationship ends. The terror is that of a young child who is frightened about sheer survival, a most unpleasant sensation to feel as an adult. The feelings will pass, if the individual has the tenacity to feel them and not numb them out with a substance or addictive behavior. During these times of regression, try to be as gentle with yourself as you would be if you found a lost child at the airport.

Join Groups According to Your Interests

One way to find a compatible mate is to participate in various adult groups that run parallel to your deepest interests. Maybe you are passionate about travel. Attend travel lectures at the local travel specialty store. Travel as much as you can, even solo, and you will likely find interesting single people along the way.

If you are a book lover, join the local friends of the library association and mingle with other book people, organizing sales, or work in the used bookstore. Scan the local newspaper for events with a literary focus and go to them, even if you're confident the perfect person won't be there and you aren't perfect enough anyway. Just have fun, and view it as practice.

Maybe genealogy is your passion. Find others with a similar bent and compare notes. You can connect with people from lost branches of your family, forming significant friendships over the Internet. Some of these new friends may have a connection with someone who could be the perfect mate for you.

Groups that meet for an extended period of time work well for those who are quiet and rather slow to warm up to the opposite sex. A class at the local community college will enable you to observe others over a period of time, as will volunteer efforts along the line of whatever interests you. It is possible to get to know a person rather well just by observing and listening for a period of several weeks. You can decide whether the person might be a potential mate after you have seen plenty of positive qualities.

FACT

Although catering somewhat to the older crowd, Parents Without Partners is helpful to many singles who are looking for wholesome family activities. Long-term friendships form, perhaps with the possibility of romance and marriage. Through participation in events, it is possible to learn a person's character over time.

Keep in mind that some of your dating may feel odd and unnatural if you want to find a person who is quite different from your parents. That initial chemistry may not be there because you are wired in a different way, but over time, if there is emotional compatibility, the relationship can blossom.

Remember to ask questions about a person's relationship history. Are there patterns of brief, turbulent involvements? A lot of blame on the previous partner? Continuing anger? Red flags such as these can prevent you being a part of the person's story a couple of years in the future. Don't imagine for a minute that your caring for the individual will solve all those past problems. Instead, more than likely, over time those past difficulties will be 100 percent projected onto you. Keep looking.

Managing Anxiety

It can be very difficult to function in life while carrying a load of high anxiety. One loses sleep, avoids social situations, feels averse to risk of all kinds, and may spend a lot of money and mental energy in trying to manage the symptoms.

Detective Work

Look for the underlying emotions and beliefs in each situation that are terrifying you. Be patient with yourself, as such difficult parts of the psyche are often buried. Sit with your journal and jot down what you are feeling or what those voices are saying to you that makes a situation fraught with danger. Are you getting ready to board an airplane and you suddenly can't breathe normally and feel that you have to flee the airport? Patiently sit with that and see what comes to mind. Maybe you don't like confined spaces. Why would that be? Did your older brother trap you in a closet, tormenting you and ignoring your protests? Ease yourself through the memory of the past situation, and the present will become okay. Breathe. Don't forget to breathe, as the body relaxes with deep breathing.

A young woman, May, had nightmares that came with anxious emotions. She would wake up in a sweat and wonder where she was and what happened. The repetitious nightmares soon started to center around the theme of eyeballs. It was as if eyeballs were everywhere, looking at her and making her frightened. She talked about it with friends and was reassured that she was not crazy. Something would emerge. She remembered after a few months of the eyeball dreams and childlike terror that her brother and his buddies looked through a hole in the bathroom wall and watched her go to the bathroom. They sexually molested her, events that May had repressed until she was mature enough to handle the emotions accompanying such trauma. This example shows that such difficult emotions are there for a reason. Sitting with them until the root emerges takes tremendous personal courage, and the result is freedom.

Increase Your Exercise

As mentioned in other sections of the book, exercise contributes greatly to an overall sense of well-being. The body is meant to be used. If you can ramp up that use, doing things that you like to do, the anxiety lessens. That raw energy gets used up in a physical way so it doesn't hover around causing problems. Try swimming laps, walking around a track at a nearby school, bicycling, or dancing. Think about whether you want your exercise to be solitary or social and choose accordingly. You might like to have a running partner or, on the other hand, use the time in the outdoors to strengthen your spirituality. There is no one right way to do it. The main thing is to do physical things that you enjoy and repeat them enough that a positive habit is formed.

One Thing at a Time

It might seem superefficient to juggle the phone, the child, the stroller, the car keys, and the car, but this style does not create serenity. Deliberately do one thing at a time and see how your mind calms down. The brain can actually only handle one thing at a time, and the constant switching gears and direction contributes to anxiety. Breathe deeply, turn off the phone, take the child's hand, strap her into the car seat, load the stroller, and then check your keys before starting the car.

Multitasking is a popular skill these days, but it's to be avoided in your work or personal life if you wish to be free of anxiety. Doing several things at once is not something to aspire to, even if an attractive job description makes that a part of the package. Remember, you have a choice about what to do and how to live, and you don't have to be a multitasker to earn your living. Seek a situation where you can complete tasks from beginning to end, and there will be less anxiety.

What Can You Do Instead?

The National Alliance for the Mentally Ill (NAMI) has local and state branches, and often can refer you to other mental health organizations in a local or regional area. It is helpful to connect with others who have similar issues, especially the unique experience of growing up in a family with a mentally ill person.

Support groups such as Emotions Anonymous provide wonderful camaraderie and a structure for working through emotional difficulties. Strong friendships result from the common experience of having mental illness or surviving a family with a mentally ill member.

No Electronic Gadgets

Set aside a time period without a cell phone, e-mail, texting, or cruising the Internet. Turn off iTunes and just be. At first, see if you can manage an hour without anything digital. Then increase to two hours. Gradually increase your time away from gadgetry to see if you can enjoy an entire weekend of silence. You will discover new regions of your mind that are quite interesting. You may discover some freedom from perfectionism.

Spiritual Relief

Depending on how you conduct your spiritual life and the nature of any belief in a deity, you may find considerable solace by simply handing over stresses connected with perfectionism and mental illness to that higher source, however you envision it. You can sit quietly and imagine the negativity and fear flowing out with each breath. You can develop personal rituals that make sense to you, such as writing down difficult memories, entrenched habits, and stressful interpersonal situations on paper; burn them; and bury them as you say a few calming words. Truly imagine those past memories and emotions going into the earth completely apart from you from this moment forward.

CHAPTER 11

Perfectionism and Disease

It may be alarming to think of perfectionism actually having a part in health or illness, but it might possibly be the case. Think of the examphobic college student who breaks out in hives and cannot hold down food during finals week. She drinks coffee and suffers through insomnia, only barely able to take tests because her hands quiver so relentlessly. Consider the long-suffering person who had been the Rock of Gibraltar for her family, making herself the last priority, succumbing to cancer. Consider the patriarchs of the ice cream company Baskin Robbins who suffered early deaths from diabetes, inspiring the son, John Robbins, to teach consumers about health and a sane lifestyle.

But Isn't It about Germs?

It has been said that medicine is both an art and a science, but in Western cultures in recent decades, the trend has been skewed toward the scientific aspects of the human body. Alternative approaches abound, but they are usually not covered by insurance and are thus affordable only by those at the top of the earning curve.

ESSENTIAL

On a historical note, nurses who worked during war efforts found that patients healed better if caretakers washed their hands before working with their charges. Soon hand washing became a necessary part of preparation, and sterile, antiseptic conditions are required by the law and policing health organizations.

During past centuries it was not known that diseases were connected with microbes in the water, and, horrifying by today's standards, sewers were not kept separate from drinking or cooking water. Gradually, however, these pieces of relevancy came to light, and conventional standards of cleanliness have more or less eradicated some of the old diseases. Standard inoculations for children have also eradicated many common diseases.

Don't Germs Cause Illness?

According to the Mayo Clinic, germs are another name for bacteria, of which only 1 percent are harmful. Bacteria are in the human body all the time, and most of them are beneficial to the bodily processes. How then did germs get such bad press? Health education in elementary schools stresses the scary, negative aspects of germs, and children think of them as something like cooties, that you want to avoid at all costs. The importance of these little microbes gets blown out of proportion, and perhaps an obsessive hand-washing habit ensues.

Germophobia

Germophobes are people with obsessive-compulsive disorder who are compelled to act out rituals of washing and cleaning, sometimes to the detriment of being able to live a normal life, although many are able to contain the condition and function fairly well.

FACT

Mysophobia is another term for germophobia with Greek word components of "uncleanliness," and "fear." It is a pathological fear of contamination. Some observers think the United States has become obsessed with germs because hand sanitizers and alcohol handwipes are available at the entrance of every store and supermarket. Are we paranoid?

Some famous germophobes are the late Howard Hughes and Saddam Hussein, who reportedly sometimes required visitors to disrobe and wash with antiseptic solution. Comedian Howie Mandel makes fun of his germophobia in his routines, but he studiously does not shake hands with people, regardless of the situation.

Perfectionism and Stress

According to Alice Domar, perfectionists have a higher risk of various stress-related illnesses. For example, perfectionists are more vulnerable than the average person to postpartum depression, popularly called "the baby blues." A new mother expects that she will be the perfect mother and is discouraged when she feels tired and afraid. She assumes that she should instantly know how to breastfeed, change the baby, and understand the meaning of the baby's fussing.

As mentioned earlier in the book, perfectionism is a factor in the stress of eating disorders, as people have unrealistically high expectations of themselves in terms of appearance, exercise, and weight. They count calories, purge, and overexercise in order to attain a mythical perfect weight.

Stress and Illness

Stress is a factor in insomnia and gastrointestinal disorders. A mother with a special needs child is so stressed about the extra attention her child needs that she develops irritable bowel syndrome and temporomandibular joint disorder (TMJ).

Stress and Cancer

Cancer is a complex disease, and it is the focus of immense research and effort in the medical community. It is feared because of its unpredictability and how it seems to take on a life of its own once it starts. Even people with outwardly healthy lifestyles can find themselves with cancer. For example, a young graduate student, a vegan marathon runner and nonsmoker, came down with cancer. Though she was outwardly healthy, she was also perfectionistic about her body, doing everything possible to maintain a perfect weight and shape.

Some researchers found that those who were diagnosed with cancer often had a traumatic life experience within the previous eighteen months before the diagnosis—loss of a friend, severe financial loss, victim of a crime, or other life trauma. It is unknown exactly why some people's bodies succumb to cancer but not others. Some say it has to do with personal resiliency and the ability to remain relaxed under most conditions.

One survivor of breast cancer admitted that before cancer she was a perfectionist, but she changed her ways after overcoming her illness. She left dishes in the sink, left junk in the garage, and let the laundry go undone. Her children learned to make their own lunches, and she focused on rest and healing. She found that having cancer reduced her perfectionism. She now relaxes more, makes time for her children, knits, exercises, and cherishes times of doing nothing.

Perfectionistic people tend to blame themselves for the illness, going over past occurrences trying to determine where they went wrong. Perfectionists are accustomed to blaming themselves for everything, so why not cancer? Getting this dreaded disease seems like a breach of trust, and the entire house of cards falls down. How could everything go wrong when they did everything right? Perfectionists hate to be out of control, and cancer is definitely a situation where one has little control.

Dr. Harold Benjamin notes that prolonged stress is a component in the development of cancer. The body adapts to what is perceived as a worrisome situation with the fight-or-flight response, and it makes no difference whether the situation is real or imaginary, physical or emotional. The prolonged adaptation breaks down the normal bodily processes, and unhealthy cells have more room to maneuver. The healthy cells, which are the protectors, are unable to do their work, and the unhealthy cells start to reproduce.

More Research on Disease and Stress

Researcher and author Jim Rubens reports that a feeling of social defeat (not achieving as much as hoped for) leads to stress and disease. It has been found that when a person feels threatened, adrenaline surges, followed by cortisol, the master stress hormone. Cortisol is a steroid that helps people get through stressful situations, but it also suppresses the immune system, possibly to help reduce inflammation. One can see that a continuous stream of cortisol would not be good for one's health.

Glucose is released to prepare the person for an emergency. Blood pressure rises, heart rate increases, and breathing becomes rapid. Digestion and sex drive are diminished. Blood vessels constrict and the white blood cell count increases. Rubens quips that this may be helpful in escaping a buffalo stampede, but it is not useful in today's world.

The paradox is that today's experience of traffic jams, impossible work deadlines, conflicting roles, pressures for ever-increasing status, and the demands of constant contact with various communication devices cause enormous stress on the body, equal to that of the primitive man running from the tiger or bison.

ALERT

Cartoonist Scott Adams advises entire days of "multi-shirking," just sitting around feeling mildly guilty for not keeping up with all the electronic communications. Enjoy a bit of sloth.

The brain rearranges itself to accommodate the stress load, resulting in the menu of modern diseases—obesity, insomnia, diabetes, atherosclerosis, depression, and decreased bone density. Other diseases related to stress are arthritis, allergies, and asthma. Another unfortunate result of prolonged stress is the brain's distortion of the emotion of fear, making the person chronically anxious.

Additional illnesses that are estimated to be 40–50 percent caused by stress are chronic fatigue, colds, flu, viruses, headaches, and migraines. Some persons in the medical community are skeptical about the relationship between stress and disease, only going so far to say that stress *contributes* to disease. Chronic stress makes a person *susceptible* to illness. These statements are somewhat different from the direct cause-and-effect supposition.

Are Stress-Related Conditions Inherited?

The United States has the seemingly positive myth and belief that anyone can make it to the top, creating a culture of high achievement, or at least the potential for such. What are some of the attributes that seem strongly related to genetics? According to Jim Rubens, the following conditions are connected to inheritance:

1. Depression
2. Extreme narcissism
3. Self-hatred
4. Autism
5. Schizophrenia
6. Bipolar disorder
7. Inclination toward addictions
8. Illegal drug use
9. Alcoholism
10. Obesity
11. Vision problems
12. High blood pressure

Rubens feels that these estimates are low, and that other physical and psychological difficulties may be highly connected to ancestry as well. So what's a perfectionistic person to do? Blame it on Mom and Dad and Uncle Charlie? It could be a case of forewarned is forearmed. Such knowledge may help you realize your propensity toward certain conditions. This does not mean that you should accept that developing these conditions is inevitable, but that you should create a lifestyle that will help ward off the genetic inclination.

The Immune System

The immune system is a delicate system of protection, finely tuned to destroy your body's invaders, such as microbes that enter through a cut in the skin, with something eaten, or negative influences in the air you breathed. The advent of AIDS made the general public more aware of the importance of a healthy immune system.

The immune system becomes depressed and weaker during times of prolonged stress and is thus unable to do its job of destroying unhealthy cells in the body. Thousands of medical studies have shown a correlation between stress and illness, although not everyone is convinced of a cause-and-effect relationship. In other words, stress and illness are present at the same time, but it is unknown whether stress is actually the cause of disease.

ESSENTIAL

Writer Martha Beck describes her mind as being like a "supercomputer possessed by the soul of a demented squirrel. It's constantly calculating, anticipating, remembering, fantasizing, worrying, hoarding, bouncing frenetically from thought to thought." Author Dwayne Dyer estimates that the human mind thinks about 60,000 thoughts a day.

The fight-or-flight response is a survival mechanism left over from primitive times when man lived very close to the earth and life was simple. If the caveman saw a tiger near his cave, he immediately got ready to fight it or run away. When danger is perceived, the mind and body work together to increase the heart and pulse rate, accompanied by a flood of adrenaline, so that the person can escape. The difficulty arises when there are numerous such incidents in modern life and everything is simply locked into the body. It's not necessary to run from the cave, but if your marriage is ending and your business is on the brink of bankruptcy, the dangers feel every bit as real as those of the caveman.

If one is still living out the aims of a perfectionistic parent (even if the parent has died) or responsible for the care of a family member with long-term illness, there is pressure on the immune system. Hormones flood into the bloodstream, the immune system is suppressed, and unhealthy conditions start to arise. Hans Selye, a researcher in the relationship between stress and illness, believes that if a lot of energy is used to handle emotional trauma, the body does not have enough resources left to take care of physical challenges. This information is good incentive to reduce mental trauma, so that energy is available to protect and heal the physical body.

The Social Component

During past generations, friends and extended family usually lived nearby, supporting all the members of a community during times of illness and stress. This is not the case in the twenty-first century, as many people live far from their blood relatives and move rather frequently during the course of their adult lives.

The experience of prolonged social defeat, as described by Jim Rubens, affects those in lower social classes with greater disease—lower birth weight, heart disease, lung disease, compromised mental health, cancer, and more days taken off from work. An unfortunate result of this lowered state of affairs is that such individuals are likely to compensate by taking up an addiction to make themselves feel better.

Don't the Doctors Know Everything?

American physicians are largely allopathic, meaning that they tend to view illness and the body in a scientific sense. Great emphasis is placed on symptoms and removing the symptoms. There is less interest in prevention and causes, and sometimes alternative methods of healing are disregarded because the physicians are not trained in these areas, and there is no way to get insurance reimbursement from approaches that are not mainstream.

Do Your Research

As the Internet has become available to almost everyone, patients have become more proactive, taking the time to research symptoms and diseases, and working with the physician as an equal team member. This can require a degree of assertiveness that is not typical when interacting with a doctor, as culturally doctors are perceived as persons of authority. However, it is your body, and you have a complete right to ask questions and pursue whatever avenue seems in harmony with your belief system.

Explore Alternatives

Perhaps you have investigated meditation, yoga, and Ayurveda medicine, wanting to add these components to the conventional prescriptions doled out by clinic physicians. It would be wise to keep your team informed of what you are doing, but they may not fully understand.

Medical schools generally do not teach nutrition, so if you want to approach an illness with changes in the diet, such as eliminating meat and trying juicing for a few weeks, the physician may minimize this effort, but that doesn't mean that it's not worthwhile. Research has found that a plant-based diet works wonders with healing, but it is unlikely that your physician will write out a prescription for broccoli.

What Can You Do Instead?

It can be helpful to aim for an accepting view of the physical body, whatever its age and appearance. Your body has not turned against you if an illness develops. Perhaps it's a signal to slow down and shift gears, devoting loving, gentle care to the marvelous human form.

Don't Buy into Flawless Appearance

The entertainment industry spends more time and attention than ever on human perfection. Makeup artists extend cosmetics to the entire body—neck, arms, and legs. Cameras are sophisticated, and every detail has to be perfect—not a single wrinkle.

Filmmakers expect to spend as much as $250,000 on postproduction work that removes blemishes and wrinkles from stars' faces, because with digital film, every imperfection is apparent.

With these images in the media, the average person is tempted to participate in the million-dollar plastic surgery industry. Consumers, mostly women, have breast lifts and augmentations, facelifts, as well as adjustments to other aspects of the anatomy. Attitudes have changed toward plastic surgery, and currently over half of the American population are in favor of such procedures. Hollywood's standards are tempting and ever-present, but what about being unique and somewhat ordinary? Individuality is always attractive and much healthier for overall wholeness and well-being.

Learn to Monitor Your Reactions to Stress

Dr. Harold Benjamin points out that everyone has stress, but one person's response might be different from another's. Keeping in mind the relationship between stress and illness, it would be quite beneficial to learn some ways to diminish the harmful bodily developments that occur because of stress.

It is possible to learn to control these emotions and behaviors, even under stressful conditions. Such control allows the immune system to do its natural work, and the body is not so apt to becoming ill. Think about which aspects of your lifestyle you have control over and make modifications wherever you can—shifting to a healthier diet, increasing exercise, avoiding ruminating over situations you cannot change, accepting the various aberrations of people and life with a sense of humor, expressing emotions as appropriate, and trying not to dwell overly long on negative feelings. Avoid self-blame and long-term resentment whenever possible.

Cultivate a degree of poise and composure that is unshakable. It will serve you well in severe emergencies and tragedies, allowing you to function in a helpful way toward others in crisis without endangering your physical health. Even if you are a fire fighter or emergency room technician, clear your mind at the end of the day and set aside your work until the next day. The technique of metaphorically putting a period at the end of the sentence would be useful. In your mind's eye, end the sentence, close the door, or put a lid on a box. Select an image that gives you the feeling of finality of the situation.

Visualization

Visualization has been found to be helpful for persons who are healing from various illnesses. This is a process, much like meditation, where the individual consciously relaxes each muscle group in the body and then imagines a vision of the location that needs to heal in its healthy form. Such a focus is powerful stimulus for the brain and subconscious mind. With repetition over time, the body responds and the healing is manifested.

Seek Out Joy

Is it possible to embrace the idea that you can be happy, even if you are healing from a serious illness? Joy does marvelous effervescent things to the immune system, quite the opposite of stress. Learn your own favorite repertoire for fun and freely indulge. Perhaps it's playing with your dog, strolling through a flea market, doodling with crayons, or tinkering with an antique automobile. Maybe you love reggae music but hardly ever go to a live concert. Make the time to find performances and attend. You will find kindred souls there, adding to the social well-being, which is a part of a healthy dynamic. Dismiss the mindset that all activity has to be purposeful.

Gather some children together—those from your family or neighbors—and make a big tub of soapy bubble solution. A little glycerin and dishwashing liquid will do the trick, and experiment with all kinds of utensils and toys to see what kinds of bubbles are possible. Have you ever made a bubble as large as a Hula-Hoop? That's an achievement!

Exercise Discernment in Relations with Others

You may find that when you are ill, some people bring you down and others build you up. There can be some surprises in the closest relationships. Some family members will bring doom and gloom to the discussion, and some of your best friends will avoid you if you are sick. It is impossible to control the emotional reactions of others, but you can make a conscious choice to interact only with people that make you feel better about yourself, those who encourage you and believe that you are fine no matter what you might be going through. You may find that it is more fun to chat with the quirky person you see at the coffee shop every week than with your relative who tells you all the scary statistics that have a bearing on your situation.

Don't Forget Sex!

Hold on to your sexuality if you become ill. Your perfectionistic voices may say that you're not attractive enough when you are sick, but your partner will feel differently. Having a disease does not mean that a person is no longer sexual. People can do sexy things together, even if intercourse is not possible because of an illness. Imagination and creativity bring new possibilities to the bedroom, if both partners are willing.

Both people may crave cuddling and embracing, especially the partner of the sick person if there has been a lengthy absence of affection. The diseased person may feel unattractive, but the genuine mutual caring will provide needed assurance.

ESSENTIAL

Not every sexual experience has to reach epic carnal heights or reverberate through history, like Antony and Cleopatra. Your perfectionism can be left outside the door so you can just focus on being together. Attention and kindness are always welcome.

Communication will help both people determine what has changed and what adaptations can occur so that needs are met. Every person, regardless of age or degree of health, has a need to be cared for and to share affection for another. You may have to be courageous and be the first to speak up. It is common to feel some loss of desire when coping with a serious illness. This can be accompanied by anxiety, as one fears the reaction of the loved one. Sometimes as healing begins, an amazing degree of tenderness and openness can ensue.

If pain is an issue, sometimes sex can be enjoyed right after the sick person has taken medication or done relaxation exercises. The couple can experiment with different positions to see what accommodates the situation.

The real challenge for the perfectionist will be the adjustment in body image. The body changes with serious illness and with age. However, the essence of the person remains intact, and that is what the partner loves: the shared experiences, memories, and emotional enjoyment of the union. This is not a time to be staring in the mirror. The partner of the sick person may be worried about hurting something or even feel guilty for having sexual needs. It seems selfish, but it is only human.

CHAPTER 12

Methods of Treatment

Even though perfectionism is not viewed as a specific disorder, there are many modes of therapy and education that can lessen the discomfort of the perfectionist. Cognitive therapy can help the individual recognize one's irrational thoughts and provide support while forming new ones. Psychoanalysis explores the roots of perfectionism, the underlying motives and issues. Group therapy is a method that provides a support system under the guidance of a trained professional, alleviating isolation. Humanistic therapy looks at the positive aspects of the situation and finds underlying meaning.

Perspective of Psychiatrists and Psychologists

Psychiatrists are MDs with a specialty in psychiatry, while psychologists hold a PhD or PsyD in psychology. Both do therapy and conduct research. Most states require that the psychologist do a supervised internship and gain licensure. Psychiatrists have attended medical school and studied further in the areas of assessment, diagnosis, treatment, and prevention of mental illness. Psychiatrists are able to prescribe medications, while in most states psychologists do not prescribe medications.

ALERT

Some tests available for measuring perfectionism are the Multidimensional Perfectionism Scale, the Perfectionistic Self Presentation Scale, the Almost Perfect Scale-Revised, and the Physical Appearance Perfectionism Scale. There is more investigative literature regarding the first three tests, compared to the final scale.

Sessions may be shorter with a psychiatrist, as they earn more money prescribing medications than doing therapy. Psychologists tend to do testing more than psychiatrists. You can expect that a psychiatrist will have a more scientific approach and perspective, and a psychologist will be somewhat broad in perspective. Of course, it is human to think that one's own perspective is superior, but the most important thing is that the patient gets the type of help desired. No one person has cornered the market on truth, and you have a right to enlist help that is in harmony with your values.

Some experts in the field believe that it does no good to encourage clients to lower their standards and try not to be so perfect. Clients have heard that from many sources already and will tend to tune out the professional. A better approach is to uncover the roots of the difficulty and focus on what is needed to feel loved, cared for, and completely okay without being perfect. Some clients have kept their imperfections secret for such a long period of time that they will stop therapy when the counselor gets close to the core of the matter.

How to Select a Therapist

Sometimes you have exhausted your inner resources and need assistance in coping with perfectionism. Ministers and mental health clinics often offer services at a nominal fee. Social service agencies may be of assistance, as well as marriage and family therapists. Clinical social workers often work as a part of a team. Psychologists and psychiatrists offer help, and the expense will be greater. When you meet with a counselor for the first time, ask lots of questions and try to determine whether you really feel comfortable with that individual. It's your prerogative to ask about the level of education, specialties, and whether the individual has experience with the specific issues you face. Investigate your insurance coverage and what documentation you will need for reimbursement.

ALERT

Don E. Hamachek of *psycnet.apa.org* discusses some differences between adaptive (normal) perfectionism and neurotic (maladaptive) perfectionism. Adaptive is believed by some to be more functional in terms of being appropriately careful, as in engineering or quality control work. Neurotic perfectionism is seen to be more debilitating. However, some professionals believe that adaptive perfectionism is harmful, as well.

Do not hesitate to shop around a bit and ask for referrals from friends and other mental health professionals in your life. The fit has to be correct in order for you to make progress with your perfectionism. Insurance may or may not cover therapy, but can you place a financial value on mental health for yourself and your future? Is it equal to a new TV or an upgrade on your car? A luxurious vacation?

In the short term, the therapist will try to tackle the immediate issues that likely brought the perfectionist in, such as difficulty maintaining relationships, obsession with success, fearful and self-critical thoughts. Then, the therapist usually begins to work on a long-term treatment strategy. The long-term strategy can involve an attempt to reshape the distorted image the client has of himself and the world around him, or to give him the skills he needs to function better.

ESSENTIAL

Psychoanalyst Heinz Kohut has suggested that children have a need to idolize and identify with their parents. They also have an equally strong need to see such worthiness reflected, or mirrored back, by their parents or other caregivers. When children do not receive this mirroring, psychological difficulties can be the result. The Kohutian approach to therapy, or working through childhood issues, can be an effective strategy. The therapist becomes the idealized parent. Through transference, the patient gets the things he missed out on at a young age.

Individual Therapy

The ultimate goal of individual therapy is to help clients to unlearn negative patterns of behavior and to learn better ways to relate to others so that all the relationships in their lives can be more intimate, enjoyable, and rewarding.

QUESTION

What is the best kind of therapy for a perfectionistic person?
The success or failure of therapy depends less on the type of therapy used than on the relationship between the therapist and client. In any therapy, patients can learn, maybe for the first time, that they can safely express anger, or any emotion, with their therapists without the risk of rejection or fear that the therapist will stop treating them. Secure and comfortable in the relationship, these clients are then able to continue to discuss intimate secrets and painful issues that were locked away and previously not shared with anyone else.

Individual therapy sessions are designed to turn the mirror inward and allow the patient to better understand what it is that drives her to be competitive, distrustful, and driven to high standards. And then, with the light shining upon her inner demons, help her to find ways to better cope with them.

Individual therapy usually has three stages:

- It begins with the client and therapist going over specific thoughts or feelings in detail.
- The therapist and client work on identifying distorted views.
- The therapist works with the client to entertain new nondistorted ways of thinking.

Each week the therapist will likely give the client some specific home-work assignments.

Psychotherapy

Another approach to individual therapy is the more classic method orig-inated by Freud: psychoanalytical therapy. Classical Freudian, or psychoan-alytic, therapy is not used as frequently today as other styles.

Psychoanalysis based on the psychodynamic model has changed some-what since the time of Freud, but basically the Freudian model states that emotional disorders are based on inner unresolved conflicts between dif-ferent aspects of one's psyche—the id, the ego, and the superego—or, more simply, between the conscious and unconscious mind. The goal of individ-ual psychodynamic therapy is to reduce these conflicts, and in doing so, modify the personality of the individual for the better.

The therapist takes a less active role in this form of therapy. He remains fairly quiet and relies on the patient to reveal increasing amounts of distress buried in her subconscious.

Dreams are an important part of psychodynamic therapy. Freud believed that many subconscious conflicts are revealed in dreams. In this type of therapy, therapist and client will discuss dreams to gain insights into their meaning and what they show about the patient's inner struggles. Psycho-dynamic therapy can run from one year to as long as fifteen years or more.

Cognitive Behavioral Therapy (CBT)

The basic idea of cognitive behavioral therapy is to get the patient to rec-ognize and identify untrue beliefs and negative behaviors, and replace these beliefs and behaviors with healthy, positive ones. The basis of this therapy is that our feelings and thinking play a major role in the way we behave and interact with people and the world around us.

The goal of cognitive behavioral therapy is to get patients to realize that while they cannot control every aspect of their lives and the world around them, they do have power over how they interpret and choose to deal with people, events, and objects in their environment.

With perfectionism, the thought patterns and feelings that cognitive behavioral therapy is trying to change are those of impossible expectations for the self and others. In order to deal with these destructive thoughts and behaviors, cognitive behavioral therapy begins by helping the client to see her problematic beliefs.

This first stage of the process is called functional analysis. The goal in this stage is to get the person to understand how thoughts, feelings, and situations contribute to negative behaviors. This can be a tough process, but when the therapist can break through the client's defenses and gain her trust, the self-discovery and insight that are essential to the treatment process can be achieved.

The second stage focuses on the actual behaviors that are making life miserable for the person and those around her. For example, the focus on perfection is creating a huge body image and appearance issue for her children. This stage can be especially difficult, as the client tends to believe there is nothing wrong with his behavior, and if those around him are taking offense, it's simply because they are too sensitive or even jealous. However, through intense cognitive behavioral therapy, a perfectionist can realize that not everyone shares her worldview and that her actions are harmful.

In the third and last part of the process, the client begins to learn and practice new skills that can be used to get different outcomes in real-world situations. For example, working on being average can be a goal. The CBT therapist can use several techniques to address this issue.

Role-playing, including role reversal, has been shown to be an effective technique. In these role-plays the therapist can get the person to see that there are other ways of relating to people and situations. Specific language will be used in the role-playing to bring about new belief statements and new thought patterns, such as "My best is good enough."

Cognitive behavioral therapy can be a challenging and rewarding method of treatment.

Find Groups of Like-Minded People

If you are looking for information about groups of people who are struggling with perfectionism, inquire at a hospital and social service agency. You may have to be creative in describing what you are looking for. The group might have a name something like "Personal Growth and Self-Esteem" or "Survivors of Trauma." Don't eliminate a group because it doesn't include the word "perfectionism." Numerous self-help twelve-step programs approach perfectionism and mental health from a variety of perspectives. There is no harm in dropping in on groups or calling the phone numbers listed on the web pages. Spending committed time in a group of people with similar suffering can lead to miracles in healing. One discovers that isolation is unnecessary, and a dozen heads are always better than one. Use your search tool and look around on the Internet to see what is available in your community.

What about Medication?

It would be unusual to use medication solely for the difficulty of perfectionism. However, if other disorders are a part of the picture, it is possible that medications could alleviate accompanying conditions, such as depression, anxiety, or other emotional distress. There isn't a known biochemistry for perfectionism, although one could expect the brain chemistry to be similar to that of the various addictions. It is unlikely that drugs will be developed specifically for perfectionism. One possible approach would be the combination of mood-stabilizing drugs for codisorders and therapy.

ALERT

Recent research suggests that some antidepressants, specifically selective serotonin reuptake inhibitors (SSRI) such as Prozac, may have the effect of creating serotonin overload. Serotonin regulates mood and levels of positive emotions. The risk is that increased levels of serotonin may also bring on false feelings of superiority.

Prescriptions could be a danger in the hands of a perfectionistic individual who also struggles with addictions. The temptation could be there to get the instant fix, even more than what is prescribed. In the long run, taking medications to feel better can result in feeling worse.

If you or someone you know tends toward depression, watch for the tendency to hoard medications for a possible suicide attempt. The prescribing physician will often suggest medications that are not addictive when such dangers are present. Throw out medications that are outdated, prescriptions for a different condition, or prescriptions for someone else.

There is no magic pill for dealing with core issues. Drugs alleviate symptoms, such as anxiety and mood swings. Persons with comorbid disorders may require medication to stimulate the brain so it reaches a normal balance and can function properly.

There is a tendency in today's medical field to overprescribe. A person who takes four or five medications has to be constantly on the alert for interactions and side effects. There is also the temptation to become overreliant on the drugs, avoiding psychotherapy that would help to unearth the underlying issues. Drugs tend to dull a person over time, leading to a situation where more and more is required for the same effect. It is important to recognize that some drugs cause challenges in thinking and performing certain tasks, such as driving a vehicle or operating machinery. The physician and patient have to work closely together to get the right balance.

ESSENTIAL

Let the prescribing doctor know if there are drug issues, and what other medications are being taken, as there may be interactions with unexpected side effects.

What Can You Do Instead?

Martha Beck suggests a way of quieting the mind called the Ticker Tape. Sit in a relaxed position as if getting ready to meditate. It is likely that you might not like meditating because of racing thoughts and complete inability to reach a Zenlike state of blank openness. The Ticker Tape exercise is perfect for this type of overthinking. With eyes closed, let the thoughts stream by, but place them on a thin strip of ticker tape as they go by behind your eyes. No judgment, just the ribbon of one thought after another. Spend a few minutes this way, and the mind and body will relax.

What Are Your Real Desires?

Mental illness can improve or simply disappear if a person gets honest about the truth of his life. Some self-inquiry can help. Ask yourself "When was I happy? What was I doing? What do I want now? What do I want to do with my time?"

One technique for accessing buried desires is to write a conversation between yourself and your inner child in a journal. Structure the writing as if it is a play, a conversation between the grown person and the inner child. It might look something like this:

Me: Hello, there.

Child: Hi.

Me: You sound mad.

Child: I am. You ignore me all the time.

Me: I'm sorry. What do you want?

Child: I do not want to work any more!

Me: I can understand that, but a certain amount of work takes care of things for us.

Child: Well then, not so much.

Me: What else would you like?

Child: Please don't make me listen to that woman with the scratchy voice. It makes my ears itch.

Me: Okay. Anything else?

Child: I just want to be outside somewhere and mess around. Look at leaves and twigs.

Me: There's an arboretum near here. Would you like to go there? They have incredible flowers.

Child: Yes. Thank you. I love you, Mommy.

Me: I love you, too, Sweetie.

This kind of dialogue calms a person down, and the simple desires come forth, sometimes leading to a new, more fruitful direction in life.

Reclaim Your Dreams

Was there a dream that you cherished as a child before you were rebuked, humiliated, and chastised out of having any authentic aspirations of your own? Some people from difficult family backgrounds learn to bury dreams because of the mistaken belief that keeping them hidden away will prevent pain. Actually, the opposite is true. Repressing one's longings ends up deadening the entire affect. Maybe there's less discomfort, but there is also less joy. This is not a happy way to live.

ALERT

Author Martha Beck suggests that those on a quest for a better, more satisfying, less perfect life should watch for the moment of *quickening*, the term used when a pregnant woman first feels the movement of the fetus in the uterus. Intense moments of awareness can be just like that—"I must work with paint;" "I have to get a divorce;" "I must live in a different house." Life's direction will smooth out after such an awakening.

Can you remember yourself at five or six years old? What did you think about and what did you like to do? What might you have done if your family had cued into your sincere interests a little more indulgently? What if there were no addictions in your family; how might you have cultivated some of your favorite pastimes? The essence of your personhood is the same now as it was then, and it's quite likely that what you enjoyed doing as a little tyke would still be enjoyed now.

Imagine the Ideal Lifestyle

Beyond winning the lottery, what seems attractive? You may be aiming for a new career, but how does it seem to be genuinely in that new career? For example, if you aspire to be a musician who receives an armful of flowers after a successful concert, would you equally enjoy the hours of preparation for public performance? The proportion of time spent alone with the instrument honing the craft is much greater than the time in the public eye. Be sure you would enjoy the entire lifestyle.

Maybe you want to travel all the time. Being an airline attendant might be fun. The travel privileges and always being on the go could be the lifestyle that satisfies you. Imagine going up and down the aisles, taking drink orders, soothing the whimpering child, answering tedious questions. Imagine handling a drunk or a potential terrorist. All this would be a part of the entire lifestyle. If you have children, would you be content with frequent phone conversations while you are flitting from place to place? Would you feel guilty that someone else was tending to the lunches and parent-teacher conferences?

Become a Risk Taker

In order to embrace your truest desires and dreams, it will become necessary to creep out of your comfort zone. This does not mean that you will be like Evel Knievel, eager to jump a motorcycle across the Grand Canyon. Small risks will suffice. Perhaps join Toastmasters in order to overcome a fear of public speaking. Sing karaoke while the club is still quiet enough to hear you. Then sign up at a neighborhood open mike. Agree to serve on the board of your favorite nonprofit, even if you have no patience for interpersonal politics.

The crux of risk taking is that you are afraid, and you face the fear and move forward. The fear subsides. Small successes and failures will make risk taking somewhat more palatable, and your life starts to blossom. You'd like to make a quilt from lovely vintage fabric handed down from the family ancestors, but machines frighten you. What if you sew your fingers to the fabric and ruin it with blood stains? It's likely that you can find a class with a patient teacher who would guide you through the process of crafting a new family heirloom.

Be Willing to Create

When you start claiming your true wants and desires and start taking risks, it becomes apparent that you are a creative person. In order to be happy you *must* create. Society has become so specialized that we imagine only a few people are unique enough to make something original. In actuality, everyone is creative. Unfortunately, this treasure of a human trait becomes stunted when too many people tell you to color within the lines.

Protect yourself from the naysayers and go forth with whatever it is that makes your soul sing. If it is ceramics, take a class and make little Zuni-style fetishes for all your friends. If it is real estate, buy a house and flip it. It's just arithmetic, right? If that's your love, go in that direction. Create a profit. The challenge will get your synapses buzzing again, and you will forget what it was like being depressed and immobilized with procrastination.

Be prepared for repetitious hard work.

ESSENTIAL

Hard work was a part of artist Michelangelo's life. Imagine laying on scaffolding under the ceiling of the Sistine Chapel for hours at a time, smelling paint fumes. He is quoted as saying, "If people knew how hard I work, they wouldn't find my achievements so remarkable." Artist Thomas Hart Benton made three-dimensional clay figures of each image in his massive murals. This was to ensure that the proportions would come out correctly.

Break Some Rules

A fair amount of self-inquiry eventually unearths one's personal rules. They may have come from parents, teachers, or the prevailing culture. It doesn't hurt to be aware of one's overriding values, as these are the beliefs that keep society from being completely chaotic. However, being a cookie-cutter person, someone with no individuality or character, could mean the death of your soul.

Maybe there's a family rule that it is not nice to outdo one particular person. The unspoken contract is agreed upon by everyone. Uncle Charlie always has the last word, and everything that is said about him is something positive. It might be fun at the next family reunion to say something after him, every time. A quiet comment to no one in particular, "Isn't Uncle Charlie a lovable bag of wind?" Say it again. Sit solidly while people look your way with a sharp intake of breath. It can be fun.

During holiday festivities, eschew the traditional tree and decorate your entire house in hues of purple. Go all out with candles, swags, blinking lights, and burgundy wine. Joke with friends who come over that you were stricken by the Sugar Plum Fairy and were obligated to fulfill her wishes until January 1. The strange looks won't hurt you.

FACT

Milarepa, a great hero of Tibetan Buddhism, encountered a host of demons, most of which he overcame with compassion. The meanest one simply would not leave. Milarepa climbed into the dragon's mouth and allowed himself to be swallowed. The dragon disappeared.

Be Naive

As you explore further and further afield outside your comfort zone, you might meet interesting people and wonder about certain aspects of their lives. Even if you don't usually strike up conversations with strangers, there is no harm in giving it a try. Ask your favorite barista how his day is going and ask what is selling well that day.

Ask a favorite (or feared) authority figure how she decided to go into her particular career. Did a certain mentor inspire her and help her? What was the path? Most people enjoy talking about themselves, and there could be something important to learn. When you're talking with someone and she uses a name or a word that is unfamiliar to you, stop and ask who that is or the meaning of that word. She will be happy to enlighten you.

Brag about Yourself

Find at least one person with whom you can exchange immodest bragging. Maybe it's a therapist, or maybe it's a best friend. Tell him in great detail how you slayed that dragon and got your proposal approved. You spoke up to your meddling neighbor. You made the dreaded phone call to the ex and apologized for your heinous behavior. You made a cake in the shape of a fire engine for your favorite nephew, without any pattern or instruction. When it's the other person's turn to brag, wholeheartedly cheer them on. Listen attentively and ask for details. You might even have a standing ovation at your little table for two in your favorite coffeehouse.

Be Childlike

There are situations in life where it is not necessary to be perfectly responsible and task oriented. It can be quite fun to occasionally set down the load of grown-up accountability and just be foolish. A woman takes her grandchild to the circus and wears a clown nose all day. A high-level architect has a secret collection of windup toys, and after especially stressful days of working with blueprints and specifications, she clears the dining room table and winds up all the little toys at the same time, enjoying the melee of color, sound, and collision.

Cultivate Partners in Crime

In order to enjoy yourself, you may need support during times when you experience opposition from significant others. Perhaps you just don't want to go across country to the wedding of the third cousin once removed, but it seems like a family obligation. Call up your friend and listen to her say, "If you don't want to go, don't go." Some of the objection may be within yourself, as you learn to align your actions with newly forming beliefs about what you want. At times it may feel like throwing the gears into reverse while you intend to move forward. Another person provides support in the new direction. Be careful in associations with those who might criticize or judge.

Perfectionism versus Authenticity

Perfection is an illusion; no one, or no thing, is or can ever be perfect. This is one of the realities that a person with perfectionism often has difficulty accepting. You have to learn to accept and embrace the imperfections in yourself, in others, and in your relationships.

This concept emphasizes authenticity as opposed to perfectionism. It stresses living authentically: having the strength and the courage to accept your own imperfections and vulnerabilities as being part of the "real you." In many ways it is a manner of living that also opposes everything perfect. When you are authentic in your own self-assessment, which includes flaws, fears, and things you may be ashamed of, you are able to be truly compassionate and empathetic toward others.

CHAPTER 13

A Thorough Self-Examination

It's fairly difficult to change something about yourself, such as modifying perfectionism, unless there is a grounded knowledge of your history and what has gone into making your personality. Instead of stumbling through a dark room without a flashlight, imagine being fearless as you look at all the parts of what has made you who you are today.

Family Rules and Values

It's not always easy to realize the truth about one's values and internalized rules because they seem so very true and normal! In fact, they are your norm and have been for many years. Often these deeply imbedded aspects of the self come to light when you start becoming close to other people and you discover how very different they are from you and each other. Their beliefs about what is important vary from yours. The variety can be interesting but unnerving.

Politics

Think about the political orientation of your parents and whether you have gone the same direction or veered the complete opposite. Maybe you're apolitical. Does your family have a tradition of becoming deeply involved with fundraising and campaigning for a particular party or person? Are politics discussed around the table during meals? Did your parents have divergent beliefs regarding politics, and did one defer to the other during election years? Did they discuss voting and informing themselves about the issues? Think about whether they read newspapers and magazines or listened to radio and television to formulate their voting strategies.

Recreational Patterns

How would you characterize your heritage in terms of having fun? Was it an Archie Bunker type of household with entertainment consisting of talking about the neighbors and bickering among the family members? What was a weekend like during your childhood or a typical holiday? Did your family travel, and were the children included?

ESSENTIAL

If you are in touch with older relatives in your family, it can be rewarding to talk with them about what sort of things they did for fun when they were young. Before media became the prominent source of entertainment, people were marvelously inventive in occupying themselves. You may hear about a vacant lot baseball team or a favorite country fishing hole.

Think about your mother's favorite things to do and your father's favorite pastimes. It's likely that you view these pursuits in a favorable light. What if you had wanted to start something completely different as a child, such as embark upon the study of sharks or collect bone fragments? How would this have been received? These types of questions help you to determine the attitudes in your household.

What were the tastes in music? Think about whether the norm in the household was Scarlatti or Johnny Cash, and where you place yourself in musical taste. Try to remember the pictures on the walls of your family home—portraits of family members, Currier and Ives prints, cherished children's art, Degas and Picasso prints, or original art created by friends or family members.

Some families are all work and no play. Children growing up in this type of environment can become perfectionistic in completing all the required tasks before allowing themselves to have fun. The dichotomy between work and pleasure can bring a negative attitude toward work, as it often is never done. Self-criticism about pleasure and being joyful in one's work are prevalent in these types of families.

Your Cultural Mandates

How would you describe the culture in which you grew up? What is your ethnicity? Are there particular "musts" that go along with being a part of that particular tribe? One of the best ways to become aware of one's culture is to visit another one! If you have been lucky enough to have an extended visit in a foreign country, think about what you learned in contrast to those local people. You can learn as much by becoming close friends with someone from a different culture.

Gender Rules

How are men and women taught to behave in your culture? Are there specific things that are expected and other things that are discouraged? Describe those things. For example, in Mexican culture, women are often taught to cater to men. Men are expected to work hard and provide for the entire family. Extended families are large and everyone is in on everyone else's news. Men are given more freedom, and women are expected to be good cooks.

FACT

Although the present generation is somewhat flexible, for years in South Korea it was tradition that once a woman married, she would no longer work outside the home. The man was the "outside person," and the woman was the "inside person," caring for all the domestic aspects of the family, including managing the finances.

You might be wondering how this could be important in this day and age, when so much is available to everyone. Gender stereotypes were eased during the social revolutions of the 1970s, and now each person can do what he or she wants. In general, that is true, but attitudes are handed down generationally, and your parents or grandparents may exert quite a lot of pressure or perhaps disapproval about certain aspects of your life. For example, if you are a woman coming from a Latina background, you might find yourself criticized if you opt for a career instead of marriage.

Education

What are the beliefs about education coming from your culture? Is it assumed that you will have an opportunity to attend college or university? Do the parents provide such an education for their children or are the children expected to work and search out scholarships? What careers are encouraged and what lines of work are scoffed at? If you decided to become a professional mime, how would that go over? Is there a cultural tradition of particular trades that are acceptable to your clan? What are they, and are you pressured to go in that direction? What happens if you want to learn something completely different?

ALERT

The Jewish culture has historically placed a great deal of emphasis on education, including girls' education, by the late nineteenth century and early twentieth century. However, people from other cultures, especially those of blue-collar socioeconomic groups, experience a particular type of discomfort if they are the first college-educated person in the family. This phenomenon is termed the imposter syndrome. Such individuals sometimes feel alienated from their families and have a sense professionally of being "found out," a bit defensive about the status they have achieved.

Is there a particular college that is favored by your family? Have many from your family or city gone to a certain university? What topics are considered useful to study and what is considered frivolous? Are you expected to get straight As, or are you encouraged to socialize and join a lot of campus clubs? Are you expected to excel in sports or in the arts?

What are your expectations regarding your children's schooling? Will they attend public schools or private? Do you home-school? What is your opinion about grades? Do you reward your children's good grades, or do you assume that they will excel because that is their job at school? These questions can help you tease out attitudes of perfectionism and high expectation concerning this aspect of your life.

Religion

In some cultures religion is synonymous with the culture. Think about your religious leanings and whether they came from your parents or your own self-inquiry and exploration. Automatically adhering to the religious beliefs of the culture in which you were raised can be a comfortable way to go, as you will have plenty of company. At the same time, it can be rewarding to acknowledge that foundation and deliberately try a different path, just out of curiosity, perhaps for a specific length of time.

Money

In your culture, what would be the prevailing beliefs about the importance of money? Do people generally save a certain portion that is earned, and what are the uses of the savings? At what age do children start to have their own money in your culture, and how do they spend it? Think about attitudes toward business—large corporations, small entrepreneurial efforts, and working from home. Some cultures favor one avenue, and others are inclined toward another. Think about a typical household within your culture and envision how the financial decisions are made.

ESSENTIAL

Money and power conventionally go hand in hand. It is good to be aware of the dynamics of power connected with money within one's family and within the culture. Such prevailing preferences can be changed within a relationship, but it will take considerable effort.

Who participates in the discussions and who has the final word? If teenagers need money to participate in school activities or other peer activities, how would the culture feel about that? Think about the prevailing cultural attitudes about banking and retirement and where you fit in terms of those cultural guidelines.

Blind Spots within Yourself

There is no foolproof way to discover blind spots, because, of course, they are hidden from your awareness! One way to think about this is to consider what friends and significant others have pointed out to you, either in exasperation or as a compliment. Think of comments that have included the words "You always . . ." or "You never . . . ." Are you always late because unconsciously you believe your time is more valuable than the other person's time? Do you think one sex is more important than the other, catering to one or the other in business settings? Should children be seen and not ever heard? Would you spend thousands of dollars on another college degree but have difficulty buying a new suit when yours becomes frayed? These are only a few examples. Try to be alert to what others say or their unspoken reactions when you relate to them. Over a period of time you may discover some blind spots.

Guidelines for Exploring Your Beliefs and Values

Writing is a good way to explore your history, background, beliefs, and values. Some people keep a separate journal for each aspect of their quest, and others devise a three-ring binder arrangement with separate categories for each part of their work. Yours will evolve over time as you get comfortable with the process. It is helpful to have a therapist, mentor, or close trusted friend to share your discoveries with as you progress through this important task. Spend a number of months to do the work, as realizations will occur to you along the way. One discovery leads to another, and momentum will build as the knowledge grows.

ESSENTIAL

Writing at the computer is somewhat different from handwriting in a journal. Handwriting seems to come from a deeper place in the brain and is useful for easing out unknown, buried attitudes, feelings, and memories. Keyboard writing is faster and a bit more analytical, perhaps using more of the left hemisphere of the brain. Make a conscious choice about which you prefer.

The twelve-step programs have an inventorying process that may work for you. The inventory can be a straightforward life story or a detailed listing of the chronology in each aspect of your life—relationships, career, spiritual growth, financial experiences. One woman remembered in a vague way that she had tremendously liked some of her homes and not so much others. She wrote a house inventory and discovered the interesting pattern that while living in the homes she did not like she was involved with dysfunctional mates! The mind is clever in how it stores information, and the writing process can tease it out in a highly beneficial way.

Your Autobiography

It may seem redundant to think of your life story again, especially if you have had years of therapy and other kinds of help. What else could possibly come to light? It never hurts to take a fresh look, as at different stages of life and maturity odd pieces of one's history are remembered with a new perspective and can be just the missing piece of the puzzle that helps you understand the perfectionistic patterns.

In her book, *Vein of Gold*, Julia Cameron recommends that the reader first write a timeline in five-year increments. "What?" you say in horror! Go ahead. Think about it. Consider making such a timeline with significant events noted under each section of your life. Then with a notebook or journal designated especially for this effort, write a thorough life story, focusing in five-year time blocks. Of course, you will not do it all in one sitting. This autobiography could take months to complete. Write about the significant happenings of each five-year increment. Were there tragedies? Traumas? Who were the significant people? What were you doing and how did you feel about it? What were your successes and failures? It will be interesting to complement your writing with photos of the places and people that were important for that time, as well as pictures of yourself. How did the six-year-old look as he went off to school? What are your memories of first driving a car? All these things are important aspects of your life story. When did you become perfectionistic? Whom did you hope to please? Were your efforts successful?

Feeling and Setting Aside Sorrow

Dr. Elisabeth Kübler-Ross brought the process of grief into mainstream awareness, mostly in connection with death, but the process is similar in facing injured and buried aspects of the self. If you lost a favorite nanny when you were five but were never allowed to grieve her exit from the family, the emotions that spew forth when you think about that will perhaps be that of a five-year-old. It will feel devastating. The same goes for the loss of a cherished pet, your trusty friend that would protect you and listen to all your stories.

American culture does not readily face or acknowledge the process of grief. Other cultures allow people to wail and take lengthy times away from usual responsibilities. It is unusual for Western workers to take more than a day or two when a family member is lost or there is some other major trauma. The stiff upper lip is expected as the worker quickly resumes normal responsibilities. Friends and coworkers may feel awkward, not knowing what to say to their peer. The truth is, difficult losses, even the loss of a fantasized idea of a perfect background, can take quite a long time to grieve—months or years even—as important anniversaries recur.

Following are the stages of grief that one can expect during a time of major transition:

- Shock and denial. You may feel numb and act as if you are on autopilot.
- Pain and guilt. This is a stage of unbelievable pain.
- Anger and bargaining. You may rant and rave, making deals with God.
- Depression and loneliness. The situation has happened and the loss is irrevocable.
- The turning point. The pain and depression begin to lessen.
- Reconstruction, adjustment, and working through. You start to look at practical considerations. With your new situation and new understanding, what has to change now? Is there a need for a financial overhaul? Do you want to sell your house and travel? Decisions are easier to make as you are more able to logically look at preferences and ramifications of each new direction.
- Acceptance and hope. At this stage the loss becomes integrated. It does not mean that you are thrilled with the loss, but you are calm and able to function in your life, even with a brand new set of circumstances. You no longer are preoccupied every waking moment with the devastation of the loss. You start to feel more comfortable about making plans for your future and actually believe that you will have a future, even without the old, previous misconceptions about where and how you are supposed to be perfect.

Complicated grief is a deeply entrenched sorrow that has been stuck in the personality. The person was unable to complete the stages of grief. A person who is seemingly permanently sad should seek professional help to move the process along.

The grief process may not be as orderly as this list. There can be some looping back and being in more than one stage at a time. How long will it last? For major losses, it can take years, and the length of time increases if a person is unwilling to face the more difficult emotions. Those feelings of unresolved grief will pop up unexpectedly when there is another loss in the future. Then you will be grieving several things at once. It is better to be courageous and face each one as it occurs.

What Can You Do Instead?

Life does not have to be an uphill battle between the self or outside environment. It's unnecessary to be sad and tired all the time. Even if there is a background of difficult experiences, it is entirely possible to work them through and claim a joyful life. This shift in lifestyle does require effort and a willingness to set down habits of negative thinking.

ESSENTIAL

Researcher and life coach Brené Brown, PhD, LMSW, has coined a way of living authentically as being "wholehearted." Wholehearted people, as Dr. Brown describes, realize that what makes them vulnerable is also what makes them beautiful and allows them to connect to all of humanity, which shares similar pains, struggles, and vulnerabilities.

A Clear Look at Your Life

Here are ten ways you can learn to live more authentically:

- **Understand your purpose.** Does it feel like your life lacks direction? Do you think that health and prosperity will just come to you? You need to identify your life purpose. Think of it like a corporation's mission statement. Knowing your purpose means you will always have a way to find your authenticity.
- **Recognize your true values.** Make a list of the five things you value most. Then think about your goals. If your goals do not match up with your values, you are not living as authentically as you can or should be.

- **Embrace your own needs.** It is not a selfish act to take care of yourself. Having unmet needs can keep you from living authentically.
- **Know what you love or feel passionate about.** Recognize and embrace the things that make you genuinely happy. Whatever it is, from writing poetry to karaoke singing, if it makes your heart soar, do more of it!
- **Try living from the inside out.** Use yoga, meditation, or any other relaxation technique that can increase your awareness of your innermost thoughts and wisdom.
- **Accept your vulnerabilities, but respect your own strengths**. Recognize yourself for your positive traits and special talents. Make a list of at least three things that you know you are really, really good at. Honor your true self by doing things that express the strengths on your list.
- **Take time to relax.** You cannot be true to yourself or anyone else if you are burned out. Give yourself time to recharge by doing things just for fun, or by doing nothing at all.
- **Get rid of negative self-talk.** Listen to your internal dialogs. Are they supportive and encouraging, or negative and self-deprecating? Choose your mind's voice. Change negative messages into positive daily affirmations.
- **Inspire and encourage yourself.** Keep a journal of all your accomplishments, big and small, every day.
- **Do unto others as you would have them do unto you.** It is not just the Golden Rule, it is the way to live authentically. And once you are living authentically, giving to others becomes your natural state of being. Because if you are true to who you are, living purposefully and sharing the best of yourself with the world around you, you are giving back in every possible way.

Living more authentically will improve your own emotional health and will likely help you live better with others. Beyond that, once you have embraced living authentically, you will also be a good role model for others in your life.

The problem with trying to achieve any kind of perfectionism is that it negatively affects and impacts every effort. Take even an Academy Award–winning film or performance that has achieved Best Picture or Best Actor. There is something in that film or that performance that could still be judged as less than perfect. Ultimately, perfectionism, as opposed to authenticity, can be just a way to feel bad inside, no matter how great a job you may have done.

Perfectionism can be the enemy of everything good, because to the perfectionist, even the very good is not good enough. To someone who is able to live authentically, on the other hand, doing something very well will likely feel great!

Laughter Is Healing!

Writer and coach, Martha Beck, endorses laughter as a route to relaxed self-acceptance. She and her family are of Nordic ancestry, so when they get together for holidays, they don ridiculous Viking hats! An activity she suggests is to make collages with odd-looking photographic images and combine them with contradictory headlines from magazines or newspapers. For example, an innocuous photo of a tired, elderly grandmother could be combined with the caption, "The Colorless, Odorless Killer: In Cold Pursuit."

Self-deprecating humor is always attractive and endearing. Could it be fun to start to laugh at your perfectionism? Instead of shame and fear, bring it out into the open and embrace others in your humanness. You will be surprised at how others will identify with you and want to draw you closer as you own up to the frailties that accompany perfectionism.

Slay the Dragons

You do not need to be frightened by the labels—for example, "Here be dragons"—that were once put on maps to describe uncharted territories. According to whom? You may have heard the adage that the way out is through. Sometimes facing the dragons and not cowering to their hot breath brings on a huge spurt of energy and new level of growth. If you have a good idea for a new business and have fleshed out a good business plan, face the angel investors. Face the venture capitalists. What is the worst that could happen? They may decline the opportunity. This does not mean the same as verbally berating you for wasting their time with such a ridiculous idea. You will survive whether they say yes or no.

Physical Awareness

Along with the five senses, there is a kind of sensitivity that has to do with awareness of bodily position. Perhaps as you work, you can stop and do a few yoga stretches. During your daily walk, pull yourself up a little more erect and take longer strides. Swing your arms and enjoy the feeling of air on your skin.

If you like to dance or swim, take a particular delight in the awareness of your muscles as they harmoniously go through the paces of a smooth crawl or a finely executed East Coast Swing. The knowledge of where your body is, what it is doing in space, and the aesthetic and physical wonder of the rhythm and symmetry of it can be an unexpected source of joy.

Cultivate Intimacy

If you come from a background that created perfectionism, it is unlikely that true intimacy is a comfortable topic. This isn't necessarily sexual intimacy, although that might be included. Emotional intimacy is the elusive holy grail that is completely absent in a dysfunctional family. If you are perfectionistic, it is likely that intimacy is challenging for you.

Try being completely honest at first with just one or two completely warm, trustworthy people—perhaps a therapist or someone you have met in a support group. Test the waters. Tell them some of your darkest secrets, for example, that you have a ritual of lining up all the spice containers so the labels all face one direction.

Perhaps you check the coffeepot and the stove several times before leaving the house, and sometimes you call your spouse or neighbor to check if they are off because you cannot remember if you truly checked them or merely thought about it.

What else would you not want to share with another? These are the things that can be carefully shared as you discern the response of the trusted other. Is there any judgment? If not, you can proceed with what could be a truly intimate relationship. As you learn how to do this, you can slowly expand your social circle by adding more trusted friends.

ESSENTIAL

> ". . . Love for and understanding of one's own self cannot be separated from respect for and love and understanding of another individual. The love for my own self is inseparably connected with the love for any other self." —Erich Fromm

It is possible to be intimate with children, if you keep the perfectionism in check. No need to correct anything about them. Ask some interesting open-ended questions. What was the best part of your day so far? What would it be like to be invisible? Where would you go and what would you do? If you could travel in time, who would you like to visit?

It can be very rewarding to have long talks with elderly people. Open-ended questions yield much wisdom and perspective on life. What was your most memorable moment in your life? Who impacted you—public or private figure? If you could have done anything differently during your life, what would it have been? What was your most interesting mistake, and how did you recover? Ask them about perfectionism.

CHAPTER 14

Rebuilding Self-Esteem

Some persons from troubled backgrounds discover that they never actually *had* self-esteem, so it is a case of building esteem from ground zero. This stark realization gives the individual clarity, and new decisions are ready to be made. Some have said that esteem comes from doing esteemable acts. You may find that the old motivations for perfection subside somewhat as new, fresh actions move to the forefront of your life. The former frantic overachievement with its fleeting accolade is no longer as appealing as an honest, authentic moment with a treasured pet, friend, or relative.

Taking Back the Initiative in Your Life

The grips of perfectionism take away true control of your existence, as you are at the mercy of the old, outdated voices, whether yours or those of former authority figures. If you can muzzle those voices, it becomes possible to make decisions about your life that result in greater satisfaction.

Start Small

Perhaps you have been dominated by your spouse's lifestyle and social expectations that go along with a particular career. It has been seductive because there are many perks. First, select your own clothing when you are forced to attend one of those command performances. Maybe the invitation called for semiformal, but your favorite cardigan is calling to you. Snaz up the rest of the outfit to balance out the soft sweater, and see how comfortable you are truly being yourself. On another occasion, opt out completely and take a class or go to a cultural event that is more to your liking. Help your spouse fabricate a plausible excuse for your absence and promise some quality time together as a reward.

Take Bigger Initiatives

The confidence gained with small steps in your true direction lead to bigger steps toward your own happiness. You may find resistance among those closest to you. This is to be expected, as they are comfortable in their relationships with you and fear losing you to the new self that is emerging. It sometimes helps to keep plans quiet and let the actions speak for themselves. That way there is less room for arguing.

During your meditations and writing, new directions will emerge. Your essence will call to you once the heavy burden of perfectionism has been laid down. Do you long for the company of others who love flowers and other exotic plants? Spend some time haunting local nurseries and public gardens. Ask a lot of questions of the workers in such places. Offer to be of assistance in some way. Perhaps the local arboretum has a yearly sale and help is needed to publicize the event. The nursery manager may need a bookkeeper.

ESSENTIAL

George Washington Carver made the inspiring statement, "If you love something enough, it will reveal its secrets." Think of this when you feel a new direction calling. Spend time with it and see what secrets might be revealed.

There is something mystical about the process of going in a new direction. Doors open and a world is revealed that was formerly mostly unknown.

Being Part of the Human Race

Perfectionists try so hard to be good enough, better than, or the very best, when lurking in the psyche are the beliefs that one is not good enough at all. It is tortuous to keep doing things perfectly to quiet the demanding directives. As one lets go of perfectionism in the self, other people become more interesting and attractive. Fewer traits are annoying, and one can go forth and be a human among humans.

But I've Always Been an Alien!

Remember how lovable E.T. was? Being an alien might not be so bad, but joining the human race can be a comfort, as well. If you are on a treadmill from dawn until midnight crossing things off your "to do" list, set that aside and hang out in a public place with some fellow earthlings. Maybe go to a concert in the park and share your picnic with the family on the next blanket. Browse at your favorite bookstore and ask a fellow browser his opinion on a particular writer or subject. Try a lecture or seminar on a topic that seems intriguing but not your usual forte. Strike up conversations with other attendees about why they happened to be there. Follow up on interesting points with the presenters. When you're out for a walk in your neighborhood, take the time to exchange pleasantries with the neighbors about their remodeling projects or new puppies.

Without Competition I'm Nobody!

Others will find you infinitely more appealing as you become less perfect. This is hard to accept when one has lived an entire life on the treadmill of achievement and people pleasing. Try to reveal your foibles to others in small increments. If you burned the bagels one morning, tell everyone you encounter for the next hour or two. They will laugh and tell you of their own kitchen disasters.

Think of people in your world who make you feel absolutely fabulous. Is it the waitress at your favorite restaurant? How interested is she in your highest achievements? She wants to know what you would like to eat and likely already has something in mind for you because she knows your tastes. Neither of you are competing. Perhaps another favorite person is the custodian at a club you frequent. He cautions you to wait a moment while he cleans up a spill on the floor so you won't slip. He is never rushed and always has time to exchange a few pleasant words. This is not a competitive person and he is not interested in your achievements. Do you have a favorite cab driver who tells marvelous stories about his family's integration into American society? This person is not interested in your achievements, but you feel infinitely cared for as he amiably philosophizes on the way to your destination. Mutual respect is present when people are equals.

Giving Up Self-Punishment

Eventually your self-inquiries will lead you to recognize the critical voices within your mind, and the connection is made to perfectionism. It helps to write down the specific sentences that others said to you that have become a part of how you talk to yourself.

Critical Voices

Others have discovered sentences similar to the following:

1. You'll never amount to anything.
2. Nothing you do is important.
3. Your purpose is to support me. Don't bother me with your stories.
4. Why can't you be more like your sister?

5. You always were too much trouble.
6. You're just crazy.
7. Why don't you give up these strange things and just be normal?
8. Everything you do reflects upon the family.
9. Can't you see I'm busy? There's no time for you. Go away.
10. How dare you do that without discussing it with me!

These statements amount to verbal abuse, and the scary thing is, as an adult, those things continue to be said! Noticing the specific statements is a good first step. Then stop saying that specific thing when you catch it. It won't be instantaneous, as you undoubtedly have practiced the litanies for years.

Craft Some Affirmations

A good way to make use of critical statements is to write them down and then write down the exact opposite. The new sentence is your affirmation. For example, the criticism of "How dare you do that without discussing it with me!" becomes "You are an intelligent person who is free to create a life you love." "I'm too busy for you," becomes "You're important. Let's take the time to think about this together."

It is interesting to experiment with the voice of affirmations. Some people crave the affirmative directive, as if it is coming from the other person. Those "you" statements give the feeling of giving permission to think and feel in a new way. Others like to put the affirmation in the first person. The strong "I" statement gives the person a sense of centeredness and control.

Release Anxiety

As a person shifts from self-criticism to self-affirmation, the old nameless fears subside. The result is a much greater degree of calm as one moves through the day. Strangely enough, without the perfectionism, there are fewer real or imagined emergencies. It may feel odd not to be hyped up a lot, as if you are not important and your various tasks are not important. Anxiety can be a habit, and there is a bit of an adjustment in giving it up. When you feel that familiar tense posture and shallow breathing coming on, along with the racing thoughts, work with your breathing, tame your thoughts, and emphatically shift gears. It really is okay to be a calm, peaceful person.

Balancing Various Aspects of Your Life

If you tend toward perfectionism, it is quite likely that different parts of your life are out of balance. It is likely that a perfectionist works too hard or too long, spends too much time at the gym, or haunts the department store sales much too much. Compulsivity can take many forms. One way to approach a better balance is to think about what is being neglected. Have people in your life complained about something to you? Maybe you need to spend more time with friends. Strong social connections are a large component of mental health.

Possibly more leisure time is needed with the caution of not making the recreational pursuits something new to work on. It's not necessary to compete at Wimbledon to enjoy tennis.

ALERT

Beware of videogames and other role-playing online games as recreation! Jim Rubens notes that the average player clocks twenty-two hours a week in such games, and extremists play for up to eighty hours per week!

Some people find that keeping a time log for a few weeks shows where time is wasted or otherwise misspent. A simple notepad where the categories of life are listed with the length of time on each one, each day, is quite illuminating. Numbers show the graphic truth, and it becomes easier to grasp the necessity of reapportioning the currency of time. Some categories may be completely absent! It might help to look at your categories with a trusted friend or professional to get some support in shaving down the parts that are too large and reallocating time to other, neglected parts of your life. Undoubtedly, you will experience various emotions and attitude adjustments as you make those changes.

The Power of Positive Reinforcement

B. F. Skinner discovered that certain types of reinforcement are powerful conditioners for animals and humans. Now it is common knowledge that a pet can be trained to do certain tricks. So can you! You know your favorite rewards better than anyone. Be careful that your rewards are not something that could take you down another compulsive direction—overeating or shopping.

ESSENTIAL

> Claiming true desires and accepting rewards for them can bring about a great deal of emotional pain if there has been a lifetime of self-deprivation. It is like a frostbitten limb thawing out. However, the benefits outweigh the discomfort if a person can withstand the process.

The areas that you discovered had been neglected might hold some ideas for helpful rewards. For example, if you tend to work too much, each day that you stop work at the specified time, reward yourself with ten minutes of dancing to energetic music. You have not danced in months or years! This is the reason to include the possibility of this as a reward.

It can be fun to discuss with your inner child what would be some good rewards. Surprisingly, something as simple as gold stars on the planning calendar might be enough to elicit that good feeling of acknowledgement. Perhaps the inner child wants to go to a comedic movie instead of another dreary docudrama. The indulgence can be very relaxing and fun. One author discovered at a book signing that almost all of her fans carried gel pens in glittery hues, a pleasant way to reward oneself.

According to classical conditioning, intermittent reinforcement is the strongest schedule because of its longer-lasting effects in shaping the behavior. You might find that when you are forming a new habit, a treat every time is needed to change the habitual direction. As it becomes a little more comfortable, a shift to a reward every few times becomes quite powerful.

Average Is Okay

Perfectionists abhor the idea of average. Actually, average is not so bad if it is accompanied by better health, better relationships, and greater peace of mind. Being average gives a person more room to experiment and to try various directions without being so afraid of not doing things well. Being an average Sunday painter might bring enormous pleasure. Singing in a chorus might provide the camaraderie of other music lovers and the safety of numbers. Not everyone has to be a soloist.

FACT

Being average is better for the health. One worker, who figuratively chained himself to the desk like a dog, never took breaks, and ate lunch at his desk, ended up with a ruptured ulcer.

Those aspects of life that have been neglected might be just the aspects that could bring happiness with average accomplishment. A fishing outing with younger relatives is fun, even if nobody catches any fish! The memories will be of the outdoors and shared moments.

Realistically, one is probably not going to become another Michael Jordan, Yo-Yo Ma, or the next winner of *American Idol*, although millions of Americans think it is possible. This is part of the American myth, that any person can reach the top. Olympist Michelle Kwan said it rather well, "I didn't lose the gold. I won the silver." Accepting the position of average is particularly difficult for baby boomers because that generation came of age when the average American did have greater options. It is especially essential for boomers not to become disillusioned but to refashion the idea of success in a way that is personal and real.

Rekindle Former Interests

What interests have you set aside because it seemed that your perfectionistic demands on yourself were so much more important? It might be fun to do some of those things again. Take a look at your Hot Wheels collection and remember how much fun you had selecting each little car. You might enjoy attending antique auto shows and refurbishing old cars. People who frequent those events may speak your same language.

Maybe life has become so impossibly busy that you have stopped cooking. Get out the cookbooks and browse through them. Think of which treasured people you'd like to cook for and plan a gathering. Shop for the best (but not perfect) ingredients and enjoy the leisurely process of preparing a meal for loved ones. Savor the textures and flavors. Create a table setting that pleases the eye, and choose background music according to the tastes of your guests. It might be fun to select a theme—a holiday or a particular type of ethnic food. This will give you an excuse to shop for exotic spices.

Has your social life suffered because of your devotion to a demanding job? Take some time and make phone calls just to catch up with friends you haven't spoken with recently. Remember who is sick or convalescing and send out some inquiries to see how those people are doing. Perhaps you like to make handmade greeting cards. Adding birthday notes to your planning calendar can spark interest in making something creative to send out for someone's birthday or other important event.

How to Manage Your Anger

It is likely that a lot of your anger is directed at yourself, because you are not perfect and do not perform perfectly. Underneath that anger is hurt and fear. If you can bear it, spend some time with yourself and find the true emotion under the anger. Are you hurt because a friend slighted you? Are you afraid that your parents or spouse will never love you the way you want to be loved? It can be sobering to face the truth of the emotion, but strangely, a person calms down a bit when clarity is reached.

Damage Control

When you feel tremendously out of sorts with anger and rage, direct that energy in another direction. Tell whomever you are with that you are taking a time-out. Go to another location and walk energetically for awhile. If you like to jog or cycle, this would be a good time to get the extra exercise.

Sometimes it helps to plug into your favorite music and be in a different zone for awhile. Perhaps you can clean out the garage or move the boxes of stored office records that you have ignored. Eliminate any thoughts of hurting yourself or others from your mind.

If you fear hurting a child while you are angry, keep close at hand, even in your cell phone, hotline numbers to prevent child abuse. Share honestly with the crisis worker how you feel and what you fear you might do. It helps, as well, to attend support groups for parents who fear that they will abuse their children. This is actually a common inclination for adults who were themselves abused as children. As you get to know those other group members, they can support you on those very difficult days.

Make Apologies as Necessary

As your anger becomes more under control, it helps to backtrack and say that you're sorry to each person that has been harmed by the outbursts. This will be quite difficult at first, as the anger seems so justified. However, with practice, getting back to the person right away humanizes the situation, and others can see that you own up to not being perfect. This can be a breath of fresh air for everyone concerned. It is especially important to make amends to children and others in very close relationships. Such sincere apologies keep the relationship channels clean and harmonious.

What Can You Do Instead?

It has been said that happiness is having something to do and someone to love. This could also be true of self-esteem. Enjoyable activities add so much to life, whether paid or unpaid, and being with persons who are genuinely cared for brings dimension and warmth to days that otherwise might be empty and barren. Perfectionists tend to suffer from loneliness.

ESSENTIAL

Maturity is the ability to work and the ability to love. Some aspects of maturity are accepting ambivalent situations and being able to cooperate with others, sometimes letting them have the final say in a decision.

Catch yourself on those good days and do a few more of the things that seem to enhance your self-esteem. As you let go of perfectionism, you will discover more about what truly makes you feel good about yourself. One good thing can lead to another, and these fine days compensate for the days when it seems that nothing goes according to plan.

Being of service to others is a sure route to self-esteem. In your work, think of the end result and how it truly meets the needs of the customers or clients. This is the heart of self-esteem—using your energy to provide something for another person who needs just what you deliver. If you are not currently employed, find a situation that cries out for your talents and give some time to others. It might be exercising and talking with animals at a humane society or sorting donations for a women's domestic violence shelter. If you like physical labor and construction sites, Habitat for Humanity is a possible place to do tremendous good.

On those days when it seems that perfectionism has the upper hand, one route to gaining self-esteem is to deliberately do things one at a time. Stop everything and do one simple thing—perhaps make a phone call or open the mail. People who do too much or try to do several things at once can experience nervous anxiety because none of the tasks they do feel complete or well done. Doing simple tasks around the home or workplace are good for calming down.

ALERT

Accept that each task requires a finite amount of time, and resist the temptation to try to do many things in a given span of time. It is frustrating, and leads to tension and anxiety.

Clearing out the inbox of old e-mails is mindless and calming. Sending a simple greeting card to a relative or friend bears fruit in self-esteem. Catching up on filing may not be the favorite task, but the feeling of accomplishment is a powerful reward.

CHAPTER 15

Perfectionism and the Only Child or Gifted Child

An only child or gifted child exists in an environment that can lead to the child trying to be perfect, and that situation often extends into adult years, resulting in a perfectionistic man or woman. The only child is the family's only shot at raising a child, and there can be intense pressure to get it right. The gifted child is so good at so many things that the temptation to be perfect is always there, both from within the child and from the parents. These inclinations continue into the adult experience.

Hazards Ahead!

Watch out for perfectionism! It can be deadly for the gifted child. Gifted children will likely be emotionally sensitive and easy to stunt with too much prodding or pushing. It's a good idea to remember that the quest of learning is what engages the mind, not the result. The result may be momentarily interesting, but the joy is in careening down the path to get there. Both parents and children need to keep in mind that it is the process that is valuable, not necessarily the result.

The child needs to understand that he is loved for who he is, not for what he does. The best prevention for the harms of perfectionism is to give the child plenty of unconditional love and affection. It also is sensible to let the child fail from time to time. Failure is definitely a part of life, and even a very young child can learn that he's okay, even if things don't turn out quite as expected.

Gifted Challenges

The exquisite sensitivity that enables gifted children to note subtle differences in texture, movement, color, and shape means that what others perceive as a blank wall can appear to them as a vibrant palette. Because they are constantly bombarded with sensory stimuli, they are more stressed. The extreme interpersonal sensitivity causes some children to tune into other people's feelings. They are aware of hints of criticism and displeasure that other children don't notice. Ironically, the combination of extreme sensitivity, high energy level, and reduced need for sleep are characteristics of children often diagnosed as hyperactive. There may be a lot of very misunderstood children out there! Gifted children can be perfectionistic in wanting to complete a task, but find to their utter frustration they do not have the physical strength or dexterity to carry it out.

Special Concerns for Adults and Children

From the beginning, an only child (who has only his parents for social company at home) is subject to peer pressure from parents that, in most cases, they aren't even aware they are exerting. The law of peer pressure is the same everywhere—conform to belong. Espousing the ruling norms of a group allows an individual member of that group to fit in, get along, and become a member in good standing.

FACT

Gifted adults often suffer from isolation and loneliness, and there is the temptation to dumb down, act normal and average, just to fit in with a social group. This quest can become a compulsion, trying over and over again to find the perfect tribe where the quick wit and curious mind will be accepted rather than scorned.

So the only child adjusts to parental ways, accepts parental terms, imitates parental actions, and acquires parental beliefs in order to be in good favor. In response, parental acceptance and approval is given. Gifted persons are sometimes similarly shackled, regardless of the age, feeling that everyone expects them to be a great problem-solver, charming and funny, and the one who always sees a project through. It can be a burdensome exercise in futile perfectionism.

Emotional Enmeshment

It's obvious to say, but important to remember, that parents and an only child grow extremely close emotionally. Their bonding is rooted in spending so much time together, keeping each other social company at home, caring so much for each other, and coming to know each other so intimately. Typically, their relationship is emotionally sensitized—parent and child being able to tell, without words, how the other is feeling. It is difficult to mask true feelings from each other.

If you remember the characters in the movie *White Oleander*, the mother fostered the enmeshment of the daughter in a very unhealthy way, refusing to let her develop as a separate individual. She insisted that the lost teenager remember that: "We are Viking women!" The mother said fairly often to the teenager, "You're perfect." This sets up unrealistic ideas in the child.

Feeling Tied to Each Other

Difficulty with such closeness arises when parents and child tie their own feelings to the well-being of each other. Harboring thoughts like the ones below is often a sign of emotional enmeshment.

- "I feel okay if you feel okay."
- "If you don't feel okay, then I don't feel okay."
- "If you don't feel okay, then I need to help you feel okay."
- "If I am unable to help you feel okay, then I won't feel okay."

ESSENTIAL

Emotional enmeshment comes at the expense of emotional independence, which allows one person to feel bad without the other automatically feeling bad in response. Someone who does not have emotional independence feels obliged to "fix" the unhappy other so they can both feel okay. This is a landmine for perfectionism because it is never possible to fix another person, although the youngster would like to.

Caution with Types of Reinforcement for Only Children

Since some degree of emotional enmeshment is very common between parents and an only child, the wrong comments can increase the pressure on this intense attachment. So when parents look at As on a report card and declare, "We must be doing something right!" the child links her personal performance to her parents' well-being. "How I do determines how my parents feel." This is a scary proposition, fraught with possibilities for perfectionistic thinking and behavior. Better for parents to have simply said, "Congratulations for how well you've done!" and express satisfaction for the child, rather than with themselves.

An only child or a gifted child can be quite sensitive to corrections, making you both unhappy. A parent may say, "It hurts me to give correction because I know it hurts my child." The child may say, "It hurts being corrected because that means I have failed to please my parents and now they are unhappy because of me." The child always wants to do the right thing and may try to second-guess what the parent wants, even if the parent does not clearly state what is expected.

Be careful of the temptation to attach your good feelings about yourself to the child's good behavior. Statements such as, "We're proud of you" or "You make us feel so proud" may increase perfectionistic pressure on the child to believe, "How well or badly I do determines how well or badly my parents feel about themselves." This gives unrealistic responsibility to the child concerning the parents' emotional health.

The Tyranny of Pleasing

Parents and their only child usually have mutual admiration for one another. Each side gives the other such high approval ratings that neither one can stand the thought of displeasing the other, or of not pleasing the other enough. This makes the give and take of getting along, with the inequities of age and power, especially hard to take.

Excessive pressure to please each other can create a "tyranny of pleasing." To reduce this tyranny of pleasing, parents should clarify for themselves and their only child the difference between love and approval. Love is a given. It is rooted in the parents' unconditional acceptance of the person their child is. Approval is earned. It is rooted in the parents' responsibility to conditionally evaluate their child's performance and to communicate how well or badly he or she is making decisions in life, completely separate from what the parents need from their own self-esteem.

ESSENTIAL

Explain to your child that love and approval are not the same. Love is a constant; approval varies with evaluation of the child's behavior. Love does not guarantee approval any more than disapproval means a loss of love. Keep dissipating the misconception that perfection is necessary for either love or approval.

You have a responsibility to evaluate your child's development and actions, but how you deliver your opinions makes the difference between fostering perfectionism or avoiding it. In fact, what you need to do is neutralize your evaluation when giving a correction by expressing it not as disapproval but as disagreement, as follows: "We disagree with the choice you have made, here is why, and this is what we need to have happen in consequence."

To keep the tyranny of pleasing from making it harder to assist your sensitive gifted or only child, you can communicate that your relationship will be displeasing sometimes, and that's okay.

- "We don't always have to agree with what the other believes."
- "We don't always have to like each other to get along."
- "We can disapprove of each other's actions and still love each other as much as ever."
- "We will both sometimes make decisions to please ourselves that we know will be displeasing to each other."
- "We are separate people and can please ourselves sometimes. This isn't selfish."

The tyranny of pleasing is not limited to children. Gifted adults, and adults who were only children, are similarly fine-tuned to the preferences of others, whether a spouse, close friend, coworker, or supervisor. The people-pleasing person is able to sense what the other wants, even before it is stated, and act on those things for the other person. This can be quite an attractive skill, to a point, but it sometimes gets out of hand, and the overly sensitive pleaser ends up having no life. All her efforts are extended toward others. This is especially the case if that was the dynamic in the person's childhood home.

The Expectation of Return

Parenting an only child is high-investment parenting. Everything that you have to give as parents is devoted to the welfare of a single child; all your hopes and dreams for parenthood ride on the shoulders of how that child grows through life. On the one hand, what you give, you give freely out of love. But because you are human, you do have some expectation of return for all the caring, time, energy, resources, and effort you have put in. The high investment parents make in an only child often comes with a high expectation of return. This setup includes dangers of perfectionism in both the parent and the child.

Sometimes, often in adolescence, the only child will object to the pressure he feels to make good on that return. "When you say you only want the best for me, what you really mean is that you want the best from me. The more you do for me, the more I'm expected to do for you, and most of all that means doing well! It's like I'm supposed to live my life to make you look good!" Be aware that a bright teenager in an emotionally healthy home will say such things, no holds barred!

Communicate to your only child that he or she does not owe you an unblemished and stellar performance in return for the dedicated care and support you provide. "All we expect from you is what we expect from ourselves—an honest effort to do what's right that results in a mixed performance of good decisions and bad, because none of us is perfect, only human."

Also, do not use the words "should" or "ought" when speaking to your child. Both words just encourage feelings of duty in a child who already carries a strong sense of obligation to you.

FACT

The only child's tendency to imitate and please parents who are very sensitive and understanding makes for a harmonious childhood most of the time. Come the more stormy adolescent years, however, the teenager may want to severely break out of the mold, especially if there have been tinges of perfectionistic expectations. Your good child may suddenly not be so good any more.

Unrealistic Standards of Performance

Being peers with parents not only leads the only child to develop more grown-up speaking and social skills at an early age, but all the adult association makes the boy or girl feel more adult. In consequence, the child will frequently lay claim to adultlike standing in the family.

Unhappily, this is where self-imposed performance pressure can begin for many only children. By presuming comparable standing to parents ("If I can act their equal, then I should have equal say"), the only child carries this equation one dangerous step further: "If I can act equally grown up, then I should be able to perform equally well." Does this sound like perfectionism?

But the child is not an adult, and so these standards are inappropriate and unreachable. "I can't do it as well as you," moans the only child when the more experienced parent does something better. Then, to ease this frustration, the parent may respond, "Don't be so hard on yourself, you're just a child." But this is not what the only child wants to hear, and now she feels put down and assigned inferior standing in the family.

To help keep your only child's unrealistically high standards from making it harder to relate to them, soften the stands you take by making honest explanations. "When we want you to take on additional responsibility, that doesn't mean you are not trying or working hard enough. It just means that as you grow there is more self-discipline to learn." "When we call you down for not doing what we feel you should, or for doing what we feel you shouldn't, that doesn't mean you don't do anything right. In fact, it's the exception that proves the rule: most of the time you conduct your life extremely well."

ALERT

Signs that your only child is putting unreasonable demands on himself include an intolerance of anything less than outstanding personal performance, extreme frustration with mistakes, severe self-criticism, and despondency after losing in competition or failing to achieve a goal.

Perfectionism can easily creep into the equation with an only child, as only children often are naturally high achievers. They have a lot of attention from the adults in their lives and can thrive in many ways. This is optimal, to a point, but not if the child becomes tense, absolutely *having* to be the best at everything. This is the route to an unhappy life.

Alice Miller's *Drama of the Gifted Child*

Alice Miller eloquently describes the painful hazards of a gifted child growing up in a situation where the parents have unhealthy needs that they attempt to fulfill through the sensitive, gifted child. This dynamic can be so insidious and twisted that it takes decades of therapy for the innocent individual to undo the psychological damage. Self-esteem must, by the very definition of the term, come from the self. Parents must have separate, fulfilled identities on their own, never leeching off the precious talents of the gifted child. If you have concerns about this dynamic, the book *The Drama of the Gifted Child* is a sober eye opener.

The situation is difficult for the child who wants to be perfect so the parents will feel okay about themselves. In a way, the child's personality and giftedness are hijacked by the parents, making it very challenging for the gifted child to develop self-knowledge and awareness. All she knows is that the parents depend upon her and it is best for everyone if she measures up accordingly.

FACT

According to a quotation from writer Pearl S. Buck, "The truly creative mind in any field is no more than this: A human creature born abnormally, inhumanly sensitive. To him a touch is a blow, a sound is a noise, a misfortune is a tragedy, a joy is an ecstasy, a friend is a lover, a lover is a god, and failure is death."

Adults who grow up with this kind of dynamic in their background often do not know their true interests and talents because the parents lived through them to such a great extent. The gifted adult is able to do many things very well and sometimes cannot distinguish between mastery and joy. Once the underlying dynamic has been discovered, the courageous adult can experiment with lost interests and talents, coaxing out tendrils of joy that were squelched by the needy parents.

What Can You Do Instead?

Only children and gifted children grow up in a pressure cooker environment. Conditions are likely that they can become arrogant, fearful, overly obligated, people pleasing, entitled, and perfectionistic. One has to be creative to overcome these tendencies, as everyone's aim in raising children (beyond the hope of surviving raising the child) is to raise a child who will be happy and functional in adult life.

Take a Time-Out from Only and Gifted

As paradoxical as it seems, these special children can get very tired of being special. The performance standards are intense, and everyone seems to be watching all the time. Enrichment can get tiresome. Some families have frank discussions with gifted children, asking them their preferences for placement in school or in summer programs. Some such children are remarkably self-aware and know when they need some time off. Sometimes they just want to be a kid. If grandparents are involved in the child's life, they often provide a mellow, tempering influence on the pressures of being so great.

Time Out from Parenting

Similarly, parents need time to simply be ordinary people. A weekend away alone or with the spouse provides marvelous respite from so much wonderfulness in the child. Parents can sleep when they want, eat whatever is desired, and watch shallow junky movies that might not be preferred fare for the child.

Parents who continue their own development tend to be happier at each stage of the child's growth. Eventually, when the only or gifted child strikes out on his own, the parent can still be happy, even if the favorite "project" has left the house. Passionate involvement in hobbies or work will continue, even after the most important years of parenting have come to an end.

Balance for Gifted and Only Adults

Like those special children, special adults have challenges in juggling the pleasures of a distinct status with that of being part of the human race. Sometimes such a person will set aside the braininess for a while and do something completely different, like work in a Buddhist bakery or join a volunteer crew of highway cleanup workers. Selection of a mate can be a challenge for exceptionally talented persons. Some join associations such as Mensa to find kindred souls, and others find them along the way in their professional associations.

If you happen to work with or otherwise are close with an only adult or gifted adult, compassion is always in order. Their perfectionism developed as a coping mechanism in a hothouse environment, and without it they would feel naked. After all, they didn't *choose* to be only or gifted. It was an accident of heritage.

CHAPTER 16

Deep Self-Acceptance

Self-acceptance is the antithesis of a perfectionist's usual self-critical frame of mind. However, it opens the door to the spiraling labyrinth of negativity. Self-acceptance slows down the mind, lowers the blood pressure, deepens the breathing, and eases a person into beautifully imperfect normalcy. With practice, the perfectionist catches the impossible demands on the self and mentally reframes them into something friendlier, more humane, more loving.

Julia Cameron's Ideas—The Artist's Date

Julia Cameron's books, *The Artist's Way* and *Vein of Gold*, are helpful resources for people working themselves out of a negative, unsatisfying life and into a life of creative expression and wholesome comfort. One of her marvelous suggestions is to take yourself on an artist's date once a week. The artist's date is a chance to go out alone and do something fun and nurturing for the creative inner artist. It doesn't have to cost money, but it does have to be alone, because having another person along diverts the focus of the outing.

Ideas for Artist's Dates

With practice, the artist's dates become quite fun, a little opportunity to goof off, play hooky, and generally be a little silly. Some possibilities might include the following, depending on what you really enjoy:

1. Go to the zoo and talk to the animals.
2. Buy some nice felt-tipped pens.
3. Buy stickers and put them in your journal every day.
4. Listen to and watch taiko drummers.
5. Go to an Aztec dance performance.
6. Go to a foreign market and buy foods you've never heard of before. Cook something with them.
7. Visit a stable and ride a gentle horse.
8. Check out children's books on your favorite topics and read them to yourself.
9. Ride a train to the end of the line, turn around, and come back home.
10. Attend a country auction and bid on something, and then eat homemade apple pie for lunch.

It is healing for the outings to be nonpurposeful, on purpose, as the brain and spirit relax with input from divergent directions. If you are a creative soul, as most people are, you may find that you get wonderful ideas during or following your artist's dates, but those ideas are not the purpose of the outing.

Watch for Self-Sabotage!

It is tempting to forget the artist's date, as you have too many other important things to do. This is the perfectionist-workaholic lurking around, trying to keep you from enjoying yourself. Think of it as medicine for the spirit, an IV for the soul that needs regular drips in order to keep all aspects of the balanced individual functioning well. You may have decades of self-deprivation to make up for, and the old punitive voices will try to derail your good intentions. If necessary, write the specific artist's date on your planning calendar and bookend it with someone in order for it to be a commitment that is as important as your work or doctor's appointments. Don't do the artist's date after everything else is finished, because that day never arrives.

Purpose for the Artist's Dates

How can these weekly outings be beneficial to a perfectionistic person? By definition, the artist's dates are little excursions with no purpose except to nurture the creative self. They are childlike, only intended for fun, but not a type of extravagant fun such as one would find in a theme park. A perfectionist has difficulty doing pleasurable actions for the self, and the artist's dates are a way to softly shave the edges off the perfectionism.

The artist's dates allow variety and innovation into the unbalanced obsessive life of the perfectionist, bringing respite to the digitally driven, time-driven, fast-paced life of accomplishment. There is no goal during the artist's date, except to enjoy oneself.

Comfortable in Your Own Skin

With more and more self-acceptance, you begin to find that you like yourself better, even without being perfect. There may be a time period of feeling vulnerable, slightly naked, as you go about your life with a less perfectionistic attitude, schedule, and lifestyle. You find yourself admitting errors and personal foibles to people and learn that they do not reject you. In fact, they are more accepting as your humanness evolves. Physically you become more relaxed, your mind slows down, and emotionally you are less wired.

You may find that you are apologizing less frequently. What a relief to be freer of unnecessary guilt, always beholden to others in a perfectionistic manner! When you feel the inclination to apologize, pause and check out the urge with someone else. It could be completely unnecessary.

Grieve the Perfectionistic Self

There may be a lengthy grief process for the loss of the perfect self. Actually, it is the idea or fantasy of the perfect self, as it can never be achieved. It was the effort that led to exhaustion and tremendous unhappiness. The predictable stages of the grief process may recycle a few times as the layers of false self and inhuman expectations fall away. Expect crying, sadness, and a need for extra rest. Some people find that they need extra nutrition, as grief is work. Think of it as hard labor for the spirit.

Where and How to Grieve

The American culture does not openly embrace grief, so finding safe places and people to support your grief can take some focused effort. Depending on their background and personalities, some therapists are able to be emotionally present when a person is grieving. Be alert for well-meaning individuals who are too quick to offer solutions, as they themselves are often quite uncomfortable with grief. Seek out friends who have walked a similar path and will not try to shape your experience for you.

FACT

Complicated grief is the term for a disorder in which the person who suffered a loss does not feel better after time has passed. The emotions of loss are as great as they were at the time of the loss, and the person has not resumed normal functioning.

It can be a tremendous comfort to have an understanding friend on the other end of a phone line when you need to cry or to tell a story about how your perfectionism tripped you up.

Support groups can be especially helpful during times of grief. Relationships are built over a period of weeks, months, or even years, and a network of genuine social support is the welcome result. Jim Rubens noted in his book, *OverSuccess*, that large numbers of people in the United States have no friends, at least no in-person friends. Social media may be relaxing and diversionary, but an actual person who can give you a warm hug is quite marvelous when one is grieving. Community bulletin boards sometimes display notices of special focus groups. Churches and hospitals offer various helpful groups, and neighborhood newspapers can be perused for possible groups during a time of specialized need.

I'm Afraid I'm Going Crazy!

The intense emotions of grief often frighten individuals who have kept them repressed for years. They might be the intense fear of a child who was reprimanded for demonstrating quite appropriate wants or needs. There may be intense longing for loving, aware, present relatives and experiences that should have been there but weren't. The good news is that those powerful feelings pass, if they are given time and space. If repressed, they do not pass. They pop out at embarrassing, inconvenient, inopportune times.

Some have been reassured that feeling crazy is actually a process of becoming uncrazy. It is a thawing out of frozen emotions that no longer want to be locked in. When a person reaches a place in life where the environment is safe, the people are safe, and one is resilient enough to withstand the torrents of tears, that's when the emotions come out.

Grief is rather organic, having an ebb and flow of its own. It's not something that you can schedule or sandwich in between getting married and finishing graduate school. It creeps up when the time is right. Sometimes an old grief will piggyback onto a current grief, especially if the former experience was not fully grieved at the time. At times an anniversary of a loss will precipitate an echo of the original loss.

There is certainly no harm in seeking professional help during times of intense grief. A familiar therapist can be of enormous comfort and support, or one can find a therapist with a specialty in grief work. Such therapeutic work can be short term or long term, depending on the needs of the individual.

ALERT

It can be a tempting to use therapy, grief work, and inner child work to such a degree that they become the end itself, rather than a means to an end. Focusing on these things for years, polishing the jargon, and finely honing the identity of a person who is irrevocably damaged can be an escape from the reality of adult functioning. It might be an interesting, even helpful diversion, but not a long-term way of life for a person who intends to thrive.

If the following symptoms are present, the grieving individual may be stuck in complicated grief:

1. Intense longing for the person who died; a focus on their possessions and reminders
2. Difficulty accepting the death or loss
3. Feeling numb, preoccupation with sorrow
4. Bitterness, inability to enjoy life
5. Depression, not functioning in normal life
6. Withdrawal from social activities
7. Believing that life has lost meaning
8. Loss of trust in others
9. Feelings of guilt and self-blame
10. Wishing that one had died along with the person who was lost

These symptoms mostly refer to what might occur with the death of a loved one, but the loss of the idea of who one is as a perfect person, fulfilling some unknown, nameless requirements, can be just as devastating. It is always good to be aware of danger signals and when to reach out for help.

Pamper the Young, Inner Child

John Bradshaw's book, *Homecoming*, includes helpful charts for remedial activities for each developmental age of maturation. For example, the elementary school years are when we learn how to competently get along in the environment. If a parent was absent or preoccupied during that time, the adult may have a deficit in terms of feeling confident in knowing basic competencies and learning new ones. Loving parents encourage little ones as they try new things, and you can do that for yourself.

Pampering Ideas

The exact activities that are right for you will depend on what was missing during the young years and somewhat on your inclinations and interests. It may take some trial and error to discover what is truly pampering to your inner child. The following are some ideas that others have found helpful:

1. Sleep in sheets and blankets in colors and textures that you like.
2. Wear clothing that you like, especially at home.
3. Pay attention to food cravings and honor them if they are not self-destructive.
4. Reward yourself with a light-hearted movie.
5. Protect yourself from loud, dogmatic people.
6. Let your inner child know that you will get back to him in a specific amount of time if you have to do adult things for a while.
7. Talk to yourself in a calm, low, soothing voice.
8. Do fewer things and do them slowly.
9. Include nonpurposeful things in the day.
10. Stare at things and do nothing.

Giving Up Suffering

It can be quite difficult to give up the habit of suffering. It may have been a family role or the habit of an important role model, and it will seem disloyal or quite odd to think about the mantle of suffering sliding away. Will anything be left? What will become important without the effortful drudgery? Some families have a generational pattern of suffering, and one can feel quite strange embracing a joyful life. Will there be anything to discuss during family reunions?

Martyrdom

The types of families that foster perfectionism sometimes cultivate people who believe that martyrdom is an attractive aspiration. One parent may have been long-suffering, and everyone acknowledged what a good person he was to put up with everything that occurred in the dysfunctional house. Sighing may have brought positive solicitations and offers of attention and help. It's very difficult to get angry with the family martyr who is always of service to others and never complains.

ALERT

Perfectionists who tend toward martyrdom may subconsciously believe that if they do enough commendable things for many people, they will escape criticism. It is nearly impossible to criticize a person who seems so altruistic.

However, it is quite fine to live an enjoyable life without being a grind in the service of others. Notice if there is guilt when you do what you want instead of doing something that someone else would like you to do. That could be a clue to some lingering vestiges of martyrdom. Martyrs sometimes suffer depression and physical illness, as these are seemingly the only way to be deserving of a time-out from excessive responsibility.

Buddhist Thoughts on Suffering

Relief from suffering is at the heart of Buddhist teaching. Yes, life is full of change, sometimes welcome and sometimes not, and the human condition seems fraught with gain and eventual loss. How can one manage and still remain relatively sane and serene?

The practice of meditation greatly quiets the mind and makes the regular meditator less susceptible to the stresses of life. The daily quieting experience provides a healthy haven to which the person can return, instantaneously if necessary, without being caught up in the emergency of the moment.

The idea of attachment is central to the tenets of Buddhism, and attachment causes suffering. What are some types of attitudes, mindsets, things, people, or situations that create attachment and suffering?

1. Always getting one's own way.
2. The idea that a relationship will last forever.
3. A mental construct, such as politicians should selflessly serve their constituency.
4. But we've always done it this way! Difficulty with flexibility and change.
5. Feeling abandoned when a favorite friend or relative dies or moves away.
6. Addictive pleasures result in suffering when the source is removed.
7. Overemphasis on results, especially perfect results.
8. Relentless pursuit of sensory experiences requires an escalating schedule, as it is never enough. Not getting whatever is sought brings depression and anxiety.
9. Needing a certain identity or status to be acceptable to oneself.
10. Excessive material comfort, which can lead to a constant search for a new experience, such as the characters in the film *Eyes Wide Shut*.
11. Undue importance on a certain personal image.
12. Grasping at wrong ideas, such as "A mother has to stay home full time."
13. Dependence on rigid routines and rituals.

One can see that these ways of thinking, feeling, and behaving are interrelated, and it could be possible to wrestle with several at the same time. This results in a clinging to impossible results, and a great deal of personal unhappiness. Imagine, for example, that a very young, attractive woman marries a wealthy, somewhat older man. They have little in common. She could be thought of as a trophy wife. Her security in the situation depends upon being attractive and available to her husband. She becomes worried when she notices a few wrinkles and wonders if she should start a strict regimen of facial treatments. She undertakes a strict program of Pilates. She is completely image conscious, as she believes that without a certain physical image, her marriage will be over. One can imagine the suffering, anxiety, and mental anguish involved in trying to prevent aging. In this case, the profession of being a trophy wife did not lead to freedom, personal growth, and joy.

What Can You Do Instead?

Deep self-acceptance can gradually become a habit, and you may find that what was once tolerable in terms of overworking or overindulging in anything is no longer acceptable. Your days become a little more peaceful and you find fewer crises encroaching upon your life. People become more likable and interesting as you like yourself a little more.

Compromise with Imperfect Situations

One enterprising social worker was burned out in her profession but felt that she could not leave it. The earnings were good, and retirement benefits would have been lost if she made a midlife career change. She decided instead to embrace her creative nature and set up a miniature studio right outside her office cubicle. She set up interactive tasks for her coworkers who dropped by—a doodle notebook for squiggles in different colors, collage pieces on a day she asked people to make a collage with only white materials, and a photograph longing for whimsical cartoon captions. Her working relationships dramatically improved, and she decided she liked her job after all.

Thirty-Day Discipline

It can be very interesting to try any spiritual discipline for a set time period, such as thirty days. Some have added a daily meditation or made a commitment to themselves to read a passage from a specific text each morning. Others have decided to read everything they can find by Hafiz or Rumi. Hafiz was a fourteenth century Persian mystic and poet, and Rumi was a thirteenth century Persian poet, theologian, and Sufi mystic. The translations of their work have deeply inspired countless modern day spiritual seekers.

ALERT

The ancient science and art of yoga is a timeless way to attune the physical body with the spirit. It is pleasant to undertake a yoga practice in the company of others. Such classes are available in many levels of difficulty, often in community recreation programs, senior centers, as well as in private studios. Often the first class is free, and lessons are discounted if payment is made in advance for a series.

It can be illuminating to be aware of suffering and attachments, tracing each one to the source, letting go of whatever is the root dependency. A daily walk in nature can be a way of connecting to the larger world of the earthy elements. It can be an interesting discipline to do an unseen act of kindness every day for thirty days. One spiritual seeker embarked on a written gratitude list each day, listing ten new items each day. By the end of thirty days, he was grateful for air, electricity, and blood coursing through his veins and arteries.

Ease Up on Time Expectations

Many perfectionistic people plan too much to do within a given amount of time, forgetting that each task requires a finite amount of time to complete. It can be a beautiful habit of self-acceptance to pencil in fewer activities for each day, each week, and each weekend. If there is work to be done, shave off the other activities that are not closely work related.

If you are going across town to have lunch with a friend, allow plenty of extra time for unknown traffic conditions so you will arrive refreshed and ready to enjoy yourself instead of harried and frazzled. If you have a specific task that you anticipate will be tiring or irksome—perhaps jury duty—allow time to rest afterwards.

If you are grieving the loss of what you have mistakenly invested in a life of perfection, allow time to do the work. When the waves of grief wash over you, pause and let the mind do its healing work.

Constant Reinvention

If you're not a martyr or a perfectionistic workaholic, who are you? Some interesting people cultivate a life of continuous reinvention. Madonna created an image in the eighties that took her to the top of pop culture, and each decade of her life brings a different swath of creative expression, incorporating her mature womanliness in a deliberate, self-accepting way. Who would have thought that the young singer and dancer from Detroit could end up portraying Evita with such élan and bringing the idea of kabala to a wider range of followers?

Family Activities

As your inner child heals, you may go through a stage where you enjoy cultural activities intended for children. If you have a child to help you gain access, so much the better! If not, you can often quietly participate in family activities, and no one will notice that you are the adult child. Public libraries and museums have marvelous programs in literature, music, magic, puppetry, dance, and art. A storyteller weaves a marvelous web, and in the process, your wounded young self is enthralled.

CHAPTER 17

Choices

Volition is part of the human condition. Even in dire situations such as a hurricane, earthquake, or something as drastic as the events of September 11, 2001, a range of choices are available for human response. One can become irate, hysterical, and out of control, adding to the chaos of the situation, or one can remain poised, peaceful, and composed, focusing on service to others. Usually life is not so excessively demanding, and it is somewhat easier to examine a range of possibilities.

Readjusting Expectations

The perfectionist has unrealistic expectations for the self and others. This is more or less the definition of perfectionism—having unnecessarily high standards, even standards that are impossible to reach. Such a miserable outlook can be improved by looking at the underlying beliefs of such a mental state and considering some modifications.

Relationships

Toni Raiten-D'Antonio, author of *The Velveteen Principles for Women*, suggests that readers examine unrealistic beliefs, especially in the area of close relationships. Some unrealistic beliefs would include thoughts such as the following:

1. I am perfect for my partner, and she is perfect for me.
2. I can make him or her perfect for me.
3. This union will make us both happy for the rest of our lives.
4. People who love me can read my mind.

Raiten-D'Antonio cautions people to be conservative during the process of mate selection, taking the time to look beneath the veneer and allowing the other person to know you, including your flaws. Marriages based on appearances sometimes falter when the appearances start to crumble, as they inevitably do. No one is perfect, and the whirlwind courtship, quick engagement, and mad dash to the altar can result in a strange situation of looking at the other person and wondering who that stranger might be. Taking the time to learn whether the person is kind, generous, and flexible might lead to a happier union.

Adult children often have a pattern of choosing partners who are emotionally or otherwise unavailable. This is a choice because it feels similar to the dynamic in the home of childhood. One can ask if this pattern is satisfying and perhaps try a different way. The quality of life with someone who is really there can seem terrifying to one who is accustomed to barren, distant relationships. If it is a goal to have an emotionally present partner, one can start with friendships of the same sex, moving on to platonic relations with others of the opposite sex, and ultimately a relationship that has romantic and deeply loving potential. The vulnerability and sharing will be quite different from that of the childhood dynamic.

To Err Is Divine

There has to be room for human error, whether in marriage, child rearing, personal appearance, or in work. Some high achievers believe that the way to visible success is to make as many mistakes as possible, as that direction will eventually lead to a few things that work out very well. Tolerance for error can be difficult for a perfectionist. Sometimes one can warm up with one activity, where it doesn't matter how it is done, and the relaxed, carefree approach transfers to the next thing, where one is inclined to grit one's teeth during the entire experience.

ESSENTIAL

A few weeds do not ruin the garden. The stray grasses coexist fairly comfortably with the fruits, flowers, and vegetables, giving the gardener something to do when he feels like puttering among living things.

For example, if you're dreading writing a tedious report, toss together a salad of your own wild invention using the leftovers in the refrigerator, odd delicacies from the pantry, and a few choice items from your favorite market. You can call it deep greens, mixed nuts, and pickled plums with a side dressing of sweet chutney. Such fun will help you to approach the dry report with a touch of abandon.

It can be helpful to examine your beliefs about making mistakes. Do any of the following statements ring true for you?

1. It is dangerous to make mistakes.
2. I must do things perfectly the first time.
3. I cannot ask for help.
4. People will not like me if I screw up too badly.
5. Making mistakes will harm my reputation.
6. If I allow even a few mistakes, I will fall apart completely.
7. I'll never attract a mate if they know of my most serious mistakes.

It can be helpful to keep in mind that your choices reflect your opinion of yourself. If you are unnecessarily harsh with yourself, does it mean that you do not love yourself? Would you be so harsh with a cherished child or a very close friend who might be struggling? However you would treat a person that you love and respect is a good way to treat yourself, even while experimenting with mistakes and new behaviors. A little latitude and slack allows you to be human. During the course of your lifetime, one of the most important relationships is your relationship with yourself. You are always there, and it greatly enhances the quality of life if that relationship is cordial, loving, and accepting.

One cannot choose the family one is born into, but one can certainly choose a response to those circumstances. It may take years of therapy and numerous courses of various types of study to break free from perfectionism, but the choice is there. Try to deliberately think about what may be desirable response instead of a knee-jerk reaction. Not everyone has the stamina to embark upon such diligent inquiry, but the result is a life of freedom and satisfaction, no matter what the outside circumstances might be.

ESSENTIAL

Abraham Lincoln suffered numerous failures and setbacks before becoming president. He was defeated for the state legislature. He failed in business. His sweetheart died, and he had a nervous breakdown. He was defeated for Speaker of the House in the Illinois legislature. He was defeated for nomination to Congress. Once elected, he was defeated for renomination. He was defeated in his bid for the U.S. Senate. He was defeated in nomination for the presidency. He was again defeated in his bid to become a senator. But don't forget that, in 1860, he was elected as president and became one of the most famous figures in history.

Failures can point to a new direction just as clearly as successes. If something did not work out, then it becomes clear you must try a different tactic. Actually, life might be boring with a steady diet of stellar successes. Eventually one would want to try something novel, just in order to have a new experience. Failures make a person human, providing compassion for the self and others who undergo such humbling moments.

Catch Yourself in the Moment

Perfectionists tend to unnecessarily ruminate over details, thinking about what went wrong yesterday and planning everything that has to be done tomorrow, next week, and next month. There is no harm, of course, in being on top of things and accountable for one's time and efforts. However, the only thing that is truly available is the present moment. Too much worrying eradicates any possibility of joy in the present time.

FACT

Choice is closely aligned with intention. Intention is aligned with strong desire. When these components are harmonized, life moves in the positive direction in harmony with the individual's deepest beliefs. The result is a satisfying experience, a satisfying life.

Next time you're rushing from here to there, pause and notice exact details in your environment. What types of clouds are in the sky? Do you remember those cloud names from elementary school science? Are there any shapes that remind you of an object?

What sounds are evident in the moment—traffic, neighbors, music, air conditioning? Is the coffeepot percolating? What snippets of other languages do you hear in your environment?

Shapes are interesting. Notice power lines, buildings, graffiti, even litter. What sorts of landscaping and trees are local to your work and house? Are there variations in color and texture? Notice the shapes of shadows. Observe people and their interactions. Is the young woman pregnant, and would you be able to guess her relationship to the two accompanying children? Perhaps they are a niece and nephew, or maybe first and second children awaiting a little brother or sister? Notice the types of clothing and hairstyles. This attention to detail is quite restful for the mind and gives you a needed vacation from obsessive dwelling on the impossible.

With the gift of twenty-four hours each day, how will you choose to use those hours and minutes? Segments of time are delicious morsels for you to expend however you decide. It doesn't have to be by rote or random, unconscious choice, often the unthinking way of the perfectionist. Each activity is yours alone, and it is up to you to make it satisfying, something that you can savor in memories you are creating.

Restart Your Day at Any Time

One aspect of personal choice is to start a new day at any point in the day. Who says it has to begin at 7:00 or 8:00 A.M.? This mental technique is especially useful on a challenging day. When too many requirements are colliding from too many directions, call a quick halt and make a decision to begin the day at that point. You may have some special rituals that give you the true feeling that a new day is beginning, perhaps an inspirational reading, a walk with your pets, or a tall glass of juice. Shift gears in a major way and let the day evolve from that point.

ESSENTIAL

Beware of the tendency to say that you will "try" to do something. Either you will do it or not do it. "Try" is a slippery word and one that can possibly be eliminated from the vocabulary, as it often genuinely means that you do not want to commit to whatever it is but do not want to tell the other person. It makes for more ease to simply say, "I'm sorry, but I won't be able to do that." It's a choice.

Gradually it becomes clear to a perfectionistic person that one always has the choice of attitude and response to life's circumstances. It may have become automatic for years or decades to respond in a certain passive, negative way when things don't go well, but it is enormously empowering to emphatically choose the thoughts that motivate daily actions. With this strong, centered stance, one is not blown around like a dandelion seed in the wind. It becomes much easier to negotiate quite complicated situations, and one becomes an asset to organizations of all kinds. You may find yourself being sought out for your calm demeanor under fire. A tranquil mind and a peaceful heart are always available to you.

Brainstorm When You're Stuck

Daily, monthly, and yearly choices make up the sum total of a person's character. There are large choices, such as whom to marry, where to live, what your career will be, and whether to have children and how many. Some of these choices seem irrevocable, and many cases that can be the case. At times, one has made a choice, and a new choice needs to be considered.

For example, a middle-aged woman living on the West Coast was concerned about her elderly mother in St. Louis. For several years she visited frequently, then for longer periods of time. At the end of her mother's life, she lived in the mother's home and handled the estate after the mother's passing, retaining her West Coast home to which she returned after the years of her mother's decline and death. Numerous choices were necessary during an approximate six-year time period.

ALERT

Being a victim is the opposite of having choices. Perhaps you were a victim in your family, and you had no choice but to accommodate the situation. However, in adult life, there are almost always choices, even if they seem scary or almost impossible. Victimhood is not a satisfying profession. Sometimes it helps to elicit the viewpoints of others when victimhood is lurking.

Can Change, Cannot Change

Sometimes it helps to make a list of situations in life that are irksome or uncomfortable. Then a chart can be fashioned with two columns—Can Change and Cannot Change. Looking at each item and asking the question about whether it can be changed or not sometimes opens some doors. Often the choices are opposite of what one has assumed! One cannot change the personality of the demanding boss, but a vacation or a transfer could lessen the difficulty.

It can be very helpful to bluntly ask yourself, "What is the truth of this situation?" This stark question sometimes opens doors and circumstances shift. It might have seemed that the choice was in regard to one thing, but it turns out to be something completely different.

Choices that support serenity and the well-being of the whole person are always desirable, if not easy. For example, if you have a certain relative who always dominates the conversation, irrevocably bringing the attention back to himself even when others attempt to join in, you have several alternatives. You can choose not to go to the event. You can go but interact with other people in a different room. You can sit by him and enthusiastically nod every time he makes another important proclamation and congratulate yourself on how brave you were for those few minutes. You can think of blessings for this person, as something dreadful must be going on that he continues to demand attention like a toddler in a grown man's body.

It is always possible to choose one's perspective. Each individual has a lens of perception, and it is up to the person to decide what works in life. A perspective of doom and gloom, self-righteous judgment, and perfectionistic self-criticism leads to one type of a result. A perspective of acceptance, composure, and goodwill leads to another result. The individual perspective is the choice of each separate person.

Consult the Inner Child

Another way to brainstorm some ideas for new choices is to ask your inner child. Setting aside some time and journal pages to access that pure, innocent voice is an interesting way to tease out some gems. She might want to be surrounded by blue velvet, listen to sitar music, and learn how to kayak. Although seemingly impractical, brief side trips to accommodate those raw desires can ultimately lead to the evolution of new, interesting forks in the road.

It is freeing to choose to no longer be defined by the past and any unpleasant things that happened. The essence of your person, the lively inner child, is wise, joyous, and free, and he or she is able to be spontaneous with new choices. This child is witty, smart, and resilient and wants to guide you along some paths not yet explored. You might feel that if you take the hand of this child and try something different, you will permanently abandon your adult responsibilities. This is unlikely. The time with the inner child is temporary, only for checking out some deeper preferences and interests. With practice, you can form a trusting partnership and have more fun.

It is unlikely that the inner child is a perfectionist. Let her help you with choices that provide a range of responses. You might enjoy building a tall structure with Legos or dominoes. The child is completely comfortable making a random, somewhat purposeless structure, whereas the adult will want to build a bridge or a skyscraper that is a copy of something already known.

The inner child is often a quite good judge of character. Like household pets, he or she intuitively knows who is trustworthy and kind, and who is not. When you are in a quandary about which person to date or which job to pursue, ask the inner child. The inner child has ways of gleaning information that are more primitive, based on such nonverbal cues as eye contact, tone of voice, and physical mannerisms. Your inner child might not like the furtive edginess of the new potential client. She would prefer that you avoid such a cagey person.

Facing Fear of Outcomes

If one approaches choices with the confidence that things will evolve in a way that is ultimately positive, it becomes less unnerving to make a decision and move forward. Becoming locked up with fear of making a wrong choice leads to procrastination, immobilization, and depression. It is usually better to make any choice and see how it turns out.

ALERT

Whenever possible, choose to have an open mind. A closed mind limits the range of choices quite drastically, and an open mind allows room for miracles and astounding new experiences.

Usually it is not too difficult to shift course, even if the result is something unexpected and unwanted. The movement through the consequences of the choice brings new information, and a different course becomes apparent along the way. It is somewhat like a courageous vacationer who takes off on country roads with no set destination in mind. She stops at roadside fruit stands, antique shops, and lavender farms, completely delighted at each juncture. This type of excursion has a completely different flavor from a highly planned outing where the traveler is white-knuckling it through the hour-by-hour schedule, looking more at the clock than the details of the sights.

Learning to be less fearful of outcomes frees up other people to be more relaxed with you and in their lives. Your social life and family life are an organic whole, and when one part improves or relaxes (you), others are somewhat let off the hook. They become less hard on themselves with you as an example. These shifts will not happen overnight, but even the possibility makes the effort very much worthwhile.

Trust is often an issue for persons who originate from troubled childhood homes. Often their perceptions were discounted, trivialized, and minimized, making it quite difficult to make discerning choices in later years. The environment may be chaotic, violent, and centered around the needs of the addicted adult. The child learns that inconsistency is the norm, making quick adaptation a more useful skill than trust in decision-making. Often for such children, what works one day to calm down the difficult parents or other family members will bring quite a different response another day. No wonder adults from such backgrounds have difficulty making choices when the outcome is unknown.

One way to gradually build confidence is to make choices in situations where the outcome is not especially important. For example, would the pasta taste better with tomato sauce or alfredo sauce? It really doesn't matter. Any choice will be fine. Sometimes choices of clothing or a movie to watch can be approached in a like manner. It doesn't matter what outfit is worn, and the choice of movie will be fine if everyone in the party reads the synopsis and a review or two. Even in the worst-case scenario, if the movie turns out to be terrible, everyone in the group can agree to leave the theater and do something else during the evening.

What Can You Do Instead?

Often choices are easier if one turns momentarily within, checking with the intuitive knowing aspect of the self. This could be called prayer. It might be a momentary meditation. It could be noticing the gut feeling about what should be next. These mental pauses require a bit of time, often something in short supply for the perfectionist, but the result is a course that is in greater harmony with the whole person.

Freely Choose Your Values

After considerable self-inquiry, one becomes at home with one's own values, even if there is somewhat of a departure from the beliefs of closest relatives or one's spouse. Most religious disciplines have a set of values, such as the Ten Commandments, that might have been the cornerstone for childhood morals, but are the beliefs up to date? Is killing ever permissible—perhaps when defending a child?

Writer Toni Raiten-D'Antonio suggests that thoughtful persons examine a whole range of values and determine what is appropriate at that particular stage of life. Some possibilities could include:

Love	Honesty	Self-Reliance
Moderation	Flexibility	Restraint
Tolerance	Commitment	Wisdom
Acceptance of Others	Devotion	Strength
Faith	Self-Awareness	Compassion
Dependability	Interdependence	Interest in Others

A few moments of pondering the topics of adultery, theft, and lying might be useful in determining true beliefs, not the ideal that is unattainable.

Write a Mission Statement

You might cringe at the idea of a mission statement, thinking that would be the domain of MBAs from Ivy League universities, but actually, the endeavor of choosing a life that is satisfying to you is completely worthy of a serious statement, perhaps crafted over a period of time. If you are close with a mentor, coach, therapist, or deeply trusted friend, it will be useful to share the mission statement, after you have completed several drafts. You will want to address major life areas such as family relationships, financial stability, creative expression, health, service, and leisure. What do you see as your legacy? Some people go so far as to imagine an epitaph on the headstone of a grave, wondering what might have been said about a life well-lived.

FACT

It is a choice to turn one's perfectionistic willfulness over to a spiritual source. It does not matter which personal faith one has, if any, but that alignment with the divine frees up the person to live in a more relaxed way, without the inclination to play God over every detail of life and the lives of others.

A genuine calling can emerge from such a focus. Where do you feel generous, or where would you like to be generous? Writing and revising a mission statement over a time period of a few months or years enables a person to release old goals that are no longer appropriate. Maybe they were someone else's idea of what is important but no longer fit. Maybe the goals have been attained and something new would be more interesting and challenging.

Writer and world traveler, Rita Gelman Goldman, author of *Tales of a Female Nomad*, left an unsatisfactory Beverly Hills marriage when she was in her forties and embarked on a life of cross-cultural inquiry and tremendous service to needy children of other countries. Elizabeth Gilbert, author of *Eat, Pray, Love*, embarked on a parallel journey at a younger age, finding physical and spiritual health and a new life partner. Both of these women chose to depart from unsatisfactory lives and make something completely new.

Try Something Opposite

Perfectionists tend to do things in a habitual, somewhat rigid manner, as those ways seem to be the right ways. It can be fun to choose something completely opposite from time to time, just to see how it feels and decide if the outcome is enjoyable. Such experimentation frees up the synapses and tensions are released.

For example, if a person always journals and does spiritual reading in a particular chair, it can be interesting to take the journal and books to a neighborhood coffeehouse and start the day in a different place. If you always celebrate your birthday with a particular friend, it can be stimulating to choose a different friend and a different way of marking the importance of the day. The previous friend would probably be happy to celebrate with you over the phone. If you always read self-help books, pick up some diversionary fiction. If you usually watch serious dramatic films or television, try something completely shallow. You might enjoy it.

ALERT

Holidays can be problematic for persons from difficult families. Instead of doing the same dreary and unsatisfying round of dutiful fiascos, plan something completely different for yourself and a few cherished, close people. You might enjoy having a Cinco de Mayo party or a Day of the Dead celebration instead of a sugary Halloween. Instead of overeating on Thanksgiving, it might be interesting to join a group who serves a fine dinner for the homeless. It is your choice to mark these days however you choose.

Perfectionists often turn down personal invitations because they are too busy doing everything that seems especially important. One can be courageous and accept every invitation for a set length of time, perhaps a month, and see what adventures ensue. It is a practice of saying yes instead of no. One friend may invite you to hear a duo of folk musicians at a neighborhood bistro. Another wants to take you to the beach for a middle-of-the-week holiday. Another is involved in a group show and wants you to help with the guest book. The owners of your favorite ethnic restaurant may invite you to visit their relatives in a foreign country the next time they visit! Say yes, and mark the dates on your calendar.

Choose Transformation and Love

When you find yourself at a fork in the road and are genuinely in a quandary about which direction would be best, think of the long-term consequences of each choice. Think broadly in terms of what would be most transformational for you and most loving for others. That might be the course toward a more pleasing life.

CHAPTER 18

Decision-Making

Conscious decision-making and follow-up actions are the crux of a satisfying adult life. Perfectionists tend to be at the mercy of hidden, subconscious motives and drives, but with considerable self-inquiry, those fall away and the deliberate nature comes forth. Each day is a series of decisions— some small and some momentous. The key is awareness, the awareness that as an independent, volitional person, you have the power and right to make decisions that are good for you.

Clear the Slate and Start Anew

To a certain degree, life is cumulative, with each phase built upon the consequences of a previous phase. One decides on a basic set of values, chooses a profession and prepares for it, chooses a mate and general lifestyle, and life follows in the wake of those early adult decisions. Occasionally, though, you are thrown a curve ball that irrevocably changes everything. Perhaps a friend is lost in an accident, or someone close becomes seriously ill. A completely different opportunity is offered, somewhat from left field. The ability to quickly clear the slate and start fresh leaves you unencumbered to accept the surprises of life.

You might find it invigorating to move to a different state or country if you or your spouse is offered an interesting job. Children who have an opportunity to travel and experience other cultures become marvelously versatile. You might receive a grant, scholarship, or fellowship to study something completely different. A stimulating opportunity sometimes gives a person new energy and vigor.

Decide to Accept Sanity

No matter what occurred in the past or what traumas pile up in the present, one can always choose a rational, sane series of responses. As mentioned in previous paragraphs, it can be tempting to make a lifestyle of various diagnoses, learning the detailed language of all the disorders, but there aren't many job descriptions available for those particular qualifications. It can be a huge diversion, eating up precious decades of life. Instead, decide to dramatically shift gears and go the way of mature, intelligent living. It might feel like shedding a skin in order to move into new roles, but more than likely it will feel like releasing a weight of burden. It requires energy to hold dysfunction and limitation in place. Decide to be free of the seduction of the old ways.

Anticipate Positive Consequences

Instead of worrying about what could go wrong, with practice the procrastinator learns to look at the options and move toward the result that seems best at the moment. Gradually, anticipations become positive instead of negative. A liberating lifestyle ensues without the shackles of constrained perfectionism. It is as if blinders have been removed and the sky is bluer, the horizon wider, and life is a little sweeter. People seem more attractive and interesting, and every decision is not so momentous. Confidence grows and there is a sense of being carried along by the positive, unseen forces of life instead of being dragged down by darkness.

Think of Each Day as Moment by Moment

Perfectionists tend to overplan, jumping ahead mentally to the next hour, the next day, week, month, and year. A string of "what-ifs" rob the individual of the precious seconds of life. Details escape notice because of the cerebral preoccupation with planning and control.

ESSENTIAL

Different cultures have different perspectives on time. For example, Navajo Native Americans do not relate to the Caucasian fast-paced lifestyle. The language has no names for the time preoccupations of English-speaking people. Latino cultures are much more flexible with time commitments, taking each thing as it occurs and adjusting when necessary for unforeseen developments.

Within the framework of your own culture, think about time in some new ways—instead of strictly linear in finite blocks, perhaps little pearls or bubbles floating along. You can juggle the pieces in a playful way instead of being caught in the rigid chain of digital figures. Experiment with ignoring the clocks and time indications of computers and cell phones, perhaps for an entire Sunday afternoon. The body relaxes and breathing is easier. Such a moment-by-moment awareness opens the possibility for more spontaneous interaction with the environment, both within and without. Without a time obsession, the creative forces may bring you a new idea with great potential for development, and you have an adept nature to shift your course of direction.

The necessity for planned time zones instead of sun time or solar time arose in the late nineteenth century, especially in the United States and Canada, because of trains traveling rapidly across the continent. It was impossible to plan schedules without an agreed-upon system. Sir Sandford Fleming, a Canadian railroad planner, initiated the time zone system, resulting in the Meridian Conference of 1884 with delegates from twenty-seven nations. Because of the conference, now twenty-four time zones encompass the globe.

Automatic Pilot—Correct, Correct, Correct

The automatic pilot or robot pilot device on a plane serves to correct the course according to a preset set of instructions. In other words, the plane is flying exactly on course a small percentage of the time, but the automatic pilot constantly corrects, and the result is a landing at the desired destination. Humans, however, often have the delusion that it is necessary, or even desirable, to be 100 percent on target. Such unrealistic thinking creates tension and harsh perfectionism.

What would happen if you let up a little on yourself and think of decision-making as smaller bites of correction, like a plane moving thousands of miles in smaller bits of a corrected course? The quality of your thinking and actions shift a bit. You might have a general long-term or short-term aim in mind, but the increments to get there are smaller with considerable correction along the way. The corrections do not mean that something is wrong, only that the aircraft is jetting along with frequent adjustments.

Make a Vision Board with New Goals

Vision boards are an interesting way to create focus and direction. This goal-setting method, termed the Wheel of Fortune by metaphysical writer Catherine Ponder, has enabled many people to achieve manifestation of their hopes and dreams. No particular skill is required—merely the willingness to make decisions about images that represent aspects of various goals.

Materials for Your Vision Board

You will need some type of background. Poster board works well. Some people like large pieces of craft paper because it rolls up and is easy to transport. Others like foam core, and some ambitious planners enjoy working with a trifold display arrangement with hinges. You might enjoy browsing at an art supply store or office supply superstore to see what seems inspiring.

ALERT

Risk is a component of making decisions. The unknown looms, and results are unpredictable. However, without risk, there is no growth and development. The result might be worth the temporary discomfort.

Next, gather magazines representing topics that interest you—travel, homes, health and fitness. For example, an enterprising young man who hoped to get married, collected bride magazines. You will need scissors, glue, space to work, and a reasonable length of time, so you are not hurried.

How to Create a Vision Board

There are a couple of ways to approach the vision board task. Some prefer to make it conscious and focused, for example, choosing items that have to do with a beautiful work environment. Using this approach, you might look for pictures of furniture, perhaps a gorgeous loft studio, maybe a mockup of a profit and loss statement. Cut out those images and words that pertain to that goal and glue them down in whatever arrangement seems right to you.

Another way is to gather images that are appealing but seemingly unrelated. Choose pictures that speak to your soul—a gorgeous flower, a couple embracing on the beach in the sunset, a dolphin kissing a child. This approach is intuitive, letting the images come to you as if they need to be chosen. Collect them in a free, spontaneous way and group them however you wish on the solid background. This method is more like a collage. Sometimes the juxtaposition of items can surprise you. Relax and let your subconscious work with you in terms of relatedness that might not be available to your conscious mind just yet.

How to Use Your Vision Board

Keep your vision board in a visible place in your home, yet away from prying eyes of those who might criticize. You might like to have it on an altar, displayed as a piece of art in your office or wherever you relax at the beginning or end of the day. If there is a spot where you gaze and daydream, that might be a good place for the vision board. Let your eyes fall on it often.

Some meditators use the vision board as a focus prior to meditating, so those images will impress themselves on the subconscious mind during the quiet moments of meditation. Over time, the manifestation occurs. Those things or experiences move into a person's life, sometimes quickly, sometimes over a period of several months. It is enjoyable to work on vision boards in a group of like-minded people, sharing successes as they come into being.

ALERT

Beware of the inclination to sabotage your vision board work. Numerous people have the experience of creating a beautiful collage only to find that they spill coffee on it or accidentally crush it in the process of moving. Be aware that it is quite difficult to let numerous positive experiences into your life. It is the internal resistance that causes these "accidents." Do whatever you can to protect your vision board from your own destructiveness.

Prioritizing

Perfectionists have difficulty understanding the relative importance of various tasks, sometimes wasting large amounts of time doing things that could be relegated to another time or even completely set aside. It is sometimes necessary to get another person's input in order to do things in a sensible order.

First Things First

When looking at your To Do list on any given day, what is absolutely paramount? Usually items that have to do with a deadline come first. These could be work obligations, due dates on payments, or a loved one's birthday. There might be smaller priorities that are a part of the dated obligation. For example, a check has to be deposited in order to have funds in the account when you shop for the birthday gift. These are the things that shift to the top of the To Do list. Others are ready for your attention when the most important things are handled. Sometimes there is a series of small things that are convenient to do first. This has the effect of clearing the mind and releasing energy for the larger tasks.

How Important Is It?

A perfectionist has a talent for putting undue importance on things that are not especially important. Again, it helps to discuss these things with others to learn what is rational to others as you learn to prioritize. One meticulous housewife arranged the folds and pleats of the draperies every day in order that they appear perfectly symmetrical. Another vacuumed the carpets every day, making sure the lines of the vacuum were perfectly parallel and perpendicular on the nap of the carpet. Perhaps these things are not really so important.

ESSENTIAL

The perfectionist has to learn to leave some things undone. As impossible expectations are shrunk to a manageable reality, there simply isn't enough time to do everything one wants to do. In fact, there never was enough time to do all those tasks, but the frantic feeling of rushing around all the time became normal. It's okay to leave things undone or delegate some to others, and accept however they wish to do the tasks.

Actually, it is a matter of personal values to decide what is truly important and what is not. Usually relationships are important. Taking care of your health, financial stability, creative expression, and spiritual sustenance are important. You may have to juggle several high-priority items over a period of time in order to see that everything is adequately covered.

Perfectionists often neglect their health, as it seems that work is much more important. It might be better in the long run to prioritize the doctor's appointment, time for the health club or spa, or at a minimum, time for a daily walk to wind down. Perfectionists sometimes drastically neglect important relationships, feeling somehow that they will get to that later, after everything else is handled. Harry Chapin's folk rock song of 1974, *Cat's in the Cradle*, poignantly describes the situation where the father is constantly too busy for the little son, and then in reverse, the elderly father asks for time with the adult son, and he puts him off, saying he is too busy.

Bouncing Back from Failures

Failure is abhorrent to perfectionists. In fact, the entire thrust of perfectionism is to prevent failure. Of course, this effort is futile, as it often propels the individual into spirals of procrastination and time wasting, never getting any momentum toward actual achievement. The entire life is based on protection from failure and criticism, whether from within oneself or perceived from others.

If you think about failure as simply an experience on the way to the ultimate goal, it is not so bad. It can be an education in the way not to do things. For example, if a person has a pattern of choosing mates exactly like his or her abusive parent, those relationships could be seen as failures. These relationships are also thorough experiences in what happens with a mate of that type. One can think of it as a homeopathic inoculation in mate selection. Some things cannot be learned theoretically.

ESSENTIAL

The old adage of getting back on the horse after falling off has some truth to it, although not many people routinely ride horses in the twenty-first century. The key is to get going again rather quickly after a failure. Too much rumination can make the situation fester in your mind.

Once one gets over the fear of failure, it is freeing to simply do things as quickly as possible to see what works and what doesn't work. If you have had the opportunity to work in the vicinity of an artist or musician, you can see this process in action. The painter slathers on some color and then changes his mind, scraping it off and trying something else. The composer taps out a tune, makes some notes on the manuscript page, hums a bit, and tries something else. He does not jump immediately from the idea of the song to renting an orchestra and time in a recording studio. A lot of trial and error, with the emphasis on the error, is necessary to create a desired result, whether the result is something creative or a life well lived.

What Can You Do Instead?

Decision-making becomes easier with practice, like any other skill. It is wise to include other trusted friends and support persons in major life decisions—whether to leave a mate or stay, whether to make a career change, or whether to move to a new location. Often those with objectivity will have an enormously helpful perspective.

It's Not Life or Death

Perfectionists tend to think of decisions as black or white, this or that, and fear the consequences of making the wrong decision. Actually, many decisions are not that important—what to eat, what book to read, and what movie to attend. It doesn't matter if you get only six hours of sleep one night if you are able to make up for it the next subsequent nights.

A willingness to simply take action, to try a little of this and a little of that, will produce results that you can look at and see if they are what you expected or even want. One sometimes listens to young college freshmen agonizing over the appropriate major course of study, when it often happens that whole professions fall by the wayside and others are created in a short period of time. Several decades ago, no one ever heard of information technology, yet at the present time, IT work is very common.

Willingness is a large component of effective decision-making and moving away from the grip of perfectionism. Each action moves a person a little more out of bondage.

Skills and Knowledge Are Transferable

Trends come and go, but if one develops an attitude that whatever is learned will ultimately be useful in most situations, the perfectionistic tension somewhat subsides. For example, an eager person gets a degree in library science only to find that libraries are becoming digital. Entire collections are in e-book format, and older cataloging systems simply do not apply. However, the degree of intelligence and literacy required to get such a degree is immediately transferrable to learning about databases, e-reading devices, and methods of educating patrons about digital books.

Decision-Making in Groups

As you gain more confidence and practice with your own decisions, you may find yourself cooperating with others in group problem-solving challenges. Leadership perhaps is thrust upon you, and others look to you for help in resolving conflict. Decision-making is slower in groups, as it takes time for each person to express thoughts and opinions. It takes time to weigh all the ramifications and to consider the consequences of each course of action. If you are able to take a calm composure into the group process, sometimes surprising creative solutions will come forth, but only if everyone in the group feels safe. If a certain few usually dominate, the quieter ones will not voice an opinion. It helps greatly if the facilitator listens to each point of view and voices it back to the group, giving equal weight to each voice.

Decide to Trust a Spiritual Source

Much perfectionistic tension is released when the individual adopts a spiritual life and seeks help in decision-making. Some people call this the Higher Self, the Divine, or God. Others turn to animal totems, angels, or ancestors. All this is a matter of personal choice and completely up to the individual. The important thing is to develop *something*, some kind of spiritual partnership so that one is not alone in making decisions.

Trust in a higher being brings amazing serenity, as that partnership becomes the most significant one. Human relationships come and go, and all aspects of life are subject to flux, but the lynchpin of self-knowledge and firm cooperation with the spiritual guide makes decisions considerably less scary.

The Now Factor

Someday isn't a day of the week. When you make a commitment to do something, write it on your calendar and share it with someone trustworthy who is interested in your personal growth. If it is a decision requiring several steps, start working on the first increments. Of course, there is no harm in making short- and long-term plans, but sometimes putting things off, even for a little while, leads to a huge case of procrastination. Willingness and decision-making go hand in hand, leading to immediate action. This is a way to eliminate too much thinking about dire, negative results.

Imaginary Protective Clothing

A West Coast radio announcer occasionally asks her radio listeners to put on their Joy Jackets and get out into the day. If you tend to be fearful, think of wearing a magic flak vest that protects you from the slings and arrows of existence. It might be fun to look through your wardrobe and designate some of your favorite clothes as good luck outfits. When you're making difficult phone calls, attending a stressful meeting, or researching a scary possibility, wear the good luck clothing, and you might feel more relaxed.

CHAPTER 19

Spiritual Solutions

Ultimately, it becomes much easier to let go of perfectionism if one embraces the idea of a spiritual life in a larger sense. Why are you here? Who are all these other beings, and what is the nature of your connection to them? How does a tree nourish itself from sunlight? How does an embryo "know" from the very beginning whether it will be a girl or a boy? These large questions about the nature of life lead one to embrace some kind of spirituality and a sense of a larger power. This can be a relief to a perfectionist. It gets tiresome being one's own God.

Meditation

Meditation is one way to develop a spiritual nature and confidence in a connection with a Higher Source. A Google search for your locale will possibly lead you to groups and teachers who are eager to help others. Churches, yoga centers, and hospitals often offer meditation classes. Be wary of taking perfectionism into the meditation experience, worrying that you're not doing it correctly. Although there are a variety of techniques and meditation philosophies, there probably is not any way a person could meditate incorrectly.

Getting Started

When beginning meditation practice, try to include the following:

1. Choose a quiet place where there will not be an interruption.
2. Silence all electronic devices.
3. Sit comfortably and close your eyes.
4. Breathe deeply and slowly, feeling the breath move into the body.
5. Relax each section of the body. It might help to contract each muscle and then relax it.
6. Quiet the mind. Notice mental chatter but do not judge it. Let it pass.
7. Aim for a "blank mind" state. Imagine a computer screen that is completely blank.
8. Notice the spaces between the thoughts and words and rest there.
9. After the meditation, thank your Higher Self for a good experience.

Meditation Tips

It is a pleasant experience to learn to meditate in a group, and even long-time meditators like being with others who meditate, as a different energy arises as individuals calm down and enter into a relaxed state of being together. A calm, focused leader with an attractive voice adds to the quality of the meditation. Some leaders offer a guided meditation with imagery that is very relaxing for the mind and body.

FACT

Scientific studies show that when a person meditates, alpha and theta waves increase in the brain. Electrodes attached to the head of the person who is meditating reveal these waves of relaxation and wakeful rest.

If you meditate at home, check that the room temperature is comfortable, possibly a little warmer than you might choose if you are physically active because the body temperature lowers somewhat during meditation. You might like to have a shawl or soft blanket nearby to wrap around yourself if you become too cool.

Start with a short meditation, perhaps ten minutes, and gradually add a few minutes as you become comfortable with the experience. Some people like to meditate for as long as an hour at a time, as there is a greater chance of experiencing visions, colorful flashes of light, and creative inspirations. It is possible, too, to divide the meditation practice with a portion in the morning and a portion in the evening.

First thing in the morning is a good time to meditate, as it quiets the mind, increasing the possibility for a peaceful day. Similarly, an evening meditation helps the individual become free of the business of the day, making it easier to invite peaceful sleep. It is beneficial to form a habit of meditating at the same time each day, in the same place, for the same length of time, as the body and mind become conditioned to welcome the quiet state of mind.

ESSENTIAL

Meditation is a spiritual oasis, available at all times. You can dip into your meditation practice in the midst of a stressful meeting at work, before an important phone call, and during family gatherings that are emotionally volatile. Your spiritual cushion is always there.

Any comfortable chair is satisfactory for meditation. Sometimes people assume that it is necessary to sit with crossed legs on the floor in order to meditate. This is a customary posture for people who come from cultures where it is common to sit on the floor. It is not a prerequisite for meditation, although floor sitting is common in many meditation groups.

Quiet music and a mat or pillow might add to your comfort. Some yoga studios or online suppliers offer special pillows and stools to complement the meditation experience.

Won't I Fall Asleep?

The meditative state is the state of consciousness that is almost, but not quite, asleep. Usually it is suggested that a person meditate sitting rather than lying down, as the reclining position does move a person into sleep rather quickly. In the sitting position, one has the quiet mind but still is aware of sounds and movement in the room, as if from a distance.

Walking Meditation

If you have tremendous difficulty sitting still during meditation, you might investigate groups that practice walking meditation. The technique is similar to the sitting meditation, but the practitioners quietly walk in a circle within a designated space during a specified length of time, usually forty-five minutes at a time, followed by a seated time of rest.

FACT

Labyrinths for walking meditation are situated in various places around the world, as well as in private locations. Some famous labyrinths include those at Grace Cathedral, San Francisco, California; Land's End Labyrinth, also in the Bay Area; and the labyrinth of Chartres Cathedral in France. Many mystics and seekers walk labyrinths as a type of pilgrimage.

Being Rather Than Doing

Perfectionists are so focused on doing so many things that the being aspect of humanness is lost. There is no harm in carving out blocks of time in a busy schedule to simply, quietly exist. This is an important time of relaxation for the mind and body to regenerate. Sit quietly with a cup of tea, watch the sunrise or sunset, listen to the sounds of the neighborhood, or just stare. This isn't the time to catch up on texting.

The first few times you attempt to do nothing, it can be jarring, as you are so accustomed to being in accomplishment mode. The intense feeling of needing to complete a task has to be reined in like a wild horse. Undoubtedly, you will feel discomfort and tremendous resistance, as if you have a plane to catch and it is taking off without you. This is the illusion of the importance of all those perfectionistic tasks that have ruled your life for a long period of time. There is freedom on the other side of that release.

Concept of a Higher Self

Most of the major world religions include ideas concerning a deity that the followers worship. It can be stimulating to learn about the beliefs of those religions, not only to understand those rich cultures, but also to inform one's own sense of a higher self.

Ultimately it is a solitary, individual process of figuring out a belief in a divine source. Many are available to teach you *their* way, but this important aspect of adult maturation cannot be borrowed from another. It is genuinely up to each person to work out a comfortable belief, one which provides a secure rudder in the maelstroms of life.

Questions for Myself

It might help to ask yourself some questions about what you believe or want to believe about a spiritual entity. The following can be a starting point for you to determine your values in this area:

1. Does my God have a gender?
2. Does my God reside in a specific place? Where?
3. Do I believe in angels?
4. Do I believe in animal totems or spirit guides?
5. What do I believe about life after death?
6. What do I think about heaven and hell?
7. Why would God bring me difficult challenges?
8. What is the difference between punishment and consequences?
9. Will I be an outcast if I reject my family's religion?
10. Does my God have form?

11. How does God indicate interest in various aspects of my life?
12. What are miracles and do I believe in them?

ALERT

Persons who grow up in troubled families may have deep-seated resistance to any type of authority, finding it difficult to trust any entity of power. From this background, it is an important challenge to begin to trust a higher power, at first with small things, and later with larger, more important aspects of life. It is a gradual process.

Daily Routine to Counter Perfectionism

It can be a great comfort to create a spiritual practice that includes various specific rituals. These aspects of a daily routine counter the chaos of perfectionism and the painful memories of a difficult childhood background, bringing order and ease into daily life.

Some people like to start the day with a meditation. It is calming to decide on the various aspects of this practice and keep them somewhat the same each day, adjusting only if you have an appointment or travel plans that require a change for a day or two. The meditation can be followed by journaling.

Personal Journaling

Ira Progoff took the practice of journaling mainstream in the 1970s and 1980s with workshops across the United States. In more recent times it is common for people to journal, as it has become an accepted part of spiritual practice.

If you are unfamiliar with journaling, think about some ways you might begin. Set aside any belief that you have to do it right, as there is no set way to journal correctly. Perhaps select a notebook for the purpose of journaling. Your local bookstore or craft store will have a wide selection. Choose one that has a design, size, and weight that you like, as it will be a part of your life for many days. Think about whether you want lined or unlined pages. Many like to doodle and sketch as a part of the journaling process.

Each day, date the entry and simply let the words flow onto the page. Your writing might include important events of the previous day, strong emotions of the moment, or decisions weighing heavily. You can write down ideas and plans for the coming day or week. Half-baked ideas are welcome! The journal is a place to let seeds of new directions freely scatter on the page.

You can write prayers in your journal, prayers you know from a particular faith or your own spontaneous conversations with your spiritual Higher Self. It is a common practice to write blessings for those you worry about or those friends and family members who are experiencing trying times. Write out detailed blessings for people who annoy you! This will free you from the mental obsession of trying to change them.

ESSENTIAL

Sleepless nights or long waits in a reception room offer opportunities for prayer. Traffic jams, being on hold on the phone, and long check-out lines in a store offer further opportunities for prayer. A creative approach brings richness and depth to your spiritual life.

It is useful to write a daily gratitude list. Focusing on the good is a sure-fire way to move from tension and resentment to relaxation and appreciation. Let the gratitude flow into the journal, and over a period of days, you will find your perfectionism diminishing. If you like things the way they are, you are not so focused on making things perfectly some other way.

Think about the place of prayer in your life and how this can be a part of your daily routine. Some people talk with God while walking in nature or even along a busy urban thoroughfare. Some play a recorded prayer in the car while commuting. Others feel a sense of prayer when listening to certain types of music. It is completely up to the individual to work out a method of communicating with the spiritual guide. If you have a yoga practice, you might experiment with including prayer within some of the resting poses, such as Child's Pose. The physical ease is quite complementary with the spiritual openness that is conducive to prayer.

Overcoming Negative Associations

Perfectionists sometimes discover that the root of their difficulty is trying to please a harsh, punitive God—a bearded old man in the sky.

Part of the maturation process is developing an individual spirituality that is exactly in harmony with deeply held personal values. The result may be the same church as the childhood church, and perhaps not.

It helps greatly to thoroughly examine the nature of learned beliefs about a deity, death, sin, heaven, and hell, and see if they truly match what the adult prefers in the here and now. Sometimes childhood experiences with churches and those who worked in the churches or parochial schools leave a harmful residue of resentment, fear, and distrust of all authority figures, including God! It helps to tell the stories to a trusted friend, mentor, or therapist in order to become free of past associations.

For example, in one situation, a person remembered that the minister of the church in the individual's very young years had extramarital affairs with members in the church, causing chaos and confusion among the congregation. The child was too young to understand exactly what was going on, but could sense distrust in church gossip. The conclusion was that church leaders are dishonest and untrustworthy. They say all the good things, but their behavior is not so exemplary. Only through this conscious memory was the person able to let go of the old association and get to know other spiritual leaders on a case by case basis.

FACT

A December 2009 study of the Pew Research Center's forum on religion found that Americans' religious beliefs and practices do not easily fit into conventional categories. An earlier study revealed that 70 percent of Americans believe in the statement, "Many religions can lead to eternal life."

Adult Children's Spirituality

Adult children of alcoholics and other dysfunctional parents may have great difficulty accepting a loving God, as the old parental traits are projected onto the spiritual authority figure. It seems that the Higher Power is neglectful, abusive, tricky, too busy, misleading, and in general, downright cruel. This mindset is challenging to unravel because with that belief life's experiences tend to appear as a self-fulfilling prophecy. This can be most disconcerting, as it seems to prove that God is, in fact, rather cold and cruel.

Over time, however, the willingness to entertain the idea of a loving, generous God will gradually open the door to loving, generous experiences in life. Some, however, cling to bitterness to the end of their days, as it makes the childhood neglect and abuse quite real. Those embittered souls wear their difficulties like a badge of honor and suffering.

In recent decades the news has been full of instances of the abuses of power within some established churches. Sometimes adults remember instances of molestation that have been buried for decades. Along with the challenges of healing from such trauma, the survivors have to decide what they believe about the churches and those who work in the churches.

Women's Spirituality

Women have a process to go through in determining the place of their gender in a spiritual context. If one affiliates with a conventional church, where much of the power and control is held by men, it is difficult to feel comfortable with the growth process. It always seems that the men have to approve the direction and the women need permission. This subtle conditioning has to be faced. Some women opt out and seek spiritual centers with female leaders or fashion a personal, eclectic spiritual practice that does not depend upon any particular person. It might bring more of a sense of female spirituality to investigate the Tara figures of Tibetan Buddhism, the female saints of Catholicism, the Greek goddesses, and pagan beliefs concerning goddesses.

What Can You Do Instead?

A life with a spiritual connection is more peaceful and manageable than a life in which the individual tries to orchestrate everything alone. In fact, in some personal growth circles, living without a divine source of some kind is termed "edging God out," or living with too much emphasis on the ego.

Create an Altar

Having an altar in your home is a beneficial way to support your spiritual practice. You might find good ideas in your library or bookstore. A simple table can offer a beginning. Cover it with a cloth that is attractive and appealing to your spirit. Over a period of time gather objects and photographs that have meaning to you. It is not necessary to have a guru to have a spiritual life, but if someone has been especially inspiring to you, a photo of that person could be a nice addition to your altar.

You may have souvenirs of special times, places, and experiences that made you feel especially close to God. Group those objects in a way that is pleasing to your eye. Incense is an interesting sensory addition and can add to the ritual of spiritual centering. You might want to gather physical representations of material things that you want to manifest in your life, making your altar a sort of three-dimensional vision board.

Some cultures use candles, flowers, and grains to represent the abundance of the earth. You might enjoy putting a few ears of dried corn or a small bowl of rice on your altar to elicit a feeling of gratitude for the abundance of the earth.

Keep your altar clean, and change the arrangement from time to time to keep your response and interest fresh. You might want to include your vision board in your altar arrangement.

Browse in Bookstores and Libraries

It is invigorating and enjoyable to linger in the spiritual section of your favorite bookish place, tasting some of what is available from the wide range of spiritual disciplines and philosophies. You may find an author that you enjoy and read everything else that person has written. There is nothing to say that you have to accept a particular religion merely because you read books about it.

It can be interesting to explore Zen, Islam, Christian history, Native American shamanism, and Hinduism. Take a look at agnosticism and atheism and make up your own mind about what you believe. It might happen that you develop a personalized spiritual faith that draws bits and pieces from various cultures and various aspects of your own cultural background.

Listen to Lectures and Form New Friendships

It is stimulating to go to various spiritual centers and listen to speakers. Usually such places are quite welcoming to visitors, and you do not have to commit just because you are there. You might feel more secure visiting a very different kind of place with a friend who is a member.

Having friends from a variety of different spiritual orientations is a very enriching experience. One can learn firsthand the meaning of different rituals and practices and discern the effect in the person's life. Are they comforted by their beliefs? Do they seem confident in their lives?

ESSENTIAL

As you build your social network with new spiritual friends, search out those individuals who seem to welcome challenges, as they understand that a person's character flexes and grows with exercise. These people do not react with resentment when life throws them a curve ball. They dig in and put their spiritual practice to work and share what they learn with others along the way.

If you are not Buddhist, it can be very exciting to attend a temple on Buddhist's Day of Enlightenment. The lanterns, lights, feasts, and sense of celebration convey the joy of Buddha's experiences. Similarly, a non-Christian can attend a Christmas Eve candlelight service in a mainline Christian church and marvel at the candles, sense of new beginning, and the mere fact that every person in the congregation seems to know the words to the hymns, joining voices in song.

My Business, Your Business, or God's Business

Having a trusting relationship with a higher source clarifies areas of control for the perfectionist, and it becomes easier to discern what is really and truly your domain and what is not. When you have done all you can on a particular issue, it is time to release it to the spiritual ether. Meddling in others' business will no longer be as appealing as you learn the effects of your perfectionism. People generally do not like that in the long run, although some who are inclined to be dependent will bask in your solicitations. Such helpful diversions ultimately prevent you from flourishing in your own life as you are too busy living other lives.

Experiment for a set length of time. For example, it may be helpful to, for one week, make conscious contact with a spiritual source and give to that source all the parts of your life that are not working—the preoccupations, the perfectionist nature, difficult relationships, and challenging situations and decisions. Visualize the process of handing them over, again and again if necessary, and after the length of time has passed, determine whether you feel more peaceful. Is it better to have a spiritual partner? The perfectionist wants to do everything alone because nobody else's efforts really measure up, but a hand-in-hand relationship with a spiritual entity of your choice brings a higher-quality daily existence. It does take practice, especially after decades of trying to be perfect.

Dream Work

Many people work with their dreams as an important aspect of their spiritual practice. If you are a person who dreams frequently and remembers your dreams, this may be a way to attune yourself to a course that is informed by your subconscious mind.

There are many dream books available, and you may find them helpful; however, dreams are so laden with images that are specific to each individual that it can be useful to learn how to interpret dreams without running to a dream dictionary. Here are some suggestions for working with your dreams:

1. Keep a journal near your bed so you can write down dreams as you awaken.
2. Write down the dream as you remember it, like a scene or story.
3. Notice any strong emotions as you awaken and remember the dream and write those down.
4. Is the dream one that you have had repeatedly? Note that in your journal.
5. Use the margin of your journal to free associate from powerful images in your dream. Let the mind be very free in this process and completely true to your background. For example, if there is a woman named Dorothy in your dream, remember all the women you have known named Dorothy and write them down. Note their personalities and significance

in your life (including Dorothy from the *Wizard of Oz!*). Was there a spider in your dream? Make a list of your honest associations with spiders—fear, dislike of insects, *Charlotte's Web*, the world wide web of the Internet, whatever comes to mind.

QUESTION

What if I have persistent, repetitive nightmares?
The subconscious mind is very efficient in storing information about your experiences and beliefs. Nightmares can be a clearing out process that occurs after you achieve a place of security and strength. Sometimes nightmares can be a warning about danger in your waking life. Deeply hidden experiences from younger years sometimes come to light first in nightmares, then later in a more linear fashion. Persistent nightmares can be taken to a therapist for help, especially if they continue for months or years.

6. Look at the flow of the associations and determine what your deeper self is telling you. It may not be evident right away. It might help to set it aside for a day or so and see if something occurs to you later.
7. Look back over your dreams as you set aside each journal to see what trends are developing in your life.
8. If you have a relationship with a helpful therapist, ask if that person is comfortable helping you with your dream interpretation. Some professionals are well informed and sensitive. If you are comfortable working with a trusted counselor on your dreams, this can be a fruitful way to determine their meaning and what you might do with the information gleaned.

God Box

One way to fine-tune your trust in a higher source is to write down concerns on small pieces of paper and put them in a God box. Any box that you choose can be your God box, or you can buy or make one for this specific purpose. It is more enticing to get into the habit of giving concerns to God if the box is attractive and has some type of symbolism for you—perhaps shells or gems from nature, colors that you especially like, or the box was a gift from a treasured relative or friend.

Small Post-it notes are good for putting worries and issues into the God box. Simply jot down the essence of the situation and put it in the box. After a few weeks or months go by, spend some time reading the notes and see what really and truly has been resolved. This simple practice will help you to trust your Higher Power to a greater degree. If there are any concerns still pending, just keep putting them in the box.

Spiritual Retreats

Most religious and spiritual groups have periodic retreats where followers of a particular belief or practice come together for a focused time. Often the change in location from the demands of home and work is healing in and of itself. Some retreats have a specific purpose, and others are more open-ended. Some are tightly structured, and some have blocks of free time during which you can rest, meditate, enjoy a library, or socialize with others.

Some retreats offer days of silence, which can be an interesting discipline for perfectionists who like to talk a lot! The long periods of quiet inform a person of how much energy is used to express verbally and to listen to others' conversation. What a lot of effort! Silent retreats in the company of like-minded spiritual seekers are quite informative about the nature of the self and the relationship with a higher self.

Retreats are a good place to rest after traumatic happenings or major losses. The meals are usually prepared and served by the retreat organizers, and you are free to heal. Some retreat centers welcome visitors who are on a solo retreat without a structured program to follow. Sometimes professionals are on staff to assist a person individually if therapeutic conversations are desired. Often quiet times in a beautiful setting bring answers from within.

An Internet search for retreats of various types in your specific region will result in many possibilities for exploration. A retreat can be combined with a vacation, making the trip quite rejuvenating and purposeful. If there is a place around the country or world that you have always wanted to see, consider doing a retreat at that location.

Being in Nature

Time spent in the beautiful outdoors can be a part of your spiritual practice, bringing deep calm and reverence for the processes of life. There is nothing quite like the majesty of redwood trees, the power of the surf, or the delicacy of a finely manicured, formal rose garden. These settings take you away from the daily stresses of personal life and work, making it easier to become attuned to your spiritual nature.

If you like to camp, this is a way to be even closer to the rhythms of the earth, spending longer periods of time away from urban noise and demands. If possible, turn off all your electronic devices and enjoy some freedom from e-mails and texts. Most of those communications probably are not truly urgent.

FACT

The lotus flower has symbolic spiritual meaning in several cultures. In the Buddhist culture, it represents faith, purity, and growth, as the beautiful blossom emerges, seemingly impossibly, from murky mud, flourishing amidst the muddy background. For centuries, thousands of Buddhists have found hope in the shape, color, and mere existence of the miraculous lotus blossom.

If you cannot get away to a quiet place in nature, investigate what is available in your immediate vicinity. A museum might offer a lovely koi pond or herb garden. Even zoos sometimes have authentic areas that are almost like home for the animals.

When you are in nature, notice the sounds and smells of the environment. Thoughtfully go back to some of those basic questions on spiritual matters. What are the plant and animal forms in that place and how are they related to each other? What do the animals eat? How do the plants get their nutrients? What are the cycles of life for the flora and fauna that you are enjoying? Can you recreate some aspects of nature that you especially love in your home or office, perhaps as a part of an altar?

CHAPTER 20

The Discipline of Forgiveness

The state of perfectionism is inherently imbued with criticisms and resentments of various kinds. Some may be deeply historical, almost a part of the personality. You might feel that it is your role in life to constantly be railing at injustices, especially those directed at you. This can become a kind of identity—the angry person done wrong. Such deeply harbored anger can provide energy and direction, but it is not positive. It is useful to imagine life without those habitual angry resentments.

But Am I Condoning Terrible Wrongs?

It is an interesting mental feat to switch gears and imagine forgiveness toward those very people who made your life miserable. You might wonder if forgiveness means that you condone those terrible acts toward you. No, forgiveness does not mean condoning, and it does not mean that you have to let those people back into your life in any relationship involvement, although you might. All you intend to do is change your mental focus from resentment to acceptance.

Acceptance

Acceptance means that you 100 percent accept the reality of what occurred in the situation. Something happened that was unjust or was otherwise to your detriment. Another person may have been at fault, but that is not the issue at this juncture. Acceptance means that, yes, it happened; you embrace that as a part of your history and go on to other experiences.

In American society, forgiveness is often seen as an act of weakness. Within a competitive society, it is the exceptional person who is able to approach a difficult situation with compassion and caring toward the person who is guilty of a harmful act. Many do not want to relinquish the upper hand in a competitive situation, feeling somehow that they are losing.

Did You Have a Part in the Occurrence?

It can be helpful to examine your resentments to see if somehow you had a part in the occurrences that have been so troublesome. Again, as with other written exercises, it helps to write it all down and think with an open mind and heart whether there was something going on within you that precipitated the action of the other person. If so, you can make an agreement with yourself to handle things differently in the future.

Believing in Spiritual Forgiveness

Research shows that those who believe that God or some other spiritual deity is forgiving and benevolent experience life in a more relaxed, less stressful manner. They are less harsh toward themselves and others. This could be a clue to embracing less perfectionism, as perfectionism includes a harsh view toward the self and others, always expecting more or different behavior.

Humility is an aspect of forgiveness. One sees and accepts that there might be a larger picture, that things happen in context, and sometimes situations play out in a way that is beneficial to more people. Sometimes humility can be an act of just showing up to participate in something, even if the relationship was problematic in the past. One can hope for a new start and be the one to make the first move.

Remembering that forgiveness is available from God prevents a person from being too self-righteous about the act of forgiveness, lording it over the other person in a falsely magnanimous manner. Such a deceitful act of forgiveness does no one any good, as it is only a ruse to look good in the eyes of whoever might be around to witness it. True forgiveness happens first within the self, then with the spiritual source, and finally with the person one is forgiving. It is definitely not a quick fix, and it will undoubtedly take some time to go through all those stages.

Forgiveness as a Shift in Focus

The poison of resentment drains away when you shift your focus from a negative preoccupation toward the wrongdoer to other aspects of your life. Perhaps the negative obsession has been a major preoccupation for years, even decades. It can be quite refreshing to reclaim that energy for more beneficial aspects of your life. You may find that a persistent fatigue lifts, and you can finally approach life with hope and vigor.

ESSENTIAL

Forgiveness is an act of release—release of judgments, hurts, grudges, anger, perceived injuries, even memories of what occurred.

Redirect Your Focus

What you want to do is redirect your thinking to something or someone else. It's like unplugging an appliance and emphatically plugging it into a different outlet. This shift in focus requires tremendous mental strength and discipline, as it may have been a part of your identity for years to habitually be angry with particular people, situations, or institutions. This undue emphasis is a type of attachment, in the Buddhist sense. It is a trap that keeps you ensnared, even as you vow that one of these days you will invoke the proper revenge toward those who were mistaken!

The best revenge is to reclaim your mental freedom and use your emotions and intellectual faculties for your own purposes and to live out your interests, goals, and dreams. Those other people and situations will, undoubtedly, take care of themselves just fine and really do not need you to explain the error of their ways. Those who do wrong endure plenty of natural consequences within themselves, and it is not up to you to straighten them out. Somehow they will find their way, and life's circumstances will bring a measure of justice in the long run, sometimes in surprising ways. Your highest and best revenge is to live a very happy life, in spite of what happened to you. If you are in a position where it is necessary to interact regularly with the one who mistreated you, that person will be mystified by your peace, tranquility, and happiness. You can have some fun with this.

FACT

Forgiveness shifts the awareness from the past to the present. Whatever happened to cause the difficulty occurred at another time. It is over. Forgiveness allows you to think about now instead of then. Pain is replaced with peace, and joy replaces hurt.

The ability to forgive is a factor in long, successful marriages. It is as if there is a larger perspective held by both parties, an ability to forgive a variety of transgressions over a lengthy period of time. Forgiveness may take some time. It does not matter if it happens instantly or not. Sometimes the situations that take a while to figure out bring a deeper degree of forgiveness.

Change your Perspective

Sometimes you may shift your focus to such a degree that you are able to relate in a loving way with those persons who harmed you. Nothing special has to be said about the change in manner. You simply start acting in a loving, caring way toward the person that you resented in the past. This shift in focus changes the tone of the relationship, and the other person may learn to meet you halfway. Sometimes the person will not be aware of what has changed but become more comfortable in your presence, as he or she does not feel defensive or frightened, as was possibly the case before you decided to forgive.

It's as if you shed an old skin, like a rattlesnake crawls out of a skin that has become too small. Your larger self does not need the rigid beliefs and emotions about what was wrong with the person or situation. Your larger, evolved self is able to embrace a spiritual view of the situation, accepting other, flawed people who are doing the best they can, sometimes with a fairly small toolbox. Those limitations do not prevent you from loving others. Others cannot genuinely prevent you from enjoying the good that you deserve, and you begin to notice this more and more as you act and behave in a more mature manner in a wide variety of situations with a more diverse swath of human beings. Your repertoire has become broad and deep.

Relationship to Physical Health

Although research in regard to forgiveness is relatively new, findings point to a correlation between forgiveness and emotional, spiritual, and physical health. It appears that the benefits are greatest when the one who forgives hopes to restore goodwill in a relationship that had been close but became estranged.

Hostility is a component of not being able to forgive and also a symptom associated with cardiovascular disease. Researchers Woodruff and Farrow found that the locus of forgiveness activity in the brain is deep in the limbic system, the seat of the emotions. It does not lie in the cortex, the seat of judgment. This is a good clue to not dwell too heavily on the logic or illogic of a situation. It is more important to get to the emotional heart of the matter and release the wrong in an emotional and spiritual sense.

What Does Research Reveal?

A two year study concluding in 2002 at Hope College showed that when people are asked to think about a grudge held against a particular person, the body responds with changes in facial muscles, heart rate, and blood pressure. Sweat gland activity increased, and the subjects felt anxious. When researcher and psychologist Charlotte Witvliet asked her subjects to think of the begrudged person in a warm, compassionate manner, the bodily responses returned to normal. Sincere apologies relaxed the facial muscles, and frowns disappeared.

A study titled, "Forgivingness, relationship quality, stress while imagining relationship events, and physical and mental health," published in the *Journal of Counseling Psychology* in 2001, revealed that in romantic relationships, those relationships that are described as generally unhappy leave the persons involved with higher levels of cortisol, the chemical associated with the fight-or-flight response, possibly contributing stress to the body.

Research also implicates a relationship between the unwillingness to forgive and compromises to the immune system, making it easier for the body to succumb to viruses, bacteria, and infection, even dental disease.

Is Age a Factor?

In general, middle-aged and elderly persons are more forgiving, possibly because they find it more difficult to accommodate higher levels of stress that result from an aversion to forgiveness. People over forty-five who are generally forgiving have fewer psychological symptoms of anxiety and depression.

Forgive Your Body

In today's fast-paced society, many view their body as a machine that is always there, ready for whatever is required. It is easy to forget about maintenance, not to mention genuine caring and appreciation for the physical self. Then when illness occurs, it is a tremendous interruption in the frantic schedule, and one feels betrayed, even angry at the body.

Needless to say, these angry emotions toward the body do nothing to help the healing processes. Better to stop everything and let a long rest provide a haven for the body to do its natural healing. Anger releases the wrong hormones, making it difficult for the immune system to function and nutrition to find its way to the healthy cells so they may do their repair work. Many who have been interrupted by a major illness realize afterward that a long rest was indeed necessary.

Ideally one would not wait for an illness in order to rest, regenerate, and heal from the daily use of the body. Self-nurturing in a physical way is always a good thing—long baths, good nutrition, exercise, massage, and whatever other pampering your time and budget allow. Gratitude is in order when thinking about the miraculous processes of the human body. Instead of annoyance, think of the marvelous organs that take care of your daily needs and how beautifully coordinated all the systems are. Even with a bit of neglect, the body functions well most of the time. It is a refined, delicate instrument that deserves excellent care and appreciation.

Examples of Radical Forgiveness

Your forgiveness challenges may be many and seemingly insurmountable. You might find it inspiring to consider stories of others who have had quite difficult instances of forgiveness in their lives.

Forgiving Criminals

Writer Aba Gayle received news that her nineteen-year-old daughter had been shot, resulting in her death. The authorities found the murderer, and Ms. Gayle focused her life, for eight years, on the just punishment of the murderer. She felt no peace in the situation and decided instead to write to the person, who was housed in San Quentin. Ultimately she decided to make the journey to visit him in person. She found that her daughter's killer, as the others on death row, were not monsters. She spoke with the individual at length, and they cried together. The result of her act of radical forgiveness was the creation of a prison ministry that focused on prisoners with looming death sentences. She doesn't focus on their crimes. She focuses on their personal freedom and relationship with God. In this way, Ms. Gayle became free from the albatross of hatred resulting from the premature death of her precious child. Her soul became free.

Forgiveness opens the way to new possibilities. A closed heart and clenched fist cannot receive something new. An open heart and open hand are able to receive new insight and new experiences.

A ten-year-old child, Chris Carrier, of Florida, was stabbed and shot by an attacker in the swamps near his home. Miraculously he survived. In his adult years he learned from a law enforcement officer that his attacker was near death in prison. Carrier chose to visit the prisoner and spend those last moments together, forgiving him and bringing peace to both parties.

Forgiving Abusive and Neglectful Parents

Eventually one heals to the point that it is possible to see dysfunctional, limited parents as flawed beings who probably did the best they could with whatever capabilities they had. They quite possibly had difficult childhoods themselves and simply repeated patterns that were generational. Seeing these people as instruments of your biological existence lets you move to a point of forgiveness toward those who treated you badly during your formative years, setting in place the mold for perfectionism.

Forgiving parents for wrongdoing opens up floodgates of love, allowing a normal relationship to develop, even if the parents never change. It is unlikely that they will change, anyway, as the motivation has to come from within the person. Once you forgive your parents, other relationships become easier, warmer, and more alive. It is possible to live in the present, seeing each person and situation for what it actually is instead of projecting the parental template on every relationship that is similar to that of the father or mother.

Apologies from the wrongdoers are not necessary for you to become free. Those apologies may occur at some point in the future, and they may not. It really does not matter because the process of forgiveness most benefits the one who forgives.

What Can You Do Instead?

There are several ways to move from resentment to forgiveness. Whatever you choose will have to do with your personal style and preference.

Write Fourteen-Day Blessings

Some have found the practice of writing out blessings for those troublesome people and occurrences quite helpful. In your journal each morning, simply write out sentences, blessing each individual that is worrisome to you. Ask for blessings in each area of the person's life—health, love, career success, relationship happiness. It does not matter if you are sincere! You may be so angry that you actually wish terrible things for them, but this is not what you write on the page. Simply go through the motions of writing out positive blessings in each area of life, for each person that festers in your mind in a negative way.

FACT

Grace is an important component of forgiveness. The forgiving person experiences grace and generosity, and the recipient receives grace and release from guilt and punishment. Grace envelopes both forgiver and forgiven in hope and renewal.

Continue the blessing writing for fourteen days for each person that you harbor resentments against. Usually, after three or four days, the preoccupation lifts, and you are able to accept them in a more positive way. Sometimes this practice brings tremendous healing in deeply troubled relationships.

You might experiment with blessing your challenges, as there might be something in the situation that will provide tremendous learning or awakening. It has been said that the way out is through, and if you bless that problem, perhaps it will reveal its secrets and illuminate the path to the other side. The challenge adds to your story, and you will have more experience to offer others who might struggle with a similar task in the future. If you have a perfect life, there really isn't any colorful texture to contribute to your relationships.

Forgive Seventy Times Seven

The conventional Christian suggestion is to forgive each wrongdoer seventy times seven times. (See Matthew 18:22, though some translations say "seventy-seven" as opposed to "seventy times seven.) If you do the multiplication, you will see that this number (490) is quite large! If you are courageous enough to approach this task, you might make it a part of your morning journaling, but of course, you cannot expect to complete it all in one day. You might select some pieces of lined paper, and see how many pages it will take to write out 490 sentences of forgiveness for one person. There usually are about sixty lines on one page. You might complete the forgiveness writing for one person in about a week.

FACT

Forgiveness does not necessarily mean that you are forgetting the incident, and it does not necessarily mean that you have pardoned the offense.

Another way is to say the forgiveness sentences out loud, perhaps as you are driving. You can complete 490 forgiveness sentences verbally in about twenty minutes. Focus on one person and use your driving time in this beneficial way, perhaps for a week, and see if you feel a lightening of the spirit.

It might be interesting to organize a group of people who have similar goals in terms of forgiveness and chant forgiveness sentences together for twenty minutes at a time. Then shift to a different person for another twenty-minute interval. An hour of this work will allow each individual to forgive three people. It can be beneficial for a few people to share their experiences with this exercise while others in the group listen.

Forgive Yourself

Ultimately, the hope of the perfectionistic person is to achieve forgiveness of the self for not being perfect. This is a tall order, sometimes seemingly impossible. Any of the techniques mentioned in this chapter can be used to forgive the self. You are worth it! When you lift the judgment, blame, and self-criticism from yourself on a daily basis, you have an opportunity to enjoy a free and interesting life, full of creative expression and fulfillment.

ALERT

The self-forgiveness process for the adult child involves acknowledging what occurred in the childhood home, grieving the loss of a normal upbringing, facing the self-hatred of perfectionism, and eventually healing the split between the disowned self and the loving mature self who is able to nurture the wounded child.

In order to achieve this, you will need a lot of courage to face the harsh self-talk directed at your own mind. This stage of awareness can be painful, but it is worth it to get to the other side. Those voices initially came from others in your life and you internalized them as your own. You can mentally reject them, just as you mentally adopted them during your formative years. You have that prerogative to decide what conversations take place in your own mind.

It is absolutely worth the effort to direct forgiveness activities inward—the fourteen-day blessings and the seventy-times-seven forgiveness work. You will definitely breathe easier at the end of such work, and you will like yourself a lot more, even if you are not perfect!

As much as possible, strive towards unconditional love and caring toward yourself. It might help to think of a small child or animal that you would want to handle with tender, gentle care. Approach yourself in a similar, forgiving, accepting way. You are doing the very best that you can, and kindness and love make your actions and endeavors much easier. No one is holding a stick over your head, although you may have felt that someone was! Remove those old critical images and embrace self-love.

Use Your God Box

If you find yourself constantly coming back to the mental preoccupation with perfectionistic demands on yourself or historical anger toward others, it is helpful to write out those instances and put them in your God box. You may need to do this more than once or even several days in a row. Forgiveness is a discipline, and you may need to face resentments and let them go multiple times. Keep in mind that you are aiming for freedom—freedom from old hurts, injustices, anger, disappointments, betrayals, and numerous situations that did not turn out as you had hoped. You can be free of it all.

If the Person Has Died

You might wonder how to manage the process of forgiveness if the person you are forgiving has died. You can write an honest letter and read it to a trusted friend or therapist. You can also go to the gravesite or place where his or her ashes were scattered, talk freely with the departed, and read a sincere letter to the person. Of course, it is impossible to know whether the person "hears" what you say. The important change takes place within you. The act of forgiveness is ultimately for you, although there are benefits for all concerned. You may find that when you forgive a parent who was neglectful or cruel, your relationships with your siblings improve.

Embrace Joy

Holding on to resentments, even if they seem justified based on the facts of what happened, locks a person into negative emotions. Releasing those old emotions with forgiveness opens up the possibility of joy in the here and now. Life and people (even with all their imperfections) add to the tapestry of your existence. An undue emphasis on everything that went wrong and continues to go wrong leaves no room for daily awareness and happiness.

As much as possible, on a daily basis, make room for joy in your life. Notice small things—a friendly exchanged greeting with a neighbor, an unexpected phone call, a beautiful flower, a song by your favorite performer, an unexpected conversation with a long-lost friend via social media. All these things are worthy of joy. Embrace it all and make a good day for yourself, however imperfect it might be.

CHAPTER 21

Moving Forward with Freedom

Perfectionism is like a veil, a shroud of gauze that hides the underpinnings and consequences of unbearably high standards. Once you have pulled those things aside, looked at the origins, and worked through the adjustments, you can confidently move into a different phase of your life. Like a birth or graduation, living and being without perfectionism, or at least claiming a lesser degree of perfectionism, requires new decisions. The old landmarks no longer apply. It is as if you see everything through a different lens.

What If Everything Turns Out Okay?

One can feel uneasy without the former mental paradigm of perfectionism. As uncomfortable as it was, the parameters were familiar. One gets used to a huge amount of tension, self-criticism, and a judgmental attitude toward external surroundings. Without all this, there is freedom, but it takes a while to adjust. Like jumping into the deep end of a swimming pool or visiting a foreign country, even after years of practice with the language, it takes a few strokes or several dozen conversations to feel truly at home in a different milieu.

If everything turns out okay, there will be no need for interminable suffering, constant complaining, and dread of the future. One can wake up in the morning and anticipate a good day instead of enduring fearful constrictions of the emotions and muscles while mentally going over lists of things that have to be done.

All will be well in the new terrain. The old map is unnecessary, and you can kiss it goodbye. Life always brings challenges and interesting problems to solve, but you have learned new techniques and approaches of self-acceptance and flexibility.

Setting Aside Former Identities

Letting go of perfectionism will likely require that you release old identities that lent themselves to trying to be perfect. This is possibly easier said than done. Perfectionists like to be right, and thinking about letting go of who you were means that your old self was wrong. This realization is uncomfortable. It doesn't mean that you were wrong as a person; it was merely a case of having many mistaken beliefs and ideas about yourself.

Who Were You?

It can be fascinating to explore those former selves. You might approach the task in a creative or artistic manner. Perhaps make a list of all the selves—scholar, career person, father, sister, coach, savior, fixer, quality control freak. Free-associate with your list and give your former selves silly names, if you feel like it. Were you Wonder Woman or Superman flying through the air with your cape? Were you Mr. Have-the-Last-Word no matter what? Honesty about your various selves will help you become free. It will be less painful if you can play with it.

ESSENTIAL

Writer Joseph Campbell said, "We must be willing to get rid of the life we've planned so as to have the life that is waiting for us." This requires some tolerance for ambiguity and the unknown.

If you like to draw or paint, it will be interesting to make pictures of your former selves, perhaps in a little cartoon booklet. If you are a storyteller or writer, jot down some essays about each of the selves and some of their more colorful escapades.

Spend some time on this exploration, as claiming the reality of the former selves, accepting their importance in your scheme of things for a number of years, and getting ready to let them go opens the way to new freedom. It is not a process that should rushed.

Say Goodbye

You may feel sadness and vulnerability as you release the old you with all the perfectionistic habits and strict structure. Whatever emotion you feel will be right for you. It might be relief, sorrow, anticipation, even love for those innovative personalities who allowed you to keep it all together for so many years.

FACT

Symptoms of withdrawal may surprise you. Nausea, anxiety, headaches, nervousness, fatigue, and the shakes are detox symptoms that are present when a substance abuser becomes clean. The process might be as profound for a person giving up a mental construct, such as perfectionism. Plenty of rest and a quiet, gentle environment will be helpful.

You might want to devise a ritual to signify the importance of the occasion. You could put them on your altar for a few days. You might make graduation caps and give each previous identity a diploma. You might create a scrapbook with a page for each one. These were important adaptations to very difficult circumstances and not to be scoffed at or treated too casually. Say goodbye, however, as the former selves have outlived their usefulness.

Is a New Career Choice in the Picture?

Releasing perfectionism may make you uncomfortable with your current or previous career choices. It is as if the perfectionism created a foggy web through which you viewed your interests and options. Circumstances change as you change, and this might include a yearning for a different direction.

ALERT

Adult children from difficult families go into the helping professions in large proportions. Some are motivated by a sincere, altruistic drive to serve others. Some are driven unconsciously to master the dynamic of the childhood home, to save others and make everything okay for someone somewhere. Such drives can be unhealthy and unrealistic. At this stage of coping with perfectionism it is helpful to take an honest look at your work life and determine whether it pleases you.

Write a Career Autobiography

It is helpful to write down your entire work history, from childhood up to the present time. Make it as detailed as you are able—whom you worked for, which aspects you liked and didn't like, how long you did that work, and why you left that work. Include the level of pay and whether you were satisfied. Try to remember tasks you did to earn money as a child and teenager.

If you attended college, how did you select your major? Think about whether someone influenced you in your choice. If that person had not had a voice, is there something else you might have enjoyed? Remember family attitudes toward various professions and honestly include those pressures in your work history.

Note especially important milestones in your work life—promotions, prizes, publications, raises, changes in professions, and geographic moves. Describe your academic programs of study and honors received. It is important to grasp the larger picture, the organic whole of your vocational life.

If there are very important hobbies or service responsibilities that are or were as important as your earning endeavors, describe those, too. Did someone nominate you to head a fundraising committee for a nonprofit organization, and you willingly spearheaded the effort? What were the satisfactions and frustrations? Did you enter your prize roses in a county competition and surprise yourself with the depth of your commitment to the task? Do you have a steady, ongoing presence in a church or community center that is pivotal to your weekly schedule? This is a part of your work life, even if it is unpaid.

Meditations and Dreams

Have new directions emerged in your meditations and dreams? Sometimes the first glimpses of something enticing can seem flitting and elusive. The perfectionistic self wants to reject anything purely joyful. As much as you are able, create a welcoming context for your subconscious mind to speak to you regarding deeply desired aims for your life. It might be important to set aside a particular journal for those visions, jotting them down in raw form so you can notice if something is taking shape over a period of weeks or months.

Dreams can sometimes seem obscure in their emotional or visual coding. Just do the best you can to write down anything that strikes you as important. As you face the fears of considering something new, the images will become clearer. The human mind has a way of protecting itself, and if you are too frightened to consider a change, your conscious mind will keep the idea away from you.

If you enjoy the vision board process, it would be possible to make miniature vision pages for aspects of a larger vision that seems to be taking shape. The form could be sleeved pages in a notebook or collaged pages in a journal.

Career Classes, Planning, and Testing

It can be very rewarding to take a career class where you are among others and can look at your values and preferences over a period of weeks. Having the companionship of other career seekers makes you feel more supported as you consider new options for your work life. Consider nonprofit career centers, counselors, coaches, and interest inventories in order to get a fresh look at the reality of who you are at this time and what your true preferences might be.

Approach this kind of study with an open mind, as your perfectionism may have skewed your studies and career choices in the past. Just think about it as someone else who did those things. A new person has shown up today, looking for joy and fulfillment in employment. Imagine you are an actor or actress, and you are ready for a new role.

Public libraries are a gold mine of helpful career resources—books, online, and free lectures. Some libraries offer weekly sessions with SCORE counselors, retired executives who are eager to help other businesspeople. Explore Internet communities for like-minded persons who are a little further along in their quest, sharing information and questions. Meetup.com (*www.meetup.com*) is active in some metropolitan areas, offering spontaneous get-togethers on a wide range of topics. Some of them might be perfect for you, enabling you to exchange tips with others on a similar path.

Create a Plan and Timeline

It is one thing to have a fantasy of doing something exotic and quite another to take action in a new direction. The fantasy might have been a convenient safe haven for a number of years, but your new career becomes quite real when you work to make it happen. Check in with yourself at every step of the way to see if you really like what you are doing. Sometimes those from perfectionistic or neglectful backgrounds need help to determine what is truly satisfying because the natural internal intuitive radar was blunted. A therapist, career coach, trusted mentor, or friend can assist with feedback and encouragement.

Create a timeline with realistic goals—perhaps six months, a year, and five years. Discuss this with others who will be a part of the change, especially a spouse or significant other. Examine the level of your prudent savings and other sources of income while you make a transition. Think about insurance and retirement and decide what you want to do in those areas.

Visualize, visualize, and visualize your target profession again! With a strong enough focus, the universe will respond.

Examining Your Relationships

With perfectionism as your daily companion, you may sense some restlessness and disquietude in your closest relationships. Did you choose a partner that you could dominate in hopes of getting perfect results? Did you hope to change that other person? Often those who come from alcoholic backgrounds choose a partner that needs serious reform, as that repeats the hope of the child with an alcoholic or substance-addicted parent. That type of relationship feels comfortable, or at least familiar. It can become considerably less comfortable when one realizes that the other person has so many issues that solving them all will take an entire lifetime. If you are considering making a major relationship change, consider joining support groups and enlisting the help of a professional who can guide you along the way. You may discover that the relationship is salvageable, if both parties are on a growth path.

FACT

Holding on to resentment is like holding your finger in a fire, even after you notice that it's burning and it hurts a lot! It probably makes sense to quickly release the cause of the pain.

In a similar manner, without perfectionism your social life may cry out for a tune-up. Do you have hanger-on friends who deluge you with woe-is-me litanies? Are they interested in you and your new directions? Do you have friends who share joy when you achieve what you have set out to do? As you let go of perfectionism, you may experience some attrition in your social life. Try not to be alarmed, as other, more appropriate friends will find you. You deserve friends who are able to relate to you in a loving, authentic manner.

Burying Perfectionism: Create a Ritual

Depending on your style and personality, you may want to create a specific ritual to let go of perfectionism. There are a variety of activities that can help you let go and move forward with freedom. Some of the following have been useful to others:

1. Write down something that represents perfectionism.
2. Make a visual representation of perfectionism.
3. Burn the representation of perfectionism and bury the ashes.
4. Make a miniature coffin and put perfectionism in the coffin.
5. Place the miniature coffin on your altar or near your God box.
6. Create affirmations of release and write them for several days.
7. Focus on release of perfectionism in your meditation and prayer practice.
8. Visualize yourself in your new life without perfectionism.
9. Create a vision board showing your life without perfectionism.

A sensitivity to your real beliefs and preferences as you create a ritual is important. You might want to do something that is very earthy, connected to the raw elements of life and death. Honor that. Perhaps words are more important to you. Scatter words about your altar or tape them on mirrors in your home. Movement might be an important aspect of how you engage in life. Burning a representation of your former perfectionism and vigorously scattering the ashes while you dance outdoors might be a good activity to connect your deeper cellular self to the changes you experience. Make it very real and authentic for yourself.

What Can You Do Instead?

Without perfectionism, life is wide open with a brand new range of possibilities. You are no longer hampered with the mistaken belief that whatever you do has to be perfect, and many more options are available.

Juggling Act

With so many tools at your fingertips to create a new start, without perfectionism, you may feel like a master juggler or aerial artist in Cirque du Soleil! Do what you are able to do, making fresh choices as they meet your needs. There is no right way to move through the process of diminishing perfectionism and creating a better life. You will discover your way with trial and error. When something doesn't seem to fit, try a different choice.

Never Too Late

It is never too late for you to undertake major improvements in your life. Some hardy people continue creative output far into their eighties and nineties, such as Louise Nevelson, Martha Graham, and Pablo Casals. Grandma Moses didn't start painting until she was in her seventies and worked well into her nineties, living to the age of 101.

Embrace Wonder

Regardless of your age and situation, without addictive emotional, mental, and behavioral tendencies, you are able to see the incredible wonder of life, partaking in pleasurable experiences in consistent ways that bring you happiness. The balance tips away from nervousness and sorrow, and you have longer series of truly good days. Each one is a creative entity that is fashioned by you and you only.

Dignity, Respect, a Slower Pace

Without perfectionism, you find yourself treating yourself and others with a higher degree of dignity and respect. Your relationship with yourself is more loving and wholesome, and you have more to offer to friends, family, and work associates. Cooperating with others is easier, and you are less afraid of disapproval from others.

As you drop obligations that are not essential, a slower pace of living becomes your norm. The slower pace allows your body to function more normally, and sometimes you are happy and relaxed, breathing deeply and truly enjoying life.

Become Like a Child

Painter Pablo Picasso said that it takes many years to become like a child. He constantly endeavored to keep a fresh perspective toward his work, eventually moving away from representation and fully embracing cubism. That childlike perspective is available to you, too!

Helpful Websites

Thirdworldpapa.com
An eclectic modern blog on many aspects of relationships.
www.thirdworldpapa.com

Davincidilemma.com
A website devoted to encouraging and helping multitalented people.
www.davincidilemma.com

Outofthefog.net
This site assists those who are coping with a friend or family member who has various psychological disorders.
www.outofthefog.net

Sober24.com
A blog devoted to issues surrounding sobriety from alcohol.
www.sober24.com

Us.mensa.org
Site for a social and networking organization for persons with a high IQ.
www.us.mensa.org

Additional Resources

Al-Anon Family Groups

757-563-1600

www.al-anonfamilygroups.org

For helping families recover from a family member's problem drinking.

Parents Anonymous

909-621-6184

www.parentsanonymous.org

For strengthening families, breaking the cycle of abuse, and helping parents create safe homes for their children.

Adult Children of Alcoholics

PO Box 3216

Torrance, CA 90510

562-595-7831

www.adultchildren.org

Twelve-step organization to help persons who come from alcoholic and other dysfunctional families.

Alcoholics Anonymous

PO Box 459

New York, NY 10163

212-870-3400

www.aa.org

Twelve-step organization that helps people stop drinking.

National Alliance on Mental Illness (NAMI)

3803 N. Fairfax Drive, Ste. 100

Arlington, VA 22203

703-524-9094

www.nami.org

This organization helps people with mental illness and family members of the mentally ill.

Overeaters Anonymous

PO Box 44020

Rio Rancho NM 87174

505-891-2664

www.oa.org

This twelve-step organization helps people who eat compulsively.

Debtors Anonymous

PO Box 920888

Needham, MA 02492

1-800-421-2383 (United States only)

www.debtorsanonymous.org

Twelve-step organization to assist persons who debt compulsively.

Gamblers Anonymous

PO Box 17173
Los Angeles CA 90017
626-960-3500
www.gamblersanonymous.org
This twelve-step organization helps people stop compulsive gambling.

Emotions Anonymous

PO Box 4245
St. Paul MN 55104
651-647-9712
www.emotionsanonymous.org
This twelve-step program helps people find emotional sobriety.

Families Anonymous

701 Lee Street
Des Plaines, IL 60016
1-800-736-9805 (United States only)
www.familiesanonymous.org
This twelve-step program assists family members who are coping with other family members who have behavioral or drug issues.

Obsessive Compulsive Anonymous

PO Box 215 New Hyde Park
New York NY 11040
516-739-0662
www.obsessivecompulsiveanonymous.org
This twelve-step program helps its members cope with symptoms of OCD.

Helpful Books and Pamphlets:

Adult Children of Alcoholics. *Newcomer* and *Identity Papers*, Torrance, California, 2004.

Alcoholics Anonymous World Service. *Alcoholics Anonymous, 4th Ed.*, New York, New York, 2001.

Beck, Martha. *The Joy Diet: Ten Daily Practices for a Happier Life*. Crown Publishers: New York, 2003.

Benjamin, Harold H. *From Victim to Victor: For Cancer Patients and Their Families*. Dell Publishing: New York, 1987.

Black, Claudia. *It Will Never Happen to Me: As Children, Adolescents, Adults*, 2002.

Bradshaw, John. *Bradshaw On the Family: A Revolutionary Way to Self-Discovery*, 1988

Bradshaw, John. *Healing the Shame That Binds You*, 2005.

Bradshaw, John. *Homecoming: Reclaiming and Championing Your Inner Child.* 1992

Camenson, Blythe. *McGraw-Hill's Careers for Perfectionists and Other Meticulous Types.* 2nd Ed. McGraw-Hill: New York, 2007.

Dolecki, Constance. *The Everything® Guide to Borderline Personality Disorder.* Adams Media: Avon, Massachusetts, 2012.

Domar, Alice D. *Be Happy without Being Perfect: How to Break Free from the Perfect Deception.* Crown Publishers: New York, 2008.

Forward, Susan. *Toxic Parents, Overcoming Their Hurtful Legacy and Reclaiming Your Life*, 2002.

Goldberg, Carey. "When perfectionism becomes a problem." The Boston Globe, March 2, 2009. Retrieved from Boston.com on June 5, 2012.

Goodman, Cynthia, and Barbara Leff. *The Everything® Guide to Narcissistic Personality Disorder.* Adams Media: Avon, Massachusetts, 2012.

Hyde, Michael J. *Perfection: Coming to Terms with Being Human.* Baylor University Press: Waco, Texas, 2010.

Norwood, Robin. *Women Who Love Too Much: When You Keep Wishing and Hoping He'll Change,* 2008.

Raiten-D'Antonio, Toni. *The Velveteen Principles for Women: Shatter the Myth of Perfection and Embrace All That You Really Are.* Health Communications, Inc.: Deerfield Beach, Florida, 2007.

Rubens, Jim. *OverSuccess: Healing the American Obsession with Wealth, Fame, Power, and Perfection.* Greenleaf Book Group Press, LCC: Austin, Texas, 2009.

Sher, Barbara. *Refuse to Choose: A Revolutionary Program for Doing Everything That You Love,* 2006.

Stoddard, Alexandra. *The Art of the Possible: The Path from Perfectionism to Balance and Freedom.* William Morrow and Company, Inc.: New York, 1995.

Whitfield, Charles L. *Healing the Child Within: Discovery and Recovery for Adult Children of Dysfunctional Families,* 1987.

Index

Adams, Scott, 153

Adaptive perfectionism, 165

Addictions, 123–37. *See also* Alcoholism
  denial of, 111–12
  in dysfunctional families, 27–30
  emotional growth and, 71
  gambling, 127–29, 135
  giving up, 76–77
  overachieving, 130–32, 136–37
  overspending, 132–33, 137
  sex addiction, 126–27, 134
  success and, 111
  workaholism, 114–15, 124–25, 133, 217, 225

Adult child
  addictions in, 76–77
  birth order and, 67–70
  concept of, 63–78
  "critical parent" syndrome, 70
  development issues in, 71–72
  dysfunctional families and, 64–67
  gratitude and, 73–74
  healing, 72–76
  impatience in, 74
  inner child concept, 72–73
  paradox of, 65–66
  reparenting concept, 72–73
  suicide and, 77
  superhero parents and, 70–74
  therapy for, 75

Affirmations, 187, 195, 288

Alcoholism, 107–21. *See also* Addictions
  causes of, 107–8
  codependency and, 110
  communication and, 113–14
  compulsivity and, 114–15
  denial of, 111–12
  in family, 27–28, 64–67, 111–15
  isolation and, 112–13
  perfectionism and, 114–15
  sobriety and, 112, 119–21

American Graffiti, 24

Anger management, 199–200

Anorexia nervosa, 91, 93–94

Antidepressants, 169

Anxiety
  alcoholism and, 114
  managing, 146–47
  mental illness and, 146–47
  overeating and, 94
  reducing, 60, 94, 195–96

Apologies, 200, 217–18, 274–76

Approval, seeking, 32, 57, 60, 207–8

Artist's dates, 216–17

The Artist's Way, 216

Authenticity, 176, 186, 188

Autobiography, 183–84, 284

Automatic pilot, 244

Average, being, 198–99

Awareness, moments of, 172, 189, 231, 243–44

Balanced life, 53–54, 103, 133, 140–41, 196, 212–13

Beck, Martha, 136, 155, 170, 172, 188

Be Happy Without Being Perfect, 60, 91

Behaviors, substituting, 45–46

Benjamin, Harold, 152, 158

Benton, Thomas Hart, 174

Berne, Eric, 70

The Betrayal Bond, 126

"Big Dream," 26–27, 33

We Have EVERYTHING® on Anything!

With more than 19 million copies sold, the Everything® series has become one of America's favorite resources for solving problems, learning new skills, and organizing lives. Our brand is not only recognizable—it's also welcomed.

The series is a hand-in-hand partner for people who are ready to tackle new subjects—like you!

For more information on the Everything® series, please visit *www.adamsmedia.com*

The Everything® list spans a wide range of subjects, with more than 500 titles covering 25 different categories:

Business	History	Reference
Careers	Home Improvement	Religion
Children's Storybooks	Everything Kids	Self-Help
Computers	Languages	Sports & Fitness
Cooking	Music	Travel
Crafts and Hobbies	New Age	Wedding
Education/Schools	Parenting	Writing
Games and Puzzles	Personal Finance	
Health	Pets	